Mac Programming for Absolute Beginners

Wallace Wang

Apress®

Mac Programming for Absolute Beginners

ISBN-13 (pbk): 978-1-4302-3336-7

ISBN-13 (electronic): 978-1-4302-3337-4

Printed and bound in the United States of America (POD)

Trademarked names, logos, and images may appear in this book. Rather than use a trademark symbol with every occurrence of a trademarked name, logo, or image we use the names, logos, and images only in an editorial fashion and to the benefit of the trademark owner, with no intention of infringement of the trademark.

The use in this publication of trade names, trademarks, service marks, and similar terms, even if they are not identified as such, is not to be taken as an expression of opinion as to whether or not they are subject to proprietary rights.

President and Publisher: Paul Manning
Lead Editor: Michelle Lowman
Development Editor: Jim Markham
Technical Reviewer: James Bucanek
Editorial Board: Steve Anglin, Mark Beckner, Ewan Buckingham, Gary Cornell, Jonathan Gennick, Jonathan Hassell, Michelle Lowman, Matthew Moodie, Jeffrey Pepper, Frank Pohlmann, Douglas Pundick, Ben Renow-Clarke, Dominic Shakeshaft, Matt Wade, Tom Welsh
Coordinating Editor: Jennifer L. Blackwell
Copy Editors: Kim Wimpsett and Bill McManus
Compositor: MacPS, LLC
Indexer: BIM Indexing & Proofreading Services
Artist: April Milne
Cover Designer: Anna Ishchenko

Distributed to the book trade worldwide by Springer Science+Business Media, LLC., 233 Spring Street, 6th Floor, New York, NY 10013. Phone 1-800-SPRINGER, fax (201) 348-4505, e-mail orders-ny@springer-sbm.com, or visit www.springeronline.com.

For information on translations, please e-mail rights@apress.com, or visit www.apress.com.

Apress and friends of ED books may be purchased in bulk for academic, corporate, or promotional use. eBook versions and licenses are also available for most titles. For more information, reference our Special Bulk Sales–eBook Licensing web page at www.apress.com/info/bulksales.

The information in this book is distributed on an "as is" basis, without warranty. Although every precaution has been taken in the preparation of this work, neither the author(s) nor Apress shall have any liability to any person or entity with respect to any loss or damage caused or alleged to be caused directly or indirectly by the information contained in this work.

The source code for this book is available to readers at www.apress.com.

This book is dedicated to all those dreamers who just needed a helping hand to turn their great ideas into a working program.

Contents at a Glance

Contents

About the Author

Wallace Wang is a former Windows enthusiast who took one look at Vista and realized that the future of computing belonged to the Macintosh. He's written more than 40 computer books including *Microsoft Office for Dummies, Beginning Programming for Dummies, Steal This Computer Book, My New Mac,* and *My New iPad.* In addition to programming the Macintosh and iPhone/iPad, he also performs stand-up comedy, having appeared on A&E's *Evening at the Improv* as well as having performed in Las Vegas at the Riviera Comedy Club at the Riviera Hotel & Casino.

When he's not writing computer books or performing stand-up comedy, he also enjoys blogging about screenwriting at his site The 15 Minute Movie Method (www.15minutemoviemethod.com) where he shares screenwriting tips with other aspiring screenwriters who all share the goal of breaking into Hollywood.

About the Technical Reviewer

James Bucanek has spent the past 30 years programming and developing microcomputer systems. He has experience with a broad range of technologies, from embedded consumer products to industrial robotics. James is currently focused on Macintosh and iOS software development. When not programming, James indulges in his love of food and fine arts. He earned an aassociate's degree from the Royal Academy of Dance in classical ballet and can occasionally be found teaching at Adams Ballet Academy.

Acknowledgments

This book would never have been written without the help of all the wonderful people at Apress who worked to make sure this book could be the best beginner's tutorial for novice Macintosh programmers. A big round of thanks goes to Michelle Lowman, Jim Markham, Kim Wimpsett, Bill McManus, Jennifer L. Blackwell, and James Bucanek for keeping this project on track and making it fun at the same time.

Another big round of thanks goes to Bill Gladstone and Margot Hutchison at Waterside Productions for always looking out for new opportunities in the book publishing and computer industry.

Thanks also goes to all the stand-up comedians I've met, who have made those horrible crowds at comedy clubs more bearable: Darrell Joyce (http://darrelljoyce.com), Leo "the Man, the Myth, the Legend" Fontaine, Chris Clobber, Bob Zany (www.bobzany.com), Russ Rivas (http://russrivas.com), Doug James, Don Learned, Dante, and Dobie "The Uranus King" Maxwell (www.dobiemaxwell.com). Another round of thanks goes to Steve Schirripa (who appeared in HBO's hit show *The Sopranos*) for giving me my break in performing at the Riviera Hotel and Casino in Las Vegas, one of the few old-time casinos left that hasn't been imploded (yet) to make room for another luxury hotel and casino designed to take money away from people unable to calculate the odds so heavily stacked against them.

Finally, I'd like to acknowledge Cassandra (my wife), Jordan (my son), and Nuit (my cat) along with Loons the parrot and Ollie the parakeet. They didn't help write this book one bit, but their presence has made the process of writing this book much more bearable.

Introduction

If you're an experienced programmer, a beginner just learning to program, or a complete novice who knows nothing about programming at all, this book is for you. No matter what your skill level may be, you can learn how to write programs for the Macintosh starting today.

What makes programming for the Macintosh so appealing is that the programming tools are free (courtesy of Apple), and by learning the basics of programming the Macintosh, you can easily apply your skills and experience to programming the iPhone, iPod touch, and iPad as well. Although this book focuses on programming the Macintosh, what you learn here can build a solid foundation to help you take the next step toward writing your own iPhone/iPod touch/iPad apps in the future.

The introduction of a new computer platform has always ushered in new (and lucrative) opportunities for programmers. In the early 1980s, the hottest platform was the Apple II computer. If you wanted to make money writing programs, you wrote programs to sell to Apple II computer owners, such as Dan Bricklin did, an MBA graduate student at the time, when he wrote the first spreadsheet program, VisiCalc.

Then the next big computing platform occurred in the mid-1980s with the IBM PC and MS-DOS. People made fortunes off the IBM PC including Bill Gates and Microsoft, which went from a small, startup company to the most dominant computer company in the world. The IBM PC made millionaires out of hundreds of people including Scott Cook, a former marketing director at Proctor & Gamble, who developed the popular money manager program, Quicken.

Microsoft helped usher in the next computer platform when it shifted from MS-DOS to Windows and put a friendly graphical user interface on IBM PCs. Once again, programming Windows became the number-one way that programmers and nonprogrammers alike made fortunes by writing and selling their own Windows programs. Microsoft took advantage of the shift to Windows by releasing several Windows-only programs that have become fixtures of the business world such as Outlook, Access, Word, PowerPoint, and Excel.

Now with the growing market for Apple products, thousands of people, just like you, are eager to start writing programs to take advantage of the Macintosh's rising market share along with the dominant position of the iPhone and the iPad in the smartphone and tablet categories.

Besides experienced developers, amateurs, hobbyists, and professionals in other fields are also interested in writing their own games, utilities, and business software specific to their particular niche.

Many programmers have gone from knowing nothing about programming to earning thousands of dollars a day by creating useful and frivolous iPhone/iPad apps or Macintosh programs. As the Macintosh, iPhone, and iPad continue gaining market share and adding new features, more people will use one or more of these products, increasing the potential market for you.

All this means that it's a perfect time for you to start learning how to program your Macintosh right now, because the sooner you understand the basics of Macintosh programming, the sooner you can start creating your own Macintosh programs or iPhone/iPad apps.

Code Conventions Used in This Book

Most of this book prints text in the font you're reading right now. However, you'll run across text formatted in different ways. To make it easy to tell the difference between explanatory text and actual programming instructions, you may see a different font like this:

```
NSString *newString;
```

This type of text highlights code that you can examine or type in. This font also highlights messages you may see on your screen.

Throughout this book, you'll be typing in sample programs. Sometimes you'll only need to modify part of an existing sample program, so to emphasize the new code you need to type in, you may see bold text like this:

```
NSString *newString;
newString = [largeString substringWithRange: NSMakeRange(5, 4)];
```

The bold text emphasizes the new code you need to add while the non-bold text represents the existing code you can leave alone. By seeing the existing code, you can easily see where you need to add any new code.

What to Expect from This Book

There are plenty of programming books on the market, but what makes this book different is that it assumes you're a complete novice with a great idea for a program but don't know the first step for getting started. For that reason, this book will minimize all the technical jargon about Objective-C, Xcode 3.2, and Cocoa frameworks and instead focus on helping you achieve specific tasks such as displaying a command button or accepting text from the user.

Of course, you will eventually need to know what Objective-C, Xcode, and the Cocoa frameworks can do, but you won't get buried in a lot of technical jargon. Since this book starts you at the very beginning, it also won't contain detailed technical information needed to create super-sophisticated programs that involve graphics or sound. If you just want to get started and learn the basics of programming using Apple's programming tools, this book is for you. If you're already an experienced Windows programmer and want to get started programming the Macintosh, this book can be especially helpful in teaching you the basics of using Apple's programming tools in a hurry.

If you've never programmed before in your life or if you're already familiar with programming but not with Macintosh programming, then this book is for you. Even if you're experienced with Macintosh programming, you may still find this book handy as a reference to help you achieve certain results without having to wade through several books to find an answer.

To help you learn the different principles behind Macintosh programming, this book also provides plenty of short example programs that you can run and study. Because each sample program is so short, you'll be able to focus just on learning a new feature of programming while reducing the possibility of typos and other errors. As a result, you're more likely to get each short sample program working right away, which can increase your confidence and enjoyment as you learn how to program.

You won't learn everything you need to know to create your own programs, but you'll learn just enough to get started, feel comfortable, and be able to tackle other programming books with more confidence and understanding. Fair enough? If so, then turn the page and let's get started.

Chapter 1

Understanding Programming

Programming is nothing more than writing instructions for a computer to follow. If you've ever written down the steps for a recipe or scribbled driving directions on the back of an envelope, you've already gone through the basic steps of writing a program. The key is simply knowing what you want to accomplish and then making sure you write the correct instructions that will achieve that goal.

Although programming is theoretically simple, it's the details that can trip you up. First, you need to know exactly what you want. If you wanted a recipe for cooking chicken chow mein, following a recipe for cooking baked salmon won't do you any good.

Second, you need to write down every instruction necessary to get you from your starting point to your desired result. If you skip a step or write steps out of order, you won't get the same result. Try driving to a restaurant where your list of driving instructions omits telling you when to turn on a specific road. It doesn't matter if 99 percent of the instructions are right; if just one instruction is wrong, you won't get you to your desired goal.

The simpler your goal, the easier it will be to achieve. Writing a program that displays a calculator on the screen is far simpler than writing a program to monitor the safety systems of a nuclear power plant. The more complex your program, the more instructions you'll need to write, and the more instructions you need to write, the greater the chance you'll forget an instruction, write an instruction incorrectly, or write instructions in the wrong order.

Programming is nothing more than a way to control a computer to solve a problem, whether that computer is a laptop, mobile phone, or tablet device. Before you can start writing your own programs, you need to understand the basic principles of programming in the first place.

Programming Principles

To write a program, you have to write instructions that the computer can follow. No matter what a program does or how big it may be, every program in the world consists of nothing more than step-by-step instructions for the computer to follow, one at a time. The simplest program can consist of a single line:

```
PRINT "Hello, world!"
```

NOTE: The sample code in this part of the chapter uses the BASIC programming language to make programming concepts easier to understand. What you'll be learning later in this book is a different programming language called Objective-C, which is a bit harder to understand than BASIC.

Obviously, a program that consists of a single line won't be able to do much, so most programs consist of multiples lines of instructions (or code):

```
PRINT "Hello, world!"
PRINT "Now the program is done."
```

This two-line program starts with the first line, follows the instructions on the second line, and then stops. Of course, you can keep adding more instructions to a program until you have a million instructions that the computer can follow sequentially, one at a time.

Listing instructions sequentially is the basis for programming, but it's not always the best way to organize instructions. For example, if you wanted to print the same message five times, you could use the following:

```
PRINT "Hello, world!"
PRINT "Hello, world!"
PRINT "Hello, world!"
PRINT "Hello, world!"
PRINT "Hello, world!"
```

Writing the same five instructions is tedious and redundant, but it works. What happens if you wanted to print this same message 1,000 times? Then you'd have to write the same instruction 1,000 times.

Writing the same instruction multiple times is clumsy. To make programming easier, you really want to write the least number of instructions that get the most work done. One way to avoid writing the same instruction multiple times is to organize your instructions using something called a *loop*.

The idea behind a loop is to repeat one or more instructions multiple times, but only by writing those instructions down once. A typical loop might look like this:

```
FOR I = 1 TO 5
    PRINT "Hello, world!"
END FOR
```

The first instruction tells the computer to repeat the loop five times. The second instruction tells the computer to print the message "Hello, world!" on the screen. The third instruction just defines the end of the loop.

Now if you wanted to make the computer print a message 1,000 times, you don't need to write the same instruction 1,000 times. Instead, you just need to modify how many times the loop repeats:

```
FOR I = 1 TO 1000
    PRINT "Hello, world!"
END FOR
```

Although loops are slightly more confusing to read and understand than a sequential series of instructions, loops make it easier to repeat instructions without writing the same instructions multiple times.

Most programs don't exclusively list instructions sequentially or in loops, but they use a combination of both:

```
PRINT "Getting ready to print."
PRINT "Program is now starting."
FOR I = 1 TO 1000
    PRINT "Hello, world!"
END FOR
```

In this example, the computer follows the first two lines sequentially and then follows the last three instructions repetitively in a loop. Generally, listing instructions sequentially is fine when you need the computer to follow those instructions only once. When you need the computer to run instructions multiple times, that's when you need to use a loop.

What makes computers powerful isn't just the ability to follow instructions sequentially or in a loop, but in making decisions. Decisions mean that the computer needs to evaluate some condition and then, based on that condition, decide what to do next.

For example, you might write a program that locks someone out of a computer until that person types the correct password. If the person types the correct password, then the program needs to give that person access. However, if the person types an incorrect password, then the program needs to block access to the computer. An example of this type of decision making might look like this:

```
ASK "Enter the password:", Password
IF Password = "OPEN" THEN
    Grant access to the computer
ELSE
    Block access to the computer
```

In this example, the computer asks for a password, and when the user types a password, the computer checks to see whether it matches the word OPEN. If the user typed OPEN, then the computer grants that person access to the computer. If the user did not type OPEN, then the computer blocks access.

Making decisions is what makes programming flexible. If you write a sequential series of instructions, the computer will follow those lists of instructions exactly the same way, every time. However, if you include decision-making instructions, also known as *branching instructions*, then the computer can respond according to what the user does.

Consider a video game. No video game could be written entirely with instructions organized sequentially because then the game would play exactly the same way every time. Instead, a video game needs to adapt to the player's actions at all times. If the player moves an object to the left, the video game needs to respond differently than if the player moves an object to the right or gets killed. Using branching instructions gives computers the ability to react differently so the program never runs exactly the same.

To write a computer program, you need to organize instructions in one of the following three ways, as shown in Figure 1–1:

> *Sequentially*: The computer follows instructions one after another.

> *Loop*: The computer repetitively follows one or more instructions.

> *Branching*: The computer chooses to follow one or more groups of instructions based on outside data.

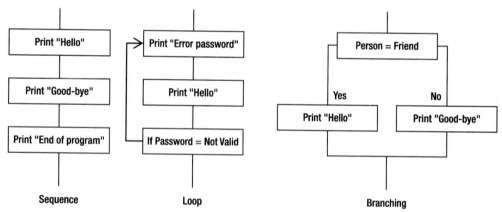

Figure 1–1. *The three basic building blocks of programming*

Although simple programs may organize instructions only sequentially, every large program organizes instructions sequentially, in loops, and in branches. What makes programming more of an art and less of a science is that there is no single best way to write a program. In fact, it's perfectly possible to write two different programs that behave the same.

Because there is no single "right" way to write a program, there are only guidelines to help you write programs easily. Ultimately what matters is only that you write a program that works.

When writing any program, there are two, often mutually exclusive, goals. First, programmers strive to write programs that are easy to read, understand, and modify. This often means writing multiple instructions that clearly define the steps needed to solve a particular problem.

Second, programmers try to write programs that perform tasks efficiently, making the program run as fast as possible. This often means condensing multiple instructions as much as possible, using tricks, or exploiting little known features that are difficult to understand and confusing even to most other programmers.

In the beginning, strive toward making your programs as clear, logical, and understandable as possible, even if you have to write more instructions or type longer instructions to do it. Later, as you gain more experience in programming, you can work on creating the smallest, fastest, most efficient programs possible, but remember that your ultimate goal is to write programs that just work.

Dividing Programs into Parts

Since small programs have fewer instructions, they are much easier to read, understand, and modify. Unfortunately, small programs can solve only small problems. To solve complicated problems, you need to write bigger programs with more instructions. The more instructions you type, the greater the chance you'll make a mistake (called a *bug*). Even worse is that the larger a program gets, the harder it can be to understand how it works in order to modify it later.

To avoid writing a single, massive program, programmers simply divide a large program into smaller parts called *subprograms*. The idea is that each subprogram solves a single problem. Connect all of these subprograms together, and you can create a single large program, as shown in Figure 1–2. This is like building a house out of bricks rather than trying to carve an entire house out of one massive rock.

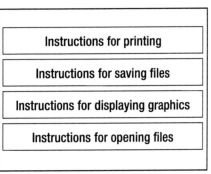

Figure 1–2. *Dividing a large program into multiple subprograms*

Dividing a large program into smaller parts provides several benefits. First, writing smaller subprograms is fast and easy, and small subprograms make it easy to read, understand, and modify the instructions.

Second, subprograms act like building blocks that work together, so multiple programmers can work on different subprograms and then combine their separate subprograms to create a large program.

Third, if you want to modify a large program, you just need to yank out, rewrite, and replace one or more subprograms. Without subprograms, modifying a large program means wading through all the instructions stored in a large program and trying to find which instructions you need to change.

A fourth benefit of subprograms is that if you write a useful subprogram, you can plug that subprogram into other programs, thereby reducing the need to write everything from scratch.

When you divide a large program into multiple subprograms, you have a choice. You can store all your programs in a single file, or you can store each subprogram in a separate file, as shown in Figure 1–3.

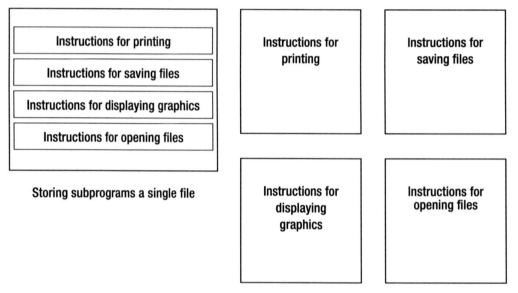

Figure 1–3. *You can store subprograms in one file or in multiple files.*

Storing all your subprograms in a single file makes it easy to find and modify any part of your program. However, the larger your program, the more instructions you'll need to write, which can make searching through a single large file as clumsy as flipping through the pages of a dictionary.

Storing all your subprograms in separate files means you need to keep track of which files contain which subprogram. However, the benefit is that modifying a subprogram is much easier because once you open the correct file, you see the instructions for only a single subprogram, not for a dozen or more other subprograms.

To write any program, most programmers divide a large program into subprograms and store those subprograms in separate files.

Event-Driven Programming

In the early days of computers, most programs forced people to use a program by typing one command at a time. For example, if you had a program that calculated the trajectory of a rocket, the program might first ask you the destination followed by the rocket's size, weight, and position from the target. If you wanted to type in the rocket's weight before typing in the rocket's height, the program wouldn't let you because such programs tightly controlled how the computer behaved at any given time.

All of this changed when computers started displaying windows and pull-down menus so users could choose what to do at any given time. Suddenly every program had to wait for the user to do something such as selecting one of many available menu commands. Since the user could do multiple actions such as typing or clicking the mouse, programs had to constantly wait for the user to do something before reacting.

Every time the user did something, that was considered an event. If the user clicked the left mouse button, that was a completely different event than if the user clicked the right mouse button. Instead of dictating what the user could do at any given time, programs now had to respond to different events that the user did. Such programs came to be known as *event-driven programming*.

Instead of following instructions from start to finish, event-driven programs divided a large program into multiple subprograms where each subprogram responded to a different event. If the user clicked the left mouse, the subprogram that handled left mouse clicks would run its instructions. If the user clicked the right mouse, the subprogram that handled right mouse clicks would run its instructions.

With event-driven programming, a large program might be divided into multiple subprograms where some of those subprograms contained instructions that ran only when a certain event occurred, as shown in Figure 1–4.

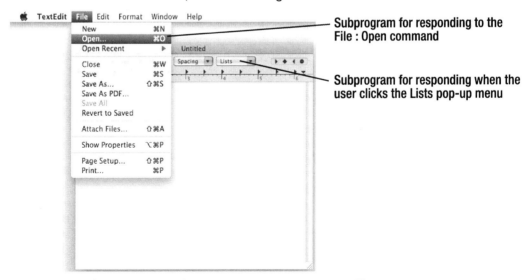

Figure 1–4. *Programs can be divided into subprograms that respond to specific events.*

Object-Oriented Programming

Dividing a large program into multiple subprograms made it easy to create and modify a program. However, trying to understand how such a large program worked often proved confusing since there was no simple way to determine which subprograms worked together or what overall task they were meant to solve.

To solve this problem, programmers grouped related subprograms and data in a single location. By using this grouped collection of subprograms and data, programmers could create objects, which represent a single element of the problem you're trying to solve.

Instead of focusing on different tasks, object-oriented programming often focuses on mimicking objects in the real world. An object-oriented video game program might divide a program into objects such as monsters, the player character, and other moving items such as falling boulders.

Each object would contain subprograms for manipulating that object along with data that defines the characteristics of that object, such as its location on the screen or the color of the item to display on the screen.

One idea behind object-oriented programming is to divide a large program into logical objects that mimic the physical problem you're trying to solve. So rather than write a bunch of subprograms that break a problem into individual tasks, object-oriented programming divides a problem into physical parts.

Suppose you need to write a program for controlling a robot. Dividing this problem into tasks, you might create one subprogram to move the robot, a second subprogram to tell the robot how to see nearby obstacles, and a third subprogram to calculate the best path to follow.

Dividing this same robot program into objects might create a Legs object (for moving the robot), an Eye object for seeing nearby obstacles, and a Brain object (for calculating the best path to avoid obstacles), as shown in Figure 1–5.

A second idea behind object-oriented programming is to make it easy to reuse and modify a large program. Suppose we replace our robot's legs with treads. Now we'd have to modify the subprogram for moving the robot since treads behave differently than legs. Next, we'd have to modify the subprogram for calculating the best path around obstacles since treads force a robot to go around obstacles, while legs allow a robot to walk over small obstacles and go around larger obstacles.

If you wanted to replace a robot's legs with treads, object-oriented programming would simply allow you to yank out the Legs object and replace it with a new Treads object, without affecting or needing to modify any additional objects.

Subprograms divide programs by tasks   **Objects divide programs by function**

Figure 1–5. *How subprograms and objects might divide a program into parts*

The Brain object wouldn't need to change since it needs to tell the Treads object only where to move, not how to move. Since most programs are constantly modified to fix bugs or add new features, object-oriented programming allows you to create a large program out of separate building blocks (objects) and modify a program by modifying only a single object.

The key to object-oriented programming is to isolate parts of a program and promote reusability through three features known as *encapsulation*, *inheritance*, and *polymorphism*.

Encapsulation

The biggest problem with dividing a large program into subprograms is that one subprogram can often access and change data that another subprogram uses. If this happens, then the entire program might not work, and trying to track down the source of the problem can be nearly impossible because you have to exhaustively examine all your subprograms.

To avoid this problem, object-oriented programming *encapsulates*, or hides, data inside an object. Each object contains both the data it needs and the subprograms allowed to manipulate that data, as shown in Figure 1–6.

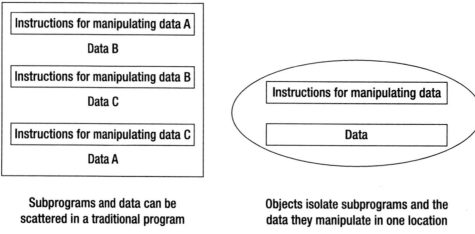

Instructions for manipulating data A	
Data B	Instructions for manipulating data
Instructions for manipulating data B	
Data C	Data
Instructions for manipulating data C	
Data A	

Subprograms and data can be scattered in a traditional program   **Objects isolate subprograms and the data they manipulate in one location**

Figure 1–6. *Objects group related subprograms and data together.*

Encapsulation simply eliminates the risk that an unrelated part of a program can change data used by another subprogram.

Polymorphism

When you divide a large program into subprograms, each subprogram needs a unique name. Normally this won't cause any problems, but sometimes you may need to create subprograms that perform similar tasks.

For example, suppose you're creating a video game where the player controls a car and the computer controls a monster throwing rocks at the car. To make the car, monster, and rocks move on the screen, you might want to create a subprogram named Move.

Unfortunately, a car needs to move differently on the screen than a monster or a thrown rock. You could create three subprograms and name them MoveCar, MoveMonster, and MoveRock. However, a simpler solution is to just give all three subprograms the same name such as Move.

In traditional programming, you can never give the same name to two or more subprograms since the computer would never know which subprogram you want to run. However, in object-oriented programming, you can use duplicate subprogram names because of polymorphism.

The reason why polymorphism works is because each Move subprogram gets stored in a separate object such as one object that represents the car, a second object that represents the monster, and a third object that represents a thrown rock. To run each Move subprogram, you must identify the object that contains the Move subprogram you want to use:

```
Car.Move
Monster.Move
Rock.Move
```

By identifying both the object that you want to manipulate and the subprogram that you want to use, object-oriented programming can correctly identify which set of instructions to run even though a subprogram has the identical name to another subprogram.

Essentially, polymorphism lets you create descriptive subprogram names and reuse that descriptive name as often as you like.

Inheritance

If you create a particularly useful subprogram, you might want to reuse that subprogram again. The simple answer is to make a copy of a subprogram and modify this copy.

The problem with copying subprograms is that you now have two or more identical copies of the same subprogram stored in different locations. Such duplication not only wastes space but, more importantly, can cause problems if you need to modify the original subprogram.

Suppose you create a useful subprogram and then make five different copies to use in other parts of your program, with minor modifications made to each additional subprogram copy. Now what happens if you find an error in your original subprogram? Fixing that one subprogram will be fairly straightforward, but now you have to fix that same error five more times in each of the five additional copies you made earlier.

Inheritance eliminates this problem because instead of forcing a programmer to create duplicate, physical copies of a subprogram, inheritance creates virtual copies of a subprogram. The original instructions remain in one physical location, but multiple objects can now access those instructions whenever they need them.

Think of inheritance like the difference between text in a printed book and text on a web page. Only one person can read a printed book at a time. If multiple people want to read that same book, you'll need to make physical copies.

However, text on a web page can be accessed by multiple people, even though there's only one copy of that text stored on a single computer.

The main idea behind inheritance is to make it easy to reuse parts of your program without creating duplicate copies.

Understanding Programming Languages

Once you understand how programming has gradually evolved and how Mac programming requires understanding all of these different programming techniques, you're almost ready to start programming. Next, you need to know that giving instructions to a computer involves writing commands using a programming language.

There are thousands of different programming languages with names like FORTH, Ada, BASIC, C#, Prolog, and Modula-3. However, the programming language you'll be learning in this book is called Objective-C.

Currently, one of the most popular programming language is C. Two huge advantages of C are its efficiency and its portability. *Efficiency* means that programs written in C are extremely small and run fast. *Portability* means that almost every computer in the world understands C. As a result,you can write a program in C and copy it to a different operating system, such as taking a C program for Windows and copying it to a Macintosh. You'll need to rewrite the C code to create a user interface that's unique to each operating system, but a large portion of your program's C code can remain intact with little or no modifications at all.

Since C is an old programming language, it lacks object-oriented programming features, which makes C unsuitable for creating and maintaining large programs. One popular variation of C is called C++, which adds object-oriented programming features. Although C++ is popular, Objective-C also offers object-oriented features and is much simpler and thus easier to learn.

To write Mac programs, you can use any programming langauge, although the most popular ones are C, C++, and Objective-C. However, Apple has officially endorsed Objective-C as the main programming language for the Mac, so if you're going to learn how to program the Mac, your best choice is to learn and use Objective-C.

NOTE: If you already know C or C++, you'll find that Objective-C is similar enough that you can learn it quickly. If you don't know any programming language at all, Objective-C may look a bit cryptic at first, but after you use it for a while, you'll soon understand how it works.

The Building Blocks of Programming Languages

Every programming language consists of special commands that are part of the language. These commands tell the computer to do something:

```
PRINT
```

In this example, PRINT represents a command that tells the computer to print something on the screen. By themselves, commands usually won't do anything interesting, so you have to combine commands with additional data to create a single instruction or a statement. A statement simply tells the computer to do something useful:

```
PRINT "This is a message from your computer"
```

Learning a programming language means learning the right commands so you can tell the computer what to do, such as print a message on the screen or add two numbers together.

To make programming as easy as possible, many programming languages use commands that look like ordinary English words such as PRINT, Writeln, or printf.

However, many programming languages also use symbols that represent different features.

Sometimes a symbol represents a command to make the computer do something. Common symbols are mathematical symbols for addition (+), subtraction (-), multiplication (*), and division (/).

Other times symbols are meant to define the beginning or end of something:

```
int age;
```

or

```
[super init]
```

Some programming languages rely almost exclusively on commands to make the instructions more readable:

```
BEGIN
    Writeln ('This is a message');
END;
```

Other programming languages, such as Objective-C, tend to rely more on symbols to make writing a program faster, but with the drawback that the statements tend to look more cryptic:

```
{
    printf ("This is a message");
}
```

Unlike human languages where you can misspell a word or forget to end a sentence with a period and people can still understand what you're saying, programming languages are not so forgiving. With a programming language, every command must be spelled correctly, and every symbol must be used where needed. Misspell a single command, use the wrong symbol, or put the right symbol in the wrong place, and your entire program will fail to work.

Programming Frameworks

Commands (and symbols) let you give a computer instructions, but no programming language can provide every possible command you might need to create all types of programs. To provide additional commands, programmers can create subprograms that perform a specific task.

Programmers can even create bigger subprograms out of commands and smaller subprograms. By creating subprograms, you can create your own commands needed to make the computer do exactly what you need.

Programmers often create subprograms unique to their particular program. However, many programmers have also created useful subprograms that provide features that other programmers might find useful. As a result, many programming languages include libraries of these other subprograms. Now when you write a program, you can use the programming language's commands and any subprograms stored in libraries.

One library might contain subprograms for displaying graphics. Another library might contain subprograms for saving data to a disk and retrieving it again. Still another library might contain subprograms for calculating mathematical formulas. By using commands to create subprograms, programmers can create an endless variety of additional building blocks for making any type of program.

To make programming the Mac, iPhone, and iPad easier, Apple has created libraries or frameworks of useful subprograms that you can use in your own programs.

There are two reasons for reusing an existing framework. First, reusing a framework keeps you from having to write your own instructions to accomplish a task that somebody else has already solved. Not only does a framework provide a ready-made solution, but a framework has also been tested by others, so you can just use the framework and be assured that it will work correctly.

A second reason to use an existing framework is for consistency. Apple provides frameworks for defining the appearance of a program on the screen, known as the *user interface*. This defines how a program should behave, from displaying windows on the screen to letting you resize or close a window by clicking the mouse.

It's perfectly possible to write your own instructions for displaying windows on the screen, but chances are good that writing your own instructions would take time to create and test, and the end result would be windows that may not look or behave identically as other Mac programs.

However, by reusing an existing framework, you can create your own program quickly and ensure that your program behaves the same way that other programs behave. Although programming the Mac might sound complicated, Apple provides dozens of different frameworks that help you create programs quickly and easily. All you have to do is write the custom instructions that make your program solve a specific, unique problem.

Mac Programming Today

Almost every program consists of three parts: a user interface, a controller, and a model. The user interface displays windows and menus to show information and let the user choose commands. The model contains instructions for accepting data, manipulating it somehow, and calculating a new result. The controller takes data from the user interface and feeds it into the model. Then it takes the newly calculated result from the model and sends it back to the user interface, as shown in Figure 1–7.

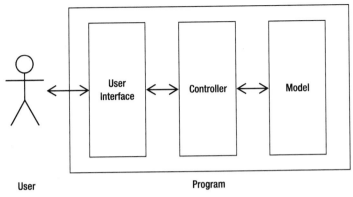

User   Program

Figure 1–7. *The three parts of a typical program*

Here's the hard way to write a Mac program. First, use the commands in Objective-C to create your user interface. After you spend time writing multiple instructions to create your user interface, you need to test it to make sure it works.

Second, use Objective-C commands to create the model for accepting data, manipulating it somehow, and calculating a new result. Now spend more time testing these instructions to make sure they work.

Third, use Objective-C commands to create the controller to link the user interface to the model. Now spend more time making sure the controller works correctly with the user interface and the model.

In the old-fashioned way of programming, you had to write three separate chunks of instructions to create the user interface, controller, and model, and then you'd test each chunk separately to make sure they worked. Finally, you had to put all three chunks of instructions together and test everything again to make sure it all worked together.

Such a process is obviously tedious, error-prone, and slow. Since you have to create everything from scratch using Objective-C commands, this can feel like trying to build a wall by pasting together individual granules of sand.

Here's the faster way to write a Mac program, which is what you'll be learning in this book. Instead of creating everything from scratch, you'll just need to focus on writing instructions that calculate a useful result. By focusing on writing instructions to create the model portion of your program, you're essentially simplifying the amount of programming work you need to do.

First, every time you create a new program, you'll get to choose from a template. A template provides the basic skeleton of a user interface that can display windows and pull-down menus found in most programs.

Since the template already provides the Objective-C commands for creating a user interface, you can spend your time customizing this user interface. Ordinarily, customizing the user interface would mean writing Objective-C instructions, but Apple provides a special tool that lets you design your user interface by dragging and dropping items on the screen such as buttons and text fields.

By eliminating the need to write a separate set of instructions for designing your user interface, you'll only need to write instructions to make your program do something useful. Even better, you won't have to waste time testing your user interface because there are no Objective-C instructions to examine since everything just works, so your program looks and behaves exactly like other Mac programs.

To create the controller and model portions of your program, you'll need to write instructions in Objective-C. Rather than rely on commands alone, you can save time by using subprograms stored in frameworks provided by Apple. By using these frameworks, you can use subprograms that have already been tested for accomplishing a variety of complicated tasks such as saving a file.

To respond to the actions of the user, you'll need to organize your instructions into subprograms that run only when certain events occur, such as when the user clicks the mouse. To further help you organize your program, you can create objects using Objective-C's object-oriented features.

The end result is that writing a Mac program eliminates as much of the tedious part of programming as possible, freeing you to focus only on the creative part that makes your program unique.

Although this may sound like a lot of information to master just to write a Mac program, don't worry. From program templates to drag-and-drop user interface designs to frameworks, Apple streamlines the programming process so you can create a fully functioning program with a minimum of effort.

Summary

To learn how to write programs for the Mac, you need to learn three separate skills. First, you need to understand the basic principles of programming. That includes organizing instructions in sequences, loops, or branches.

Second, you need to learn a specific programming language. For the Mac, you'll be learning Objective-C. Objective-C is designed more for program efficiency and less for human readability, which means that writing and reading Objective-C instructions can look cryptic at times.

Third, you need to know how to use Apple's programming tools for writing Objective-C instructions and how to use Apple's frameworks so you can focus solely on writing instructions that make your program work (which you'll learn more about in Chapter 2).

Once you learn how to program the Mac, you can easily use your skill to write programs for the iPhone, iPod touch, and iPad as well. Whether you want to write your own software to sell or you want to sell your programming skills to create custom software for others, you'll find that programming is a skill anyone can learn.

Programming is nothing more than problem solving using a particular programming language. By knowing how to solve problems using Objective-C, you can create your own programs for the Mac much easier and far faster than you might think.

Chapter 2

Understanding Apple's Programming Tools

To write a program, you need at least two tools: an editor and a compiler. An editor acts like a word processor and lets you write instructions using a programming language such as Objective-C. A compiler converts your instructions (called *code*) and compiles (or translates) them into a language that computers can understand, which is called *machine code*. When you buy a program, that program is stored in a file that contains nothing but machine code.

Every time you run a program on your computer, whether it's a word processor or a web browser, you're using a program that someone wrote in an editor using a programming language and converted into machine code using a compiler.

Understanding Editors

To create a program, you'll need to write, save, and edit instructions (your code) using a programming language such as Objective-C. In the early days of programming, an editor (also called a *text editor*) looked and behaved like a word processor, but without the need for fancy formatting commands. After you edited and saved a program in an editor, you had to exit the editor and run a compiler to test whether your program worked.

If your program didn't work, you had to load your editor again, open the file that you saved your instructions in, make any changes, and save the file once more. Then you had to run the compiler once again.

This process of constantly loading and exiting from the editor and compiler wasted time. The more time you wasted switching back and forth between your editor and your compiler, the less time you had to work on your program.

To fix this problem, computer scientists created a special program called an *integrated development environment* (IDE). The idea behind an IDE is that you need to load a single programming tool only once. You can write, edit, and save your program in the IDE and then compile it without having to exit the editor and load the compiler since everything is integrated in a single program.

Besides making programming faster and easier, IDEs had a second benefit. If you ran a compiler separately from the editor and your program had an error or bug in it, the compiler could identify the line in your program only where the error occurred. To fix this problem, you had to load your editor again, open your program, and move the cursor to the line where the error occurred so you could fix it. Once again, this process wasted time.

Since an IDE never forces you to quit and load a separate program, the moment the compiler discovers a bug in your program, it can highlight that error in the editor so you can fix it right away. An IDE simply combines the features of multiple tools into a single program.

To write programs for the Mac, you'll be using two free tools provided by Apple called Xcode and Interface Builder. Xcode combines the features of an editor and a compiler (along with other tools) so you'll be able to create and edit programs written in Objective-C. Interface Builder lets you visually design your program's user interface. By using both Xcode and Interface Builder, you'll be able to design your user interface and connect it to your Objective-C code to make the whole thing work.

Understanding Xcode

To write Mac programs, you have to use Xcode, which you can download for free from the Apple Developer Center site (http://developer.apple.com). The first time you see Xcode, it might look intimidating because of all the menu commands, windows, and icons that appear everywhere. The idea of trying to master every feature of Xcode can be as intimidating as learning to fly for the first time by stepping in the cockpit of a 747 jumbo jet.

> **NOTE:** Interface Builder is a program bundled with Xcode, so when you download Xcode from Apple's developer's site, you get both Interface Builder and Xcode in the same file.

Don't worry. Although Xcode provides hundreds of options and features, you don't have to learn them all right away, or even at all. To write a Mac program, you only need to learn how to use a handful of features. Later as you get more experienced with Mac programming, you can take advantage of Xcode's other features, but only when you're ready.

The three basic uses for Xcode are as follows:

- Creating and editing Objective-C code
- Creating and modifying your program's user interface
- Running and testing your program

Before you can start writing Mac programs, you need to understand how to use Xcode. The first task is to learn and understand the Xcode user interface. The second task is to learn how and when to use different features of Xcode when writing your own program.

Deciphering the Xcode User Interface

Unlike other types of programs you may have used before, such as a word processor or web browser, Xcode lets you customize the user interface to display only the information you want at any given time. This makes Xcode flexible enough for everyone but also means that one copy of Xcode can look wildly different than another copy of Xcode.

The part of Xcode that always remains the same is its pull-down menus, which consists of the following:

- *File*: Commands for creating, opening, saving, and printing your programs

- *Edit*: Commands for copying, deleting, and moving items when writing code in Objective-C or when designing your program's user interface

- *View*: Commands for hiding or displaying icons or windows that display additional information

- *Product*: Commands for compiling and testing your program

- *Build*: Commands for compiling your programs

- *Run*: Commands for testing and debugging your program

- *Window*: Commands for manipulating Xcode's windows that may display additional commands

- *Help*: Commands for getting help using Xcode or writing Objective-C code

In addition to commands stored on pull-down menus, Xcode also offers numerous icons that display different types of information. Since these icons are small and not always intuitive as to what they do, most icons duplicate commands already available through the pull-down menus. The idea is that once you get used to using different commands regularly, you may find it faster to click an icon that performs the same function, rather than constantly going through the pull-down menus over and over again.

The main part of Xcode consists of multiple windows that appear stacked or side by side. Windows display different information about your program, so by moving, closing, or resizing a different window, you can change what type of information you want to see.

These three parts of Xcode (pull-down menus, icons, and panes) provide you with the tools you need to create, edit, and run your programs, as shown in Figure 2–1.

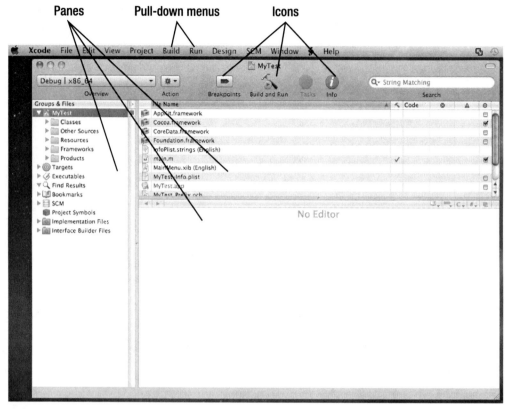

Figure 2–1. *The Xcode user interface consists of pull-down menus, icons, and panes.*

Running Xcode

When you install most programs on your Mac, such as Microsoft Word or iTunes, that program appears in the Applications folder. However, when you install Xcode on your computer, it usually appears in a special Developer folder.

To locate Xcode on your Mac, follow these steps:

1. Open the Finder window.

2. Click your hard disk icon (usually called Macintosh HD) located under the DEVICES category.

3. Choose View ➤ as List. A list of folders appears in the right pane of the Finder window.

4. Click the gray arrow that appears to the left of the Developer folder. A list of files and folders inside this Developer folder appears.

5. Click the gray arrow that appears to the left of the Applications folder. The Xcode icon appears as one of many files stored in the Applications folder, as shown in Figure 2–2.

Figure 2–2. *Finding Xcode on a Mac*

> **NOTE:** To make finding and running Xcode easier in the future, you may want to drag the Xcode icon onto the Dock. This will give you one-click access to starting Xcode whenever you need it.

Creating a New Project in Xcode

In the early days of programming, most programs were fairly small so they could easily fit into a single file. As programs grew larger and more complicated, programmers started to store different parts of a program in separate files. Each file represented a different part of a program, and all the files taken as a whole were called a *project*. A project file simply keeps track of all the files needed to create a single program.

To create a new Mac program, you have to create a new project. There are two ways to create a new project. First, when you start Xcode, a dialog box appears, letting you open an existing project or create a new product, as shown in Figure 2–3.

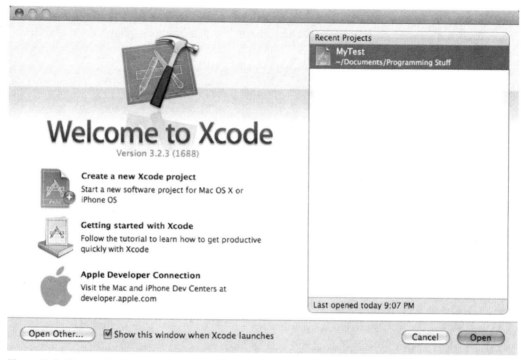

Figure 2–3. *The opening Xcode dialog box lets you choose between creating a new project or opening an existing one.*

If you've already started Xcode, a second way to create a new project is to choose File ► New Project or press ⇧⌘N. No matter how you choose to create a new project, Xcode displays a dialog box with different templates you can choose. The two groups of available templates are organized between the iPhone OS and Mac OS X.

If you want to create an iPhone/iPad app, you'd choose a template under the iPhone OS category. If you want to create a Mac program, you'd choose a template under the Mac OS X category, which displays different types of templates, as shown in Figure 2–4:

- *Application*: Creates a Mac OS X program, which is the template you'll use most often.

- *Framework & Library*: Creates your own framework of useful code that you can reuse in different programs. (This option is for advanced Mac programmers.)

- *Application Plug-In*: Creates small programs designed to work with existing applications such as the Address Book. (This option is for advanced Mac programmers.)

- *System Plug-In*: Creates small programs designed to work with the Mac OS X operating system. (This option is for advanced Mac programmers.)

- *Other*: Creates a completely blank file so you'll have to create everything from scratch. (This option is for advanced Mac programmers.)

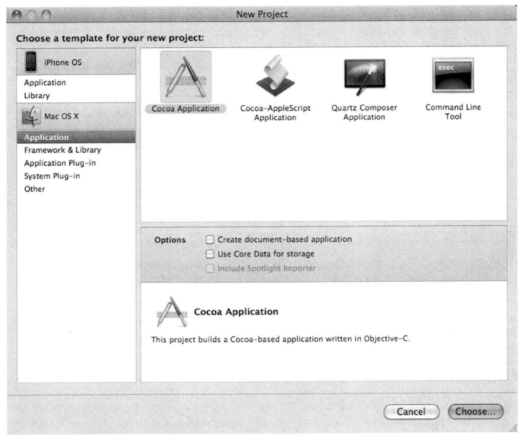

Figure 2–4. *To create a new program, you must choose a template.*

When you select the Application template, Xcode gives you the option of creating four types of applications:

- *Cocoa Application*: Creates the most common type of Mac OS X applications.

- *Cocoa-Applescript Application*: Creates an application based on the AppleScript programming language. (This option is for advanced Mac programmers.)

- *Quartz Composer Application*: Uses a visual programming language for processing and rendering graphical data. (This option is for advanced Mac programmers.)

■   *Command Line Tool*: Creates an application without the standard Mac
     OS X user interface. (This option is for advanced Mac programmers.)

In this book, you'll only be using the Application template to create Cocoa applications, which creates typical Mac OS X programs. When you create a Mac OS X program, you'll also have the option of selecting a "Create document-based application" or "Use Core Data for storage" check box. The "Create document-based application" option lets you open multiple windows to display different files, such as a word processor displaying multiple documents. The "Use Core Data for storage" option lets you use a special data management framework for storing data. For the purposes of this book, you can ignore these two options since they're designed for creating more sophisticated programs.

> **NOTE:** Cocoa is the name of Apple's framework to help you create Mac OS X programs. An older version of Apple's frameworks is called Carbon, which was designed to help programmers transition their programs from OS 9 to Mac OS X. Most new Mac programs rely on the Cocoa framework rather than the Carbon framework. If you hear people talking about Cocoa programming, they're just talking about Mac OS X programming using the Cocoa framework.

After you choose the Cocoa Application template, Xcode will ask for the name of your project. Type a descriptive name for your project, and click the Next button.

A Save dialog box appears, letting you name your project and choose the drive and folder to store your Xcode project. Select a folder, type a name (such as **Test**), and click the Save button. The Xcode window appears.

Examining Project Files in Xcode

When you choose a program template, Xcode creates a bare-bones, working program for you. To view the Objective-C code that your template already contains, you can click the list of folders displayed in the left pane of the Xcode window, as shown in Figure 2–5.

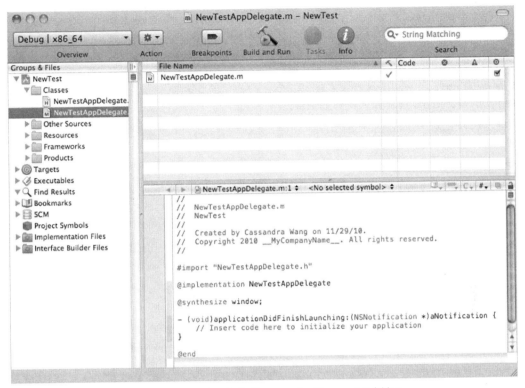

Figure 2–5. *Every Xcode project consists of multiple files organized in separate folders.*

You can actually put any file in any folder, regardless of the folder's name. However, it's a good idea to keep files stored in specific folders based on their purpose, which are as follows:

- *Classes*: Holds the files that contain Objective-C code.

- *Other Sources*: Holds Objective-C files necessary for creating your program, but you'll almost never need to look at, let alone edit, any of the files stored in this folder.

- *Resources*: Holds files containing information about your program as well as files (named *xib files*) that define your user interface.

- *Frameworks*: Lists all the frameworks that your program uses when it runs.

- *Products*: Holds the actual program file that you can give to others.

To view the contents of any folder, click the gray arrow (called a *disclosure triangle*) that appears to the left of that folder. To hide the contents of any folder, click the gray downward-pointing arrow to the left of that folder.

The two folders you'll open and add files to most often are the Classes and Resources folders. The Classes folder holds all your Objective-C code, while the Resources folder holds all your user interface files.

Each time you select a file within a folder, Xcode displays the contents of that file in the middle window. If you open the Classes folder and click a file stored in that folder, you'll see a file containing Objective-C code.

If you now open the Resources folder and click the `MainMenu.xib` file, you'll see the user interface for your program, which will initially be blank.

> **NOTE:** User interface files have the file extension of `.xib`, which stands for Xcode Interface Builder. User interface files are also called *nib* files, which stands for NeXT Interface Builder. NeXT stands for NeXTSTEP, which is the operating system that Apple used to create Mac OS X. Apple simply improved the NeXT Interface Builder program and renamed it Interface Builder.

Compiling a Program

When you create a new Xcode project and choose a template such as the Cocoa Applications template, Xcode creates a skeleton program. Without writing a single Objective-C command, your Xcode project already contains enough code to create a bare-bones user interface that consists of pull-down menus and windows that you can move, resize, close, or open.

To compile and run an Xcode project, you need to choose the Build and Run command, which you can choose by doing one of the following:

- Click the Build and Run icon.
- Choose Build ➤ Build and Run.
- Press ⌘Return.

If you choose the Build and Run command to compile and run a program, based on the Cocoa Applications template, you'll see that program's pull-down menus plus a window on the screen, as shown in Figure 2–6.

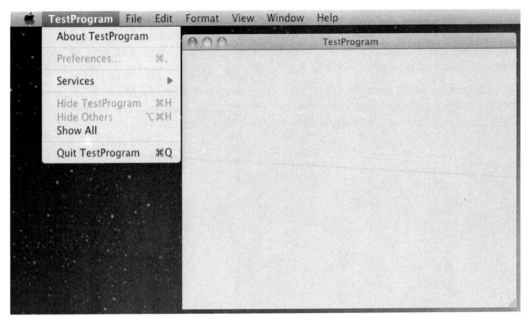

Figure 2–6. *The Cocoa Applications template creates a program with a simple user interface.*

Click any of the pull-down menus, and move or resize the window. Notice that your program behaves like a typical Mac OS X program, and you haven't even written a single line of Objective-C code yet. When you chose to use a Cocoa Applications template, Xcode created a skeleton Mac OS X program that already knows how to work. All you have to do is provide the custom instructions to make the program solve your specific task. When you're done toying with your Mac OS X program, choose the Quit command just as you would do in any Mac OS X program.

By using program templates, you can create a working program without writing a single line of code whatsoever. This is one of the ways that Xcode makes Mac programming easy for you.

Summary

To write Mac programs, you'll be spending most of your time using Xcode. With Xcode, you can write and edit Objective-C code, design a user interface, and run your program to make sure it works or fix problems if it doesn't work.

Just remember that you don't need to learn every feature in Xcode to start using it. Just as staring at all the instruments crammed into the cockpit of a 747 jumbo jet might seem intimidating, so might Xcode's initial appearance frighten you with its apparent complexity. Just focus on the features you'll need and use the most, and ignore those features you don't need until you eventually understand and want to use them.

Xcode is your primary tool for creating Mac programs, so you'll be spending a lot of time using this program. The more you use Xcode, the more comfortable and familiar the program will get. Pretty soon you'll find yourself spending more of your time using Xcode and less of your time trying to figure out how to do something useful with it.

This chapter is meant as an introduction to Xcode so you know what you're looking at and the purpose of each feature. In the next chapter, you'll actually use Xcode to create small programs that can give you a taste of what Mac programming is really all about.

Chapter 3

The Basic Steps to Creating a Mac Program

The two basic steps needed to create a Mac program involve designing your user interface and writing Objective-C code to make your program actually do something. Although you can design your user interface first and then write your Objective-C code (or vice versa), it's more likely that you'll switch between both tasks as you gradually add features to your program. Before you start writing a program, the most important first step is to decide what you want your program to do and how you want it to look. Take a moment, sit down with a pencil and paper, and decide exactly what you want your program to do.

Once you know what you want your program to do, you'll know what type of data it needs and how it needs to manipulate that data to create the desired result. After you know this crucial information, you can sketch out the user interface to accept data and display a useful result to the user.

These are the four basic steps needed to create any program:

1. Design the user interface.

2. Write code to make your program do something.

3. Connect your user interface to your code so your user interface can control your code and your code can display information to the user interface.

4. Test and debug your program until it finally works.

In this chapter, we'll focus on the first three, with an emphasis on connecting your user interface to your code in a succeeding version of a sample program. Just remember that there is no best way to create any program. Throughout this book you'll see sample programs, but these programs could have been written a million different ways. The purpose of these sample programs is to show you the basic principles of how different features of Mac programming work. Once you understand these principles, you'll be able to use them to write your own programs.

To learn any programming languages, most programmers start by creating a simple "Hello, world!" program, which displays the message "Hello, world!" on the screen. So, we'll start with one such example before addressing the basic steps. The purpose of such a simple program is to show how a complete (but short) program works in a particular programming language and how that specific language uses different methods to display data to the user.

A Bare-Bones Program Example

Creating a typical "Hello, world!" program can show you three important parts about Mac programming.

> **NOTE:** Chapter 5 will go into more detail about writing Objective-C code. For right now, the Objective-C code you'll create in this chapter will be simple enough that you'll be able to type them without necessarily understanding how they work, although you'll be able to figure out what they do.

First, you'll learn how to use Objective-C to display a message. Second, you'll learn how a Mac program can run commands based on an event that occurs. Finally, you'll start getting familiar with the basic steps and commands needed to create a program using Xcode.

To create your first real Mac program, follow these steps:

1. Create a new project in Xcode. If you start up Xcode, a dialog box appears where you can choose to create a new project (see Figure 2-3 in the previous chapter). Otherwise, if Xcode is already running, choose File ➤ New Project, or press ⇧⌘N. A dialog box appears letting you choose a project template.

2. Click Application under the Mac OS X category in the left pane of the dialog box.

3. Click Cocoa Application in the right pane of the dialog box, and then click the Next button. A new dialog box appears, asking for the product name.

4. Type any name, such as **TestProgram**, and click the Next button. A Save As dialog box appears.

5. Choose the drive and folder to store your Xcode project, and click the Save button. Xcode saves your new project.

6. Click the gray arrow (called a *disclosure triangle*) that appears to the left of the Classes folder in the left pane of the Xcode window. Two files appear named TestProgramAppDelegate.h and TestProgramAppDelegate.m. (If you named your project something other than TestProgram, your chosen name will appear as part of the file name instead.)

7. Click the `TestProgramAppDelegate.m` file. The Objective-C code in that file appears as shown in Figure 3–1.

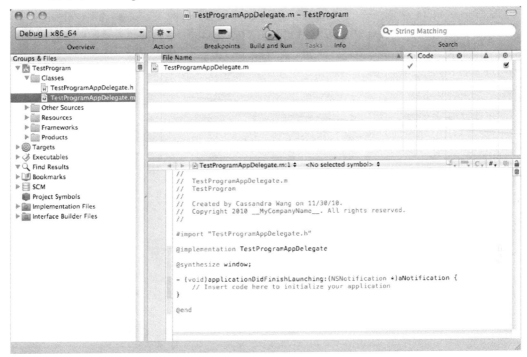

Figure 3–1. *Clicking a file displays its contents in the middle pane of the Xcode window.*

8. Move the cursor in front of the two slashes that appear to the left of the text that reads "Insert code here to initialize your application."

9. Type the following (make sure you type it exactly with the same uppercase and lowercase characters):

```
NSLog (@"Hello, world!");
```

What you're doing is adding a line of code to a subprogram named `applicationDidFinishLoading`. This subprogram runs only when a certain event occurs. In this case, this subprogram runs when your program (or application) successfully starts.

The keyword `NSLog` is an Objective-C command that displays a string of characters—in this case, "Hello, world!" The entire subprogram should look like this:

```
- (void)applicationDidFinishLaunching:(NSNotification *)aNotification {

    NSLog (@"Hello, world!"); // Insert code here to initialize your application
}
```

To help identify different parts of your Objective-C code, Xcode highlights different commands in colors. Although there are more symbols, commands, and characters that may not make sense to you at this time, the main point to learn is just that this is a subprogram that runs when your program first starts.

10. Choose File ➤ Save or press ⌘S to save your changes. To see your program work, click the Build and Run button, or choose Build ➤ Build and Run.

If you mistyped something or forgot a punctuation mark, such as the semicolon, Xcode will display an error message, as shown in Figure 3–2.

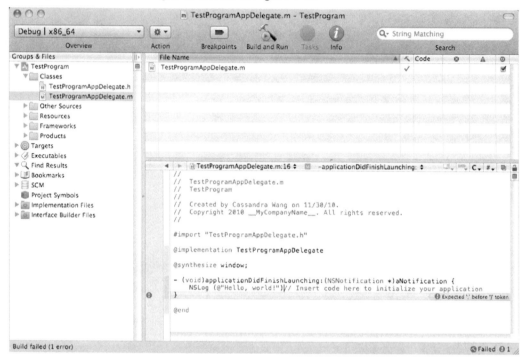

Figure 3–2. *Xcode can alert you to errors or problems in your code.*

If you did type everything correctly, Xcode will compile and run your program, displaying a window with pull-down menus at the top of the screen. In case you're wondering why you can't see the "Hello, world!" message, it's because the command you wrote prints to a special screen called the Log or Console, which does not appear on the Mac user interface. To view the log, you need to do the following:

1. Quit the currently running test program.

2. Click the Xcode icon on the Dock to make the Xcode window appear.

3. Choose Run ➤ Console, or press ⇧⌘R. The Debugger Console window displays the log window. If you look for the bold text, the "Hello, world!" message appears there, as shown in Figure 3–3.

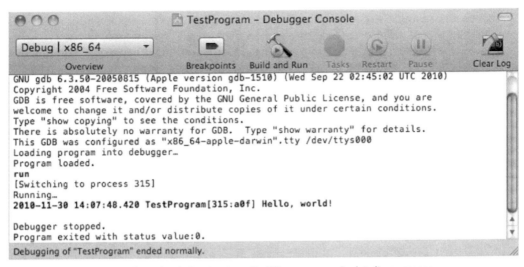

```
GNU gdb 6.3.50-20050815 (Apple version gdb-1510) (Wed Sep 22 02:45:02 UTC 2010)
Copyright 2004 Free Software Foundation, Inc.
GDB is free software, covered by the GNU General Public License, and you are
welcome to change it and/or distribute copies of it under certain conditions.
Type "show copying" to see the conditions.
There is absolutely no warranty for GDB.  Type "show warranty" for details.
This GDB was configured as "x86_64-apple-darwin".tty /dev/ttys000
Loading program into debugger…
Program loaded.
run
[Switching to process 315]
Running…
2010-11-30 14:07:48.420 TestProgram[315:a0f] Hello, world!

Debugger stopped.
Program exited with status value:0.
```

Figure 3–3. *The Debugger Console window is where the* NSLog *command prints its messages.*

There are four lessons you should learn from this brief exercise. First, you must type Objective-C code exactly right using both uppercase and lowercase characters. If you mistype a command and use the wrong case (such as uppercase instead of lowercase, or vice versa), your program will not work. That's because Objective-C considers uppercase and lowercase characters to be completely different, so a lowercase *a* is as different from an uppercase *A* as the letter *Z* is completely different from the letter *T*. Typing Objective-C commands incorrectly is the most common source of errors.

Second, to define the end of each Objective-C line, you must use a semicolon. If you forget this semicolon, your program will not work correctly. Omitting the semicolon is another common source of errors.

Third, the NSLog command displays text to the Debugger Console window, but not to the Mac screen. The Debugger Console window often displays messages that explain what your program has done, which can be useful later when you're testing your program to make sure it's working.

Fourth, a Mac program is typically divided into subprograms that respond to different types of events. In this example, you wrote a command inside a subprogram that ran only when a certain event occurred. In this case, the event is when your program first loads and runs.

Although this may seem like a simple example, it's already taught you much about how Mac programming works using Xcode.

A Simple User Interface Example

By using the NSLog command, you can verify that certain parts of your program are actually running. In a normal program, you would delete these NSLog commands before giving your program to others.

Of course, displaying messages to the Debugger Console window is meant for the programmer to see, not for the user of your program to see. In today's world of computers, nearly every program displays and accepts information through a graphical user interface (GUI) consisting of pull-down menus, windows, and buttons. In this exercise, you'll display "Hello, world!" on your program's user interface by modifying the project you created in the previous section of this chapter.

1. Close or hide the Debugger Console window so you can see the Xcode window displaying your list of files and folders that make up your program.

2. Click the gray arrow (disclosure triangle) that appears to the left of the Resources folder. A list of files appears including one named MainMenu.xib, which is the file that contains your program's user interface. (Programs can contain more than one .xib file to create multiple user interfaces, but this simple program needs only one user interface and hence only one .xib file.)

3. Double-click the MainMenu.xib icon. The Interface Builder window appears, as shown in Figure 3–4.

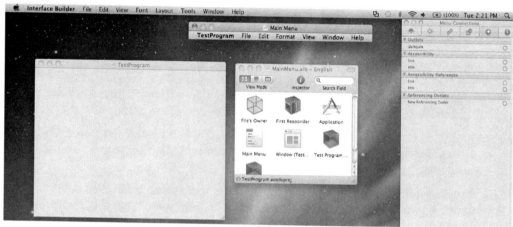

Figure 3–4. *The Interface Builder screen is where you design your program's user interface.*

4. Choose Tools ➤ Library. The Library window appears, as shown in Figure 3–5.

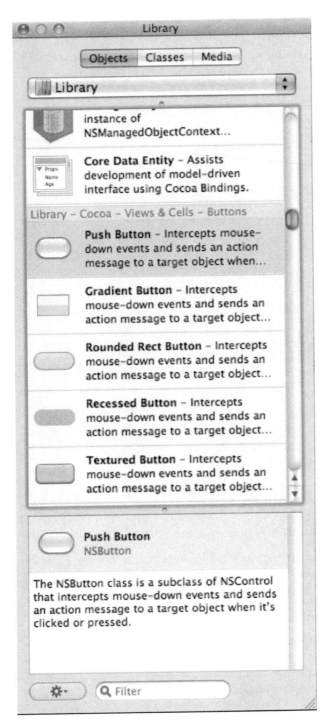

Figure 3–5. *The Library window provides objects you can place on your user interface.*

5. Scroll through the Object Library window until you find an object called Label.

6. Drag the Label object from the Library window to the inside of the window that appears in the middle pane of the Xcode window, as shown in Figure 3–6.

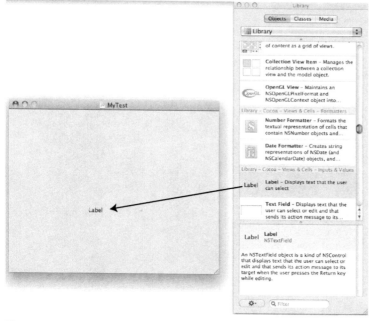

Figure 3–6. *Dragging a Label object places it on your program's user interface.*

7. Double-click the Label object you just placed on your user interface. Xcode highlights the text inside the label.

8. Type **Hello, world!** and press Return. The words "Hello, world!" now appear in the label.

9. Choose File ➤ Save or press ⌘S to save your changes.

10. Switch back to the Xcode, and click the Build and Run button or choose Build ➤ Build and Run. Your program's user interface appears, displaying the text "Hello, world!" inside its window.

11. Quit the program to return to the Xcode window.

In this short example, you learned that Xcode stores your user interface as a .xib file, stored inside the Resources folder. To view and modify your user interface, you have to open the .xib file. Large programs may have multiple .xib files, but a simple program needs only one .xib file since it needs only one user interface.

Your user interface consists of multiple parts such as a window (for displaying information) and pull-down menus. In this example, you only modified the window portion of the user interface by clicking the Window icon that appears among other icons.

To customize your user interface, you had to open the Library window and choose to view the Object Library, which contains common user interface items such as buttons and text fields. In this example, you dragged a Label object onto the user interface window and then customized the text inside that label to display "Hello, world!"

An Interactive User Interface Example

Using a label on the user interface to display text might work, but it's a static, fixed solution. To change the text displayed, you have to modify the label on the user interface. A more flexible solution is to allow the user interface to accept and display different types of text without having to edit the user interface directly.

In this example, you'll customize the same program you edited from the previous section in this chapter, but you'll add a button that users can click. When the user clicks the button, the text in the label will change.

1. Click the gray arrow (disclosure triangle) that appears to the left of the Resources folder in the Xcode window. (You may be able to skip this step if a list of files already appears.)

2. Click the `MainMenu.xib` icon. The Interface Builder screen appears (shown in Figure 3–4).

3. Choose Tools ➤ Library. (You may be able to skip this step if the Library window already appears.)

4. Scroll through the Object Library list until you find the Push Button object.

5. Drag the Push Button object and place it anywhere on your program's window near the label object.

6. Double-click the text that appears on the Push Button object and type **Good-bye**. Then press Return.

7. Choose File ➤ Save, or press ⌘S to save your changes.

At this point, you've created a push button on your user interface, but it won't do anything. To make the push button work, you need to complete two additional tasks. First, you need to write a subprogram filled with instructions or code that tells the computer what to do if the user clicks that push button. In Objective-C, subprograms are called *methods*, so in technical terms, you have to create a push button method.

Second, you need to "connect" your method to the actual push button on your user interface. Connecting your method to your user interface push button tells Xcode to run the connected method whenever the user clicks that particular push button.

Writing Objective-C Code

The goal is to make the push button change the currently displayed text in the label. To do this, you need to write two types of Objective-C code called *Actions* and *Outlets*. An Action responds to something from the user interface, such as the user clicking a push button. An Outlet connects to a user interface item such as displaying text in a label object.

To define an Action, you'll need to write a method and fill it with Objective-C code that tells the computer what to do if the user does something. In this case, you'll be creating a method to respond when the user clicks the push button.

To make your user interface display information through an Outlet, you need to declare a variable as an Outlet. Then you'll have to define which part of your user interface is connected to that particular variable.

Creating an Action Method

There are three steps to creating an Action method:

1. Declare the name of your method.

2. Write the code that makes your method work.

3. Connect your Objective-C method to your user interface object, such as a push button.

If you peek into the Classes folder of your project, you'll see two identically named files (such as TestProgramAppDelegate.h and TestProgramAppDelegate.m). The .h file is known as a *header* file, and the .m file is known as the *implementation* file.

The header (.h) file defines all the methods and variables (called *properties*) that other parts of the program need to know about.

The implementation (.m) file defines all the details of your methods, which is actually hidden from the rest of your program.

So to write a method, you'll need to first declare just that method name in the header (.h) file, and then you have to write the actual method code in the implementation (.m) file.

After you've done this, you'll be ready for the third and final step of connecting your method to your user interface object, such as a push button.

To create the Action method for the push button on your user interface, follow these steps:

1. Switch to the Xcode window, and click the TestProgramAppDelegate.h file stored in the Classes folder. The Objective-C code for this file appears.

2. Type the following bold text in the existing Objective-C code:

```
@interface TestProgramAppDelegate : NSObject <NSApplicationDelegate> {

    NSWindow *window;
    NSTextField *message;
}

@property (assign) IBOutlet NSWindow *window;
@property (assign) IBOutlet NSTextField *message;

-(IBAction)goodBye:(id)sender;

@end
```

Here's what you just typed:

- NSTextField *message: This declares a variable called message, which can display data in the Label user interface object. (The Label user interface object is based on another object called NSTextField.)

- @property (assign) IBOutlet NSTextField *message;: This defines the variable message as a property that other parts of your program can use to retrieve information out of the message variable or store information into the message variable. Note the keyword IBOutlet, which lets you know that the variable is meant for displaying information as an Outlet to a user interface object.

- -(IBAction)goodBye:(id)sender;: This declares your Action method for the push button on your user interface. The name goodBye is the name of the method and is completely arbitrary; feel free to use a name of your own choosing.

After typing these three lines of Objective-C code into the header (.h) file, you need to save this file by choosing File ➤ Save or pressing ⌘S. Then you need to finish defining your Outlets and Actions in the implementation (.m) file:

1. Click the TestProgramAppDelegate.m file stored in the Classes folder. The Objective-C code for this file appears in the middle pane of the Xcode window.

2. Type the following bold text in the existing Objective-C code:

```
#import "TestProgramAppDelegate.h"
@implementation TestProgramAppDelegate
@synthesize window;
@synthesize message;

- (void)applicationDidFinishLaunching:(NSNotification *)aNotification {

    NSLog (@"Hello, world!"); // Insert code here to initialize your application
}
 - (void)dealloc {
        [window release];
     [super dealloc];
}
-(IBAction)goodBye:(id)sender
{
```

```
      message.stringValue = @"Good-bye";
}
```

@end

The @synthesize message; line lets your program read and save data in the message variable.

> **NOTE:** In other object-oriented programming languages, you often have to write two additional methods called a *setter* and a *getter*. The setter method lets you store data in the variable, and the getter method lets you read data from the variable. To avoid making you write these two separate methods yourself, Xcode lets you use the @synthesize command, which duplicates the features of the setter and getter methods without making you write out the ugly details.

```
-(IBAction)goodBye:(id)sender
{
      message.stringValue = @"Good-bye";
}
```

This Action method (defined by the IBAction keyword) holds only a single line of code between the curly brackets. This line of code simply stores the string "Good-bye" in a message variable. The message variable is an Outlet to a user interface object, so it holds the actual string in a property called the stringValue.

Save this file by choosing File ➤ Save or pressing ⌘S. To finish, you need to "connect" this Objective-C code to your user interface to make everything actually work.

Connecting the User Interface

At this point, all you've done is write Objective-C code in the header (.h) and implementation (.m) files. However, your user interface has no idea that all of this newly added Objective-C code even exists. To fix this problem, you'll need to "connect" your Outlets and Actions.

Connecting an Outlet to a user interface means selecting a variable name and dragging the mouse to connect a line between the variable name and a user interface object to display the data.

Connecting an Action to a user interface means selecting the name of an Action method and dragging the mouse to connect a line between the Action method name and a user interface object, such as a push button object.

To connect Actions and Outlets to your user interface, you need to follow these steps:

1. Double-click the MainMenu.xib file stored in the Resources folder in the Xcode window. The Interface Builder windows appear.

Right-click the Test Program App Delegate blue cube icon inside the
MainMenu.xib window. A heads-up display window appears, as shown in Figure
3–7.

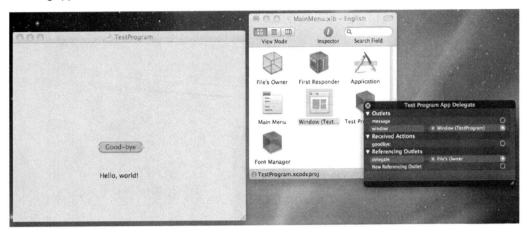

Figure 3–7. *Right-clicking an icon displays a window.*

2. Move the mouse pointer over the little circle that appears to the right of the
    message (under the Outlets heading) at the top of the window. Drag the mouse
    over the Label object on the user interface, and release the mouse button, as
    shown in Figure 3–8.

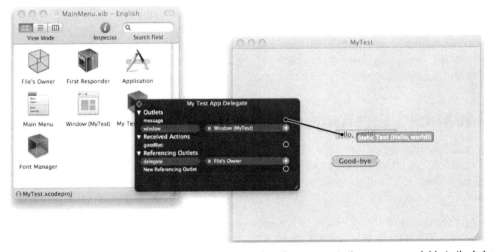

Figure 3–8. *Dragging from the Outlet circle to the user interface connects the message variable to the Label
object.*

3. Move the mouse pointer over the little circle that appears to the right of the goodBye method name (under the Received Actions heading). Drag the mouse over the push button object on the user interface, and release the mouse button, as shown in Figure 3–9.

Figure 3–9. *Dragging from the Actions circle to the user interface connects the Action method to the push button object.*

After you have connected your user interface to your Objective-C code (Outlets and Actions), save your program by choosing File ➤ Save or pressing ⌘S to save your changes.

Then switch back to Xcode, and click the Build and Run button or choose Build ➤ Build and Run. When your program's user interface appears, click the Good-bye button, and the text in the label changes from "Hello, world!" to "Good-bye."

An Advanced Interactive User Interface Example

The previous sample program showed how to respond to an Action (the user clicking the push button) and how to display data through an Outlet (displaying text inside the label object). The next step in designing a user interfaces is to learn how to retrieve information from the user.

Displaying the message "Good-bye" in the label every time you click the push button isn't very flexible. Whenever you write code that has data written directly in its instructions, that's referred to as *hard-coding*, which means the code can only do the same thing over and over again until you change the code.

Hard-coding isn't necessarily bad, but it limits the versatility of your program. A better solution is to make your code work with any type of data. In this example, you'll be adding a text field to your user interface. When the user clicks the push button, the text from the text field will appear in the label (instead of repetitively displaying "good-bye" in the label each time).

You can complete this next sample program in several ways. First, you can draw a text field on your user interface, go back and define an Outlet for that text field in Objective-C, and then go back to your user interface and connect the text field on the user interface to the Outlet you defined in Objective-C code. Constantly switching back and forth between your user interface and your Objective-C code might seem cumbersome, so a second way is to focus on one task at a time by planning ahead.

Any time you need to either display or retrieve data, you need an Outlet so you can declare an Outlet in your Objective-C code. Then you can view your user interface, add a text field, and connect the text field to your newly created Outlet.

Either method works; it all depends on how you like to work. The three basic steps are as follows:

1. Draw a text field on the user interface.

2. Declare an Outlet to hold the data in the text field.

3. Connect the Outlet to the text field on the user interface.

To create an Outlet, you need to edit the Objective-C code by following these steps:

1. Switch to Xcode, and click the `TestProgramAppDelegate.h` file in the Classes folder. The Objective-C code for that file appears.

2. Type the following bold text in the existing Objective-C code:

```
@interface TestProgramAppDelegate : NSObject <NSApplicationDelegate> {

    NSWindow *window;
    NSTextField *message;
    NSTextField *inputData;
}

@property (assign) IBOutlet NSWindow *window;
@property (assign) IBOutlet NSTextField *message;
@property (assign) IBOutlet NSTextField *inputData;

-(IBAction)goodBye:(id)sender;

@end
```

3. Choose File ➤ Save or press ⌘S to save your changes.

4. Click the `TestProgramAppDelegate.m` file in the Classes folder. The Objective-C code for that file appears.

5. Type the following bold text in the existing Objective-C code:

```
@implementation TestProgramAppDelegate

@synthesize window;
@synthesize message;
```

```
@synthesize inputData;

- (void)applicationDidFinishLaunching:(NSNotification *)aNotification {

    NSLog (@"Hello, world!"); // Insert code here to initialize your application
}

-(IBAction)goodBye:(id)sender
{
    message.stringValue = inputData.stringValue;
}

@end
```

Inside the goodBye Action method, you'll need to delete this line:

```
message.stringValue = @"Good-bye";
```

6. Choose File ➤ Save, or press ⌘S to save your changes.

After you declared your Outlet in both the header (.h) and implementation (.m) files, you'll need to modify your user interface.

> **NOTE:** When switching between Xcode to edit your Objective-C code and Interface Builder to design your user interface, always make sure to save all changes in one program before switching to the other. So if you edit your Objective-C code, save your changes before switching to Interface Builder (and vice versa). If you fail to save your changes, Xcode may not notice any changes you made in Interface Builder and Interface Builder may not notice any changes you made in Xcode. The result is that you could make a change, and then run your program but your program doesn't reflect any changes you made, which can give the illusion that your changes aren't working.

1. Double-click the MainMenu.xib file stored in the Resources folder.

2. Scroll through the Object Library window, and drag a Text Field object to your user interface. If the Object Library window isn't visible, choose Tools ➤ Library.

3. Right-click the Test Program App Delegate icon. A pop-up window appears.

4. Move the mouse pointer over the little circle to the right of the inputData Outlet, and drag the mouse over the text field you just placed on the user interface, as shown in Figure 3–10.

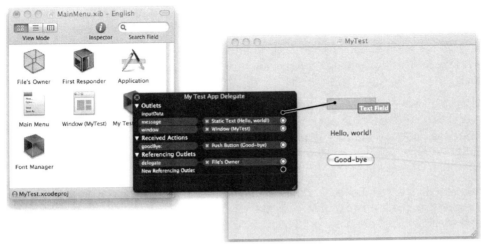

Figure 3–10. *Dragging from the* inputData *circle to the text field connects the text field to the* inputData *Outlet defined in your Objective-C code.*

5. Choose File ➤ Save or press ⌘S to save your changes.

After you have connected the text field on the user interface to your Objective-C code and saved your program, switch back to Xcode, click the Build and Run button, or choose Build ➤ Build and Run. When your program's user interface appears, click in the text field, type any text you want, and then click the Good-bye button. The label now displays the text you typed into the text field.

Summary

In this chapter, you learned how to create a simple "Hello, world!" program that displays text. Initially, you learned how to use the NSLog command to display text, although the NSLog command merely sends data to a special Debugger Console window, not to the program's user interface. Although you won't be using the NSLog command to interact with the user, you can use the NSLog command to help test your program.

With each succeeding version of the sample program, you gradually learned how to create and display data on your program's user interface. First, your program's user interface gets stored as a .xib file in the Resources folder. Larger, more complicated programs may have several .xib files to create a more sophisticated user interface, but this sample program just uses a single .xib file because it only needs a simple user interface.

Your user interface consists of pull-down menus and windows. To design the items that appear on the window, you need to click the Window icon to view the window in the Xcode window.

Next, you need to open the Object Library window and drag objects (such as labels, buttons, or text fields) onto the window of your user interface. Later, you'll learn how to precisely align user interface objects, but for now, you just need to know how to drag items from the Object Library window and place them on the user interface window.

To customize the appearance of some user interface objects, you can double-click the text they display. This lets you edit the existing text or replace it with new text altogether.

After designing your user interface, the last step is to link your user interface to your Objective-C code. For each object on your user interface that needs to either display data or retrieve data that the user typed in, you'll need to create an Outlet variable. For each Outlet variable, you'll need to write Objective-C code in the header (.h) file and the implementation (.m) file.

In the header (.h) file, you'll need to declare a variable and then declare a variable as an Outlet property. In the implementation (.m) file, you'll need to use the @synthesize command to allow other parts of your program to store and retrieve data from that variable.

For each user interface object that provides a command to the user, you'll need to create an Action method that contains one or more instructions that tell your program what to do when the user gives a command, such as clicking a push button. You need to declare the name of your Action method in the header (.h) file and then write the actual method code in the implementation (.m) file.

Finally, you'll need to right-click the icon that represents the files where you wrote and stored your Outlet and Action code. This displays a window that lets you drag to a user interface object and connect the user interface object to a specific Outlet or Action.

Although you created only a simple program and modified it, you can already see the basic steps needed to create any Mac program using Xcode. Mac programming is a combination of writing Objective-C code and designing your user interface.

Getting Help

Chapter **4**

Nobody knows everything, which is why everyone may need help writing programs once in a while. Sometimes you may need help just figuring out how to use Xcode. Other times you may need help creating your program by looking for a specific Objective-C command or using a specific user interface object.

Of course, one of the most reliable places to look for help is to search for your problem on the Internet. Most likely, someone else has already run into your problem and has already stumbled across an answer. There are also multiple programming forums where you can post questions and get a response fairly quickly, depending on the nature of your question.

Unfortunately, you can't always rely on the Internet to help you find the answers to your problems. Sometimes people won't know the answer. Other times you can't afford to wait a day or two until someone responds. In these situations, you need to know how to find help on your own right away. When you might know what you want to do but have no idea how to do it, that's when you need to turn to Xcode's help system.

Installing Help Topics

Xcode provides help on a variety of topics, but to avoid overwhelming you with all available help topics, Xcode organizes help into topics such as iOS (for iPhone and iPad programming) and Mac OS X (for Mac programming). To ensure that you have the help topics for Mac OS X, you may need to load the Mac OS X help by following these steps:

1. Choose Xcode ➤ Preferences. The Xcode Preferences window appears.

2. Click the Documentation icon at the top of the window. (You may need to scroll these icons to the right to find the Documentation icon.)

3. Click the Documentation Sets tab, as shown in Figure 4–1.

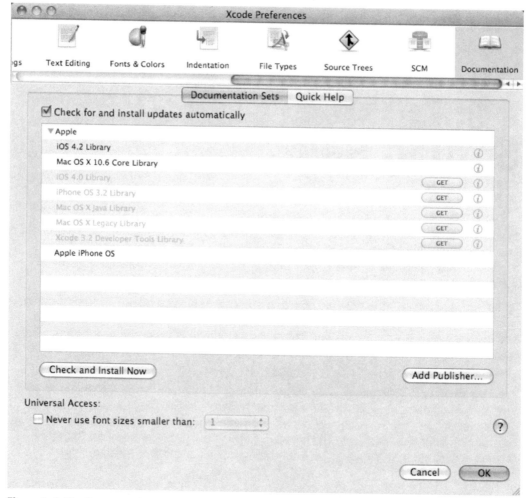

Figure 4–1. *The Documentation Sets tab reveals all the currently installed documentation topics.*

4. (Optional) Click the Get button next to a topic you want help on, such as Mac OS X Java Library or Xcode 3.2 Developer Tools Library.

5. Click the close button of the Xcode Preferences window to make it disappear.

Getting Help About Xcode

The easiest type of help to find is when you have questions about using Xcode such as how to use certain commands or how to modify the appearance of the Xcode window. When you need help on using Xcode, follow these steps:

1. Choose Help ➤ Xcode Help. The Developer Tools Reference Library window appears, as shown in Figure 4–2.

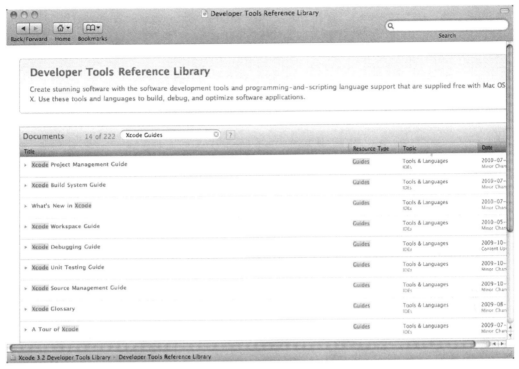

Figure 4–2. *The Developer Tools Reference Library window*

2. Click a displayed topic. The window displays details about your chosen topic.

3. (Optional) Click the Back and Forward arrows that appear in the upper-left corner of the window. This lets you quickly display information you've previously viewed.

Getting Help About Core Library

Using Objective-C and Xcode, anyone can write any type of program for the Mac. The problem is that when you need to do something routine such as saving a file to a disk or displaying a window on the screen, you would have to write your own Objective-C code to perform these common functions.

Not only does this mean you would have to spend time writing code to do routine tasks, but you'd also have to test these routines to make sure they work as well. With thousands of programmers creating their own routines, chances are good that one programmer's code to create windows won't look or work identically to another programmer's code to create and display those same type of windows.

To avoid this chaotic situation where everyone must essentially reinvent the wheel, Apple provides code stored in something called the Core Library. This collection of code performs common tasks. Just as a public library lets everyone read the same books, so does the Core Library let everyone use the same code. Any time you need to do a common task, such as save a file or play audio, chances are good that Apple has already written that code. All you need to do is figure out whether that code exists and, if it does, how to use it.

To browse through the Mac OS X Core Library, follow these steps:

1. Choose Help ➤ Xcode Help. The Organizer window appears, displaying the Xcode documentation files (see Figure 4–2).

2. Click the Home icon at the top of the left pane.

3. Click Mac OS X Core Library in the left pane.

4. Click the gray arrow (called a *disclosure triangle*) that appears to the left of the Mac OS X Core Library icon. A list of topics appears, as shown in Figure 4–3.

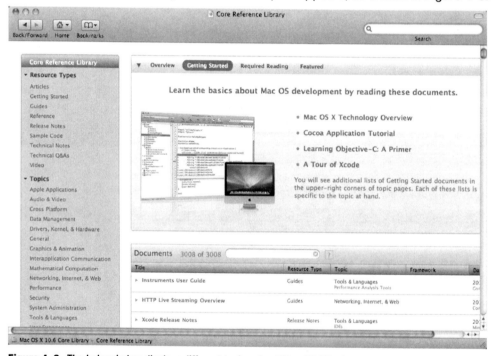

Figure 4–3. *The help window displays different topics about Mac OS X topic.*

5. Click the help you want to view. A list of help topic appears that you can choose.

When browsing through Xcode's Core Library help, you may see several different types of help screens:

Q&A

Tips

Sample programs

Class references

A Q&A help screen, as shown in Figure 4–4, answers a common question and provides detailed explanation for solving a specific type of problem.

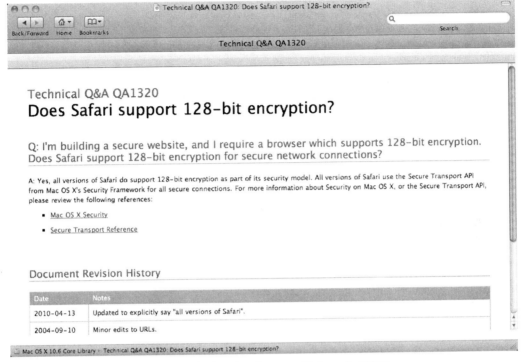

Figure 4–4. *A Q&A screen typically explains how to solve a specific type of problem.*

A tips help screen typically provides programming guidelines for designing your programs, as shown in Figure 4–5.

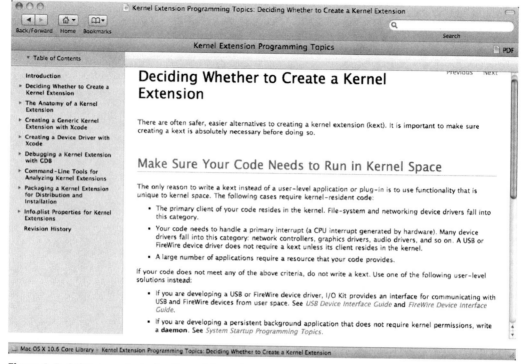

Figure 4–5. *A tips screen typically offers advice and tips for creating your program.*

A sample program help screen briefly describes what the sample program does and how it works so you can see whether it's something you want to study, as shown in Figure 4–6. Other screens might show the actual Objective-C code.

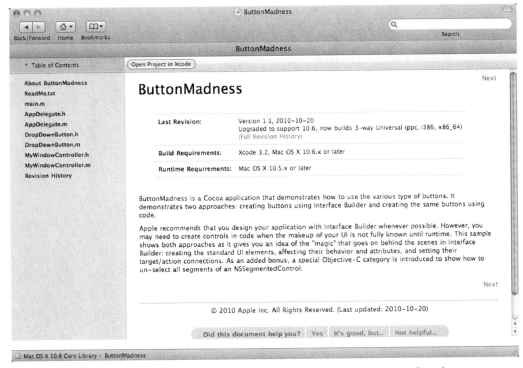

Figure 4–6. *A sample programs screen explains what the sample program does and how it works.*

A class reference screen provides detailed information about a class that performs a specific task, which you can use in your own programs. The class reference screen lists the properties and methods stored in that class as well as any related classes, as shown in Figure 4–7.

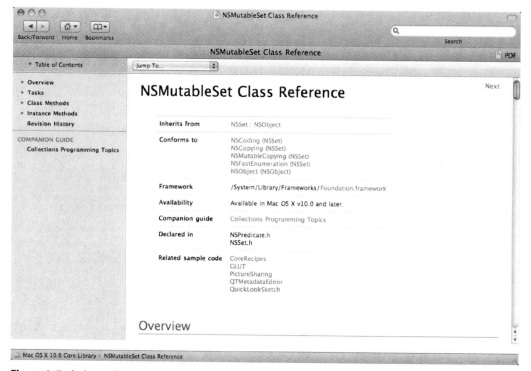

Figure 4–7. *A class reference screen provides programming details for how a particular class works and what it does.*

Searching for Help

Browsing through the Xcode help window can be a great way to stumble across interesting information about using Xcode or using Apple's Core Library. However, random browsing can be tedious and time-consuming. When you need help with a specific topic, it's much faster to search through the help screens and jump straight to the information you need.

To search for help, follow these steps:

1. Choose Help ➤ Xcode Help. The Reference Library window appears.

2. Click the Search field that appears in the upper-right corner of the Reference Library window, as shown in Figure 4–8.

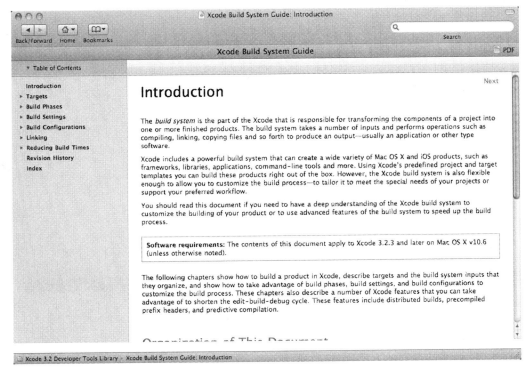

Figure 4–8. *The Search field where you can type a term or phrase*

3. Click in the Search field, type a term or phrase, and press Return. The Xcode window displays topics related to your query.

4. Click a topic to display information.

Getting Quick Help

One problem with using Xcode's help window is that you may be busy working on your program and need help on a particular Objective-C command right away. You could wade through the different Xcode help screens, or you could just use Xcode's Quick Help command instead.

Quick Help lets you select a command directly in your Objective-C code and display a tiny window of help, as shown in Figure 4–9. You can also get Quick Help by selecting an item on your user interface and choosing the Quick Help command.

Figure 4–9. *Quick Help displays a window near your selected command.*

To use Quick Help, follow these steps:

1. Click an Objective-C code file (either an .h or .m file), or click a .xib file that makes up your user interface.

2. Select an Objective-C command, or click a user interface object such as a button.

3. Choose Help ➤ Quick Help. A window appears, displaying help near your selected Objective-C command or user interface object.

Viewing Documentation for Selected Text

The Quick Help command lets you view a condensed version of information about commands or objects you select. However, if you need more detailed information about an Objective-C command, you can browse through the documentation yourself, which can be time-consuming and tedious. For a faster solution, just let Xcode show you the documentation for a specific command.

To view help for a specific Objective-C command, follow these steps:

1. Click an Objective-C code file (either an .h or .m file).

2. Select an Objective-C command.

3. Choose Help ➤ Find Documentation for Selected Text. The Organizer window appears, displaying help about your selected Objective-C command, as shown in Figure 4–10.

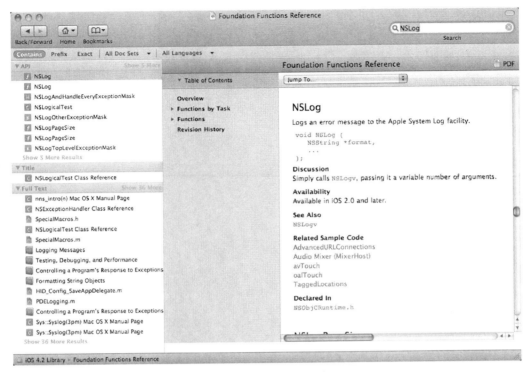

Figure 4–10. *You can highlight Objective-C code to view detailed help.*

Getting Help with Library Windows

When you're creating your program, you'll often use one of the Library windows to help you design your user interface. By clicking an item displayed in each Library window, you can view a window that explains the purpose of your selected item.

To get help with an item displayed in a Library window, follow these steps:

1. Switch to Interface Builder.

2. Choose Tools ➤ Library.

3. Click an item, and keep the mouse pointer over that item. Xcode displays a window that describes the purpose and function of your chosen item, as shown in Figure 4–11.

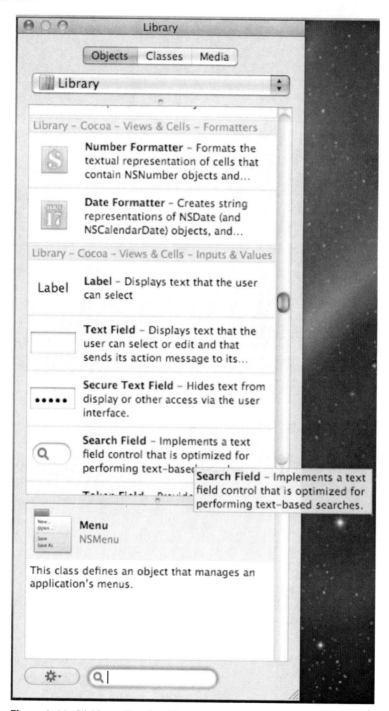

Figure 4–11. *Clicking an item in a Library window displays information about that item.*

Help While Writing Code

Even the most experienced programmer can make mistakes or forget how to spell or use a particular command. To help you write code easier and faster, Xcode provides several tools.

First, Xcode can color-code keywords and commands to make it easier to identify different parts of your code. Second, Xcode lets you modify the way the editor works so it displays code the way you like. In addition, Xcode also offers a code completion feature so you can start typing a command and have Xcode guess what command you might want to use.

Color-Coding

Xcode highlights Objective-C commands in different colors to help you identify the parts of your program. This feature is turned on by default, but you can turn it off or choose different color-coding schemes.

To modify the way Xcode displays code in different colors, follow these steps:

1. Choose Xcode ➤ Preferences. The Preferences window appears.

2. Click the Fonts & Colors icon to display the different color-coding options, as shown in Figure 4–12.

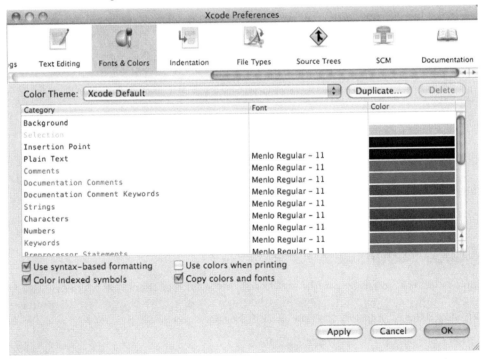

Figure 4–12. *The Fonts & Colors icon lets you choose or modify the way Xcode colors Objective-C commands.*

Customizing the Editor

The editor portion of Xcode is where you type Objective-C commands. To make editing simpler, you can turn on (or off) code completion, which is where Xcode tries to guess what command you're typing before you finish typing it all. In addition, you can also modify the way the editor displays your code such as changing how far it indents code or having the editor display line numbers to help you pinpoint a particular part of your program.

To modify the way the Xcode editor works, follow these steps:

1. Choose Xcode ➤ Preferences. The Preferences window appears.

2. Click the Text Editing icon to display the different editing options including code completion, as shown in Figure 4–13.

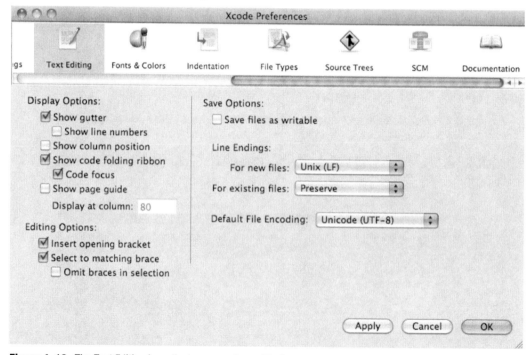

Figure 4–13. *The Text Editing icon displays ways to modify the appearance of Objective-C code in the editor.*

Using Code Completion

Code completion lets you type part of an Objective-C command and have Xcode display a likely command you may want. Then you just have to select the suggested command or keep typing if the suggested command isn't the one you want.

To use code completion, follow these steps:

1. Type a command. As soon as Xcode recognizes a valid command, it displays a possible command in faint text, as shown in Figure 4–14.

```
message.stringValue = inputData.stringValue;
NSLog( NSString *format )
```

Figure 4–14. *As you type, code completion displays a possible command.*

2. Choose one of the following options:

   a. If the suggested command is not what you want, keep typing, and Xcode may display another suggested command.

   b. If the suggested command is what you want, highlight it using the up/down arrow key, and then press Return key so Xcode types the rest of the suggested command automatically.

Through code completion, Xcode helps minimize typing errors and helps you write code faster and more accurately.

When writing Objective-C code, you often need to use curly brackets to group related code. Since multiple brackets can make identifying each pair of left and right brackets difficult, Xcode can highlight a matching bracket (or matching square bracket, or matching parenthesis) by following these steps:

1. Move the cursor to the left of a right bracket (}).

2. Press the right arrow key to move the cursor to the right of the right bracket (}). Xcode highlights the matching left bracket ({), as shown in Figure 4–15.

```
-(IBAction) goodBye:(id)sender
{
    message.stringValue = inputData.stringValue;
}
```

Figure 4–15. *Moving the cursor across a right bracket highlights its matching left bracket.*

Summary

Although there's no substitute for a book or someone by your side who can answer your question, you can often find the help you need by digging through Xcode's help documentation.

When you know what type of task you want to accomplish but don't know the exact command to use, you may want to browse through Xcode's help. By rummaging through the help documentation, you can find Apple's library of code that you can use in your own programs.

As a general rule, only write code that's unique to what your program needs to do. When you need to do a more general task, such as saving a file or displaying graphics on the screen, chances are good that Apple already provides code that does what you need, so all you need to do is find that proper command.

When designing your user interface, you'll often need to know which methods and properties are available. For example, if you want to know how to display text in a Label object, you need to know the property to use (stringValue).

To find the properties available in an object, click that item in the Library window to display a little window, which tells you what class that user interface object is based on. (In the case of a Label object, it's based on the NSTextField class.)

Once you know the class, you can search for that specific class to view a more detailed list of all the available methods and properties for that class.

Xcode tries to provide as much help as possible, but there's no substitute for just digging into your programs, making mistakes, and fumbling around for a while. Like learning any new skill, programming the Mac may feel strange and confusing initially, but the more you do it, the easier it will get. The key is to keep practicing a little bit each day until digging through Xcode's help documentation becomes second nature and understanding Xcode's help screens gradually becomes clear and actually understandable.

Chapter **5**

Learning Objective-C

In the old days of programming, you had to write code to create your user interface and then create your actual program. With Xcode, you can create your user interface without writing any code at all. However, to make your program do something, you'll still need to write code. Although you can theoretically use any programming language to create a Mac program, the language used most often (even by Apple's programmers themselves) for this task is Objective-C.

When learning any programming language, you must first learn the syntax, which defines how to write commands in a particular programming language. Then you need to learn how to do common tasks used to create a typical program.

If you're already familiar with another programming language, you can skim through this chapter to get acquainted with the way Objective-C works. However, if you've never used any programming language at all, then this chapter will explain the basics of programming the Mac using Objective-C.

Differences in Writing a Mac Objective-C Program

There's a big difference between writing a program in traditional Objective-C and writing a program in Objective-C for the Mac. When you write an ordinary Objective-C program, you have to write a main program that looks something like this:

```
int main( int argc, const char *argv[] ) {
    printf( "Hello, world!");
    return 0;
}
```

Every Objective-C program consists of a main program (identified by the keyword main). To make your program work, you have to write and store instructions in this main program.

In this example, there are only two instructions. One displays the message "Hello, world!" on the screen, and the second returns a 0, which essentially tells the operating system that the program ran successfully. In a more complex Objective-C program, you might have thousands of instructions stored in this main program or stored in multiple subprograms, which are called or run from within this main program.

A Mac Objective-C program also has a main program, but Xcode creates this main program for you automatically. Normally, you never even have to peek at this main program, let alone modify it. To examine this main program, open the Other Sources folder, and click the main.m file to view the code, as shown in Figure 5–1. This Mac Objective-C main programs looks like this:

```
int main(int argc, char *argv[])
{
    return NSApplicationMain(argc,  (const char **) argv);
```

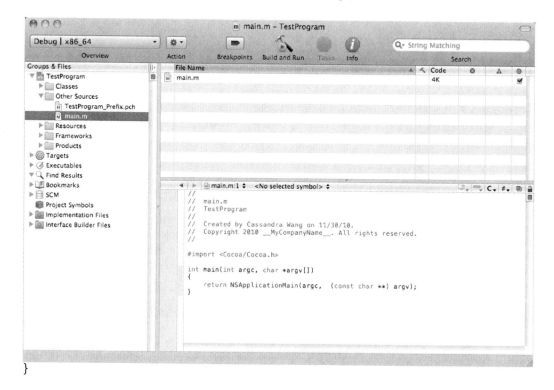

}

Figure 5–1. The main.m file appears in the Other Sources folder.

Essentially, the main program consists of a single line of code, which loads the main user interface file (typically called MainMenu.xib). When the main program runs, it also runs any instructions stored inside a method called applicationDidFinishLaunching, which appears in the AppDelegate.m file inside the Classes folder, as shown in Figure 5–2.

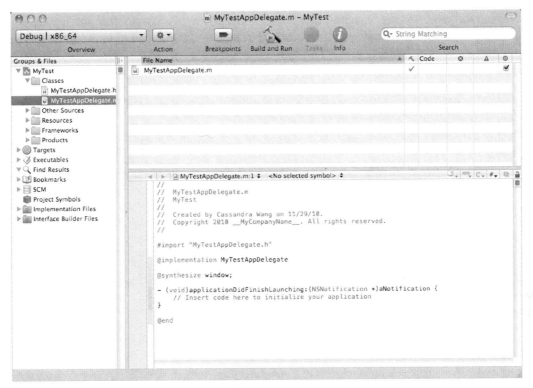

Figure 5–2. The `AppDelegate.m` file is where you can write methods for responding to events.

When you need to write code to do something right away, you need to store this code in this `AppDelegate.m` file's `applicationDidFinishLaunching` method:

```
- (void)applicationDidFinishLaunching:(NSNotification *)aNotification {
    NSLog (@"Hello, world!");
}
```

In a traditional Objective-C program, you have to write a main program and fill it with instructions written in Objective-C. In a Mac Objective-C program, Xcode creates your main program automatically, so you just need to write instructions in other files, such as the `AppDelegate` files (created automatically by Xcode) or any additional files you create.

Understanding Objective-C Symbols

In comparing a traditional Objective-C program with a Mac Objective-C program, you may notice the different commands in printing "Hello, world!" on the screen. In a traditional C program, you might use the `printf` command. In a Mac Objective-C program, you can use `printf`, but you'll more commonly use `NSLog`.

The `printf` command normally prints to the screen, but with a Mac program, you actually need to print to the user interface or to the Log or Console window, which is what the `NSLog` command does.

The second difference is that the `printf` command prints any data that appears inside quotation marks. The NSLog command does that as well but requires that the @ symbol appears in front of the data inside the quotation marks:

```
NSLog (@"This prints a message.");
```

When writing Mac Objective-C programs, you'll see this @ symbol often, which identifies commands that are unique to Objective-C and not found in traditional C programs.

Rather than just print text using the NSLog command, you may need to print different types of data. To do this, you'll have to use the % symbol followed by a single letter that identifies the type of data to print. The three most common types of data you can print are as follows:

- `%i`: Prints integer values such as `34`, `192`, and `5`
- `%f`: Prints floating-point values such as `54.903` and `2.14`
- `%@`: Prints objects such as strings like `@"Hello, world"`

When printing data with the NSLog command, you need to specify the type of data to print along with the actual data:

```
NSLog (@"Print an integer = %i", 34);
```

This command would simply print this:

```
Print an integer = 34
```

Some other symbols you'll often see in an Objective-C program include the semicolon (;), curly brackets ({ }), number sign (#), double slash (//), asterisk (*), and square brackets ([ ]). Although such symbols may look cryptic, they all serve a specific purpose. By understanding what these different symbols do, you can better decipher Objective-C code and understand how it works, even if you don't know exactly what the code does.

Defining the End of Each Line with a Semicolon

Every program consists of instructions or code. A simple program might have only one line of code, but most programs have hundreds, if not thousands or even millions, of lines of code. To help the compiler understand where each line of code ends, you have to use a semicolon:

```
NSLog (@"Hello, world!");
NSLog (@"Good-bye!");
```

The most common mistake programmers make is omitting this all-important semicolon. Omitting the semicolon from the first line, in the previous example, makes the computer think you actually wrote something like this:

```
NSLog (@"Hello, world!")NSLog (@"Good-bye!");
```

This line won't work because the computer doesn't know when the first NSLog command that prints "Hello, world!" actually ends. Semicolons may look trivial, but they're extremely important and used whenever you write Objective-C code.

Defining the Beginning and End of Code with Curly Brackets

Besides the semicolon, the second most common symbols you'll see are the left and right curly brackets: { and }. Since you'll often need to write multiple lines of code that work together to perform a specific function, curly brackets define the beginning and end of those lines of code:

```
{
    NSLog (@"Hello, world!")
    NSLog (@"Good-bye!");
}
```

You always use curly brackets in a method (subprogram) to define all the lines of code stored in that method. When using curly brackets, the ending right curly bracket typically appears on a separate line. However, the beginning left curly bracket can appear at the end of a line:

```
- (void)applicationDidFinishLaunching:(NSNotification *)aNotification {
    NSLog (@"Hello, world!");
    NSLog (@"Good-bye!");
}
```

Or the left curly bracket can appear on a separate line:

```
- (void)applicationDidFinishLaunching:(NSNotification *)aNotification
{
    NSLog (@"Hello, world!");
    NSLog (@"Good-bye!");
}
```

To the computer, both approaches are equivalent, so it's more a matter of personal style which method you prefer. You can actually mix both styles in the same program, but it's usually best to stick to one style for consistency.

You may also see nested pairs of curly brackets where one pair of left/right curly brackets appears inside another pair of left/right curly brackets:

```
- (void)applicationDidFinishLaunching:(NSNotification *)aNotification
{
    if (response == "true")
    {
        NSLog (@"Hello, world!");
        NSLog (@"Good-bye!");
    }
}
```

Each left curly bracket must pair up with a matching right curly bracket. By using indentation (which the compiler completely ignores), you can vertically align each matching left/right curly bracket pair. Since the compiler ignores indentation, the Xcode compiler treats the previous code as if it actually looked like this:

```
- (void)applicationDidFinishLaunching:(NSNotification *)aNotification
{
if (response == "true")
{
NSLog (@"Hello, world!");
NSLog (@"Good-bye!");
}
}
```

Since this code can be harder to read, it's always best to use indentation to make it visually clear where one chunk of code begins and ends. When writing your own Objective-C code, always strive to make it as readable and understandable as possible.

Defining Compiler Directives with the # Symbol

When you run a program, the Xcode compiler examines your code, line by line. However, sometimes you may need to give the compiler special instructions. To do this, you have to put the # symbol in front of these special instructions called *compiler directives*. The most common compiler directive appears in front of the import keyword:

```
#import "MyProgramAppDelegate.h"
```

This #import command tells the Xcode compiler to take any code stored in a specific file (such as the MyProgramAppDelegate.h file) and add or import that code into the current file. From the compiler's point of view, it's as if you crammed all your code from a separate file into the currently displayed file. However, from a programmer's point of view, your program remains divided into different files, which makes editing and modifying these separate files far easier than trying to edit and modify one massive file.

The #import command is one that you'll see and use often since it allows you to access all of Apple's prewritten and tested code without physically copying that code into your own programs.

Defining Comments with //

When writing code, you may need to jot down a note to yourself (or to another programmer) that explains what a particular chunk of code does or what assumptions you've made in writing your code. Rather than jot down these notes on a separate piece of paper (and risk losing or misplacing them), it's easier to write notes directly in your code.

To keep the Xcode compiler from mistaking your notes as code, you need to use special symbols. For identifying a single line as a note or comment, you can use the // characters:

```
{
  NSLog (@"Hello, world!");
  // This line is a comment
```

```
}
```

Xcode treats anything that appears after the // characters as if it doesn't exist, so the previous code looks like this to the compiler:

```
{
    NSLog (@"Hello, world!");
}
```

Comments can appear on a separate line or at the end of a line of code:

```
{
    NSLog (@"Hello, world!") ;   // This line is also a comment
    // This line is a comment
}
```

Comments are useful for writing short explanations on how your code works or for identifying the date and name of the last programmer who changed the code. If you need to write comments on multiple lines, you could use the // symbols at the beginning of each line:

```
{
    NSLog (@"Hello, world!")
    // The line above prints to the log window
    // Last modified on April 1, 2012 by Bob Smith
}
```

However, typing multiple // symbols in front of each comment can get tedious. For a faster method of turning multiple lines into comments, you can use matching pairs of the slash and asterisk symbols:

```
{
    NSLog (@"Hello, world!")
    /* These two lines are comments
        Last modified on April 1, 2012 by Bob Smith */
}
```

The /* and */ symbols tell Xcode that anything in between those matching symbols are a comment that the compiler can ignore. You can use both the // and /* and */ symbols to create comments in your code.

Identifying Objects with [and]

Many times your code will use single-word commands, such as NSLog, to tell the computer to do something. However, one benefit of Objective-C is that you can divide a large program into objects, so instead of just using the built-in commands of Objective-C, you can define your own commands and store them in objects of your own creation.

To identify when you're working with objects in Objective-C, you'll need to use square brackets in a form such as the following:

```
[object message];
```

The square brackets identify a single object and the message you're sending to that object. Typically that message sends either an object data or an instruction:

```
[textField setStringValue:@"Hello, world!"];
[personalData release];
```

The first line of code sends the message `setStringValue` using the data "Hello, world!" to an object called `textField`. The second line of code sends the message `release` to an object called `personalData`. Although you may not understand what these two lines of code actually do at this point, the square brackets identify that you're working with objects.

Just like with pairs of curly brackets, you may also see nested pairs of square brackets:

```
[[NSObject alloc] init];
```

Like nested pairs of curly brackets, nested pairs of square brackets must match. For every left square bracket, you need a matching right square bracket. Although square brackets can look unusual, especially if you're used to other programming languages, just remember that square brackets always identify when you're working with objects.

Defining Pointers with *

You can use the asterisk symbol in several ways. First, it can represent a multiplication symbol such as 54 * 11. Second, it can identify the beginning and end of a comment:

```
/* This is a comment */
```

Third, the asterisk can identify a pointer. When storing data, computers carve out a chunk of memory to hold the data. Each time you need to store more data, your program needs to use more memory.

If you need to store identical data, you could store that data in three separate chunks of memory. However, a more efficient way to use memory is to store that data once and then create pointers to that single copy of data, as shown in Figure 5–3.

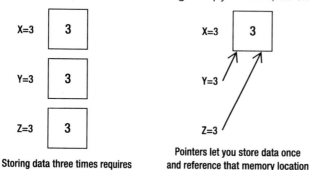

Storing data three times requires using memory three times.

Pointers let you store data once and reference that memory location multiple times.

Figure 5–3. *Pointers let you use memory more efficiently.*

In most programming languages, including Objective-C, you can store data in a variable such as assigning 48 to a variable named myAge. When you store data in a variable, that data gets stored in a specific part of the computer's memory, called a *memory address*. Each time you want to store data, your data gobbles up another chunk of memory.

As an alternative to creating a new chunk of memory, pointers work by referencing or *pointing* to, a memory address that already stores data. The power of a pointer is that it's much easier and faster to reference or point to a new memory address quickly. The drawback is that if your pointers point to the wrong memory address, your program could physically foul up the computer's memory.

When working with Objective-C and objects, you'll need to use pointers. In Objective-C, a pointer is represented by the asterisk. Since pointers are used with objects and Objective-C programming heavily relies on objects, you'll be using pointers in almost every nontrivial Mac program.

Typically you'll use the asterisk symbol (*) to declare a pointer to an object:

```
Object *pointer;
```

Oftentimes you'll see the asterisk symbol (*) used with square brackets:

```
NSObject *myObject = [[NSObject alloc] init];
```

Whenever you see asterisks and square brackets, chances are good that the code is working with pointers and objects.

Manipulating Data with Variables

All programs need to store data. In any programming language, you can store data in something called a *variable*. A variable is nothing more than a unique name that acts like a box for holding data. Variables get their name because they can store various data. One moment a variable might hold 45, and the next moment that same variable might hold 740.

To avoid mixing data up, every variable needs a unique name where each variable can hold only one chunk of data at a time. The moment you store data in a variable, any new data wipes out any data currently stored in that variable.

Declaring Variables

Before you can use a variable, you must create or declare that variable. Declaring a variable simply tells the Xcode compiler that the variable is now available for storing data. There are two parts to declaring a variable.

First, you must define a unique name for your variable. Second, you must define the type of data that the variable can hold.

The name you give a variable is completely arbitrary, although most programmers use a descriptive name. For example, if a variable is meant to hold someone's salary, it's logical to name that variable something like Salary rather than something generic and nondescriptive like X.

Although you can name variables as short as X or as long as Thisisavariablenamethatistoolong, it's common in Mac programming to create variable names that consist of two or more words combined using something called *camel case*.

With camel case, the first word of the variable appears in lowercase, but the first letter of the second and any additional words appear in uppercase:

```
variableName
numberHolder
lengthInMeters
```

After you choose a descriptive name for your variable, the second part in declaring a variable involves defining what type of data it can hold. The most common types of data are numbers, and the two most common types of numbers are integers and floating-point or real numbers.

An integer variable can hold only whole numbers such as 102, 5, or 649. A floating-point variable can hold only real numbers such as 3.125, 10.24, or 90.08.

To declare an integer variable, you need to use the int keyword followed by the variable name:

```
int myAge;
int dogsInHouse;
int peopleOnBoard;
```

To declare a floating-point variable, you need to use the float keyword followed by the variable name:

```
float stockPrice;
float averageAge;
float medicineQuantity;
```

> **NOTE:** There are actually variations of int and float data types. If you want to define only positive numbers, you can declare a variable as unsigned such as unsigned int myAge;. If you want to make it clear that a variable can hold both positive or negative, you can declare a signed variable such as signed int myDebt;. If you need to declare extremely large floating-point numbers, you can use the double keyword such as double myExtremeValue;. While you're learning to program the Mac, you'll probably only need to use the int and float keywords to declare your variables.

Besides declaring variables as int or float data types, a third commonly used data type is the Boolean data type. A Boolean variable can hold only one of two values, either 1 (YES) or 0 (NO). Boolean data types are often used to help the computer make a decision, and based on the value of a Boolean variable, the computer may follow one set of instructions or another set of instructions.

To declare a Boolean variable, you just need to use the BOOL keyword followed by your variable name:

```
BOOL doorOpen;
BOOL onTarget;
BOOL windowOpenAndDoorShut;
```

Assigning Data to a Variable

When you first declare a variable, the value of that variable is unknown. If you try to use a variable right after you declare it, the unknown value of that variable will likely crash your program or make it behave erratically. As soon as you declare a variable, it's a good idea to assign a value to that variable right away.

Assigning a value to a variable simply means using the equal sign (=):

```
Variable = value;
```

There are two ways to declare a variable and assign a value to it. The first way involves two separate lines of code:

```
int myAge;
myAge = 49;
```

A second way to assign a value to a variable is to combine the variable declaration and the assignment to a value in a single line:

```
int myAge = 49;
```

To ensure that a variable never contains an unknown value, it's usually best to use the second method of declaring and assigning a variable in a single line, but as long as you can remember to always assign a value to a variable before using it, you can use whichever method you like.

The Scope of a Variable

When you declare a variable, you also declare the scope of that variable. The scope defines which part of your program can access and use that variable. In most cases, you'll declare a variable inside a method so the scope of that variable is visible only to code stored in that same method. For example, suppose you had two methods like this:

```
- (void)applicationDidFinishLaunching:(NSNotification *)aNotification
{
    int myCats = 4;
    // More code goes here
}

- (void)countBoxes;
{
    int numberOfBoxes = 75;
    // More code goes here
}
```

Any code stored in the applicationDidFinishLaunching method could access and use the myCats variable because the myCats variable is declared inside that method. Likewise, any code stored in the countBoxes method could access and use the numberOfBoxes variable because the numberOfBoxes variable is declared inside that method.

The scope of a variable typically lasts from the variable declaration line to the end of the code block where the variable was declared. Since each variable was declared inside the code block that makes up each method, each variable's scope is valid only in that particular subprogram or method.

What happens if you try to access a variable declared in another method like the following?

```
- (void)applicationDidFinishLaunching:(NSNotification *)aNotification
{
    int myCats = 4;
    numberOfBoxes = 120;
}

- (void)countBoxes;
{
    int numberOfBoxes = 75;
    myCats = 1;
}
```

In both cases, each method is trying to use a variable that was declared in a different method. In the first method, the numberOfBoxes variable is considered undeclared. In the second method, the myCats variable is considered undeclared.

Since the scope of a variable typically extends only within the method where it was declared, it's possible to do the following:

```
- (void)applicationDidFinishLaunching:(NSNotification *)aNotification
{
    int happyPeople = 2;
}

- (void)countBoxes;
{
    int happyPeople = 75;
}
```

In this example, both methods declare a variable with the same name. Although this may look confusing, it's perfectly valid because the scope of each variable extends only to the method that it was declared in. Although this is valid, it's not a good idea to use identical variable names in different parts of your program because the potential for confusion is so high.

As a general rule, any variable you declare will likely be accessible only inside a block of code defined by the curly brackets: { and }.

A Program Example Using Variables

To get practice declaring and assigning values to variables, this sample program shows how to use the NSLog command to print data stored in two different variables. To create this sample program and see how to declare and use variables, follow these steps:

1. Start Xcode, and create a new project such as by choosing File ➤ New Project. A dialog box pops up letting you choose a template to use.

2. Click the Cocoa Applications icon, and click the Next button. A dialog box appears, asking you to choose a name for your project.

3. Type a name such as **VariableTest**, and click the Next button. A Save As dialog box appears.

4. Select a drive and folder to store your project, and click the Save button.

5. Click the disclosure triangle (the gray arrow) that appears to the left of the Classes folder in the left pane of the Xcode window. A list of two files appears. If you named your project VariableTest, these two files will be named VariableTestAppDelegate.h and VariableTestAppDelegate.m.

6. Click the .m file, such as the VariableTestAppDelegate.m file. The code for that file appears in the middle pane of the Xcode window.

7. Modify the applicationDidFinishLaunching method so that it appears as follows:

```
- (void)applicationDidFinishLaunching:(NSNotification *)aNotification {
    int myAge = 49;
    float myPaycheck = 5120.75;
    NSLog (@"This is my age: %i", myAge);
    NSLog (@"This is my paycheck amount: %f", myPaycheck);
}
```

8. Choose File ➤ Save or press ⌘S.

9. Click the Build and Run button, or choose Build ➤ Build and Run. As long as you didn't mistype anything, you should see a blank window pop up.

10. Quit the program, such as clicking the Stop button or choosing Product ➤ Stop from the Xcode pull-down menus.

11. Choose Run ➤ Console or press ⇧⌘R. You should see the printed statements created by the NSLog command such as the following:

```
2010-08-24 22:39:14.358 VariableTest[1001:a0f] This is my age: 49
2010-08-24 22:39:14.362 VariableTest[1001:a0f] This is my paycheck amount: 5120.750000
```

You may notice that when printing out a floating-point number, the NSLog command printed a bunch of extra zeroes. If you want to define how many numbers you want to appear to the right of the decimal point, you need to specify the number of digits:

```
NSLog (@"This is my paycheck amount: %.2f", myPaycheck);
```

This code tells the computer to print the floating-point number with two digits to the right of the decimal point:

```
2010-08-24 22:39:14.362 VariableTest[1001:a0f] This is my paycheck amount: 5120.75
```

> **NOTE:** If your floating-point number has more digits than you've specified, your number will be rounded. For example, suppose you have a floating-point number of 3.79 and you specify just one digit to the right of the decimal point like %.1. Then your number will be rounded from 3.79 to 3.8.

Using Constants

Variables are handy for storing data that may vary. For example, you might create a variable called yourAge where one person might type in a value of 43 and another person might type in a value of 82.

However, sometimes you may need to create a fixed value. The most common use for a fixed value, or *constant*, is when you need a specific value that represents something that will never change within your program such as defining the number of letters in the alphabet or defining a retirement age like 70.

To declare a constant, you need to use the #define command followed by the constant name and its assigned value:

```
#define CONSTANTNAME Value
```

> **NOTE:** When defining a constant, you do not need a semicolon at the end of the line.

The #define command tells the Xcode compiler that you're creating a constant name with a fixed value. Constant names can appear as a combination of uppercase and lowercase characters:

```
#define constantName Value
#define CONSTANTName Value
```

Some programmers like to use all uppercase since uppercase letters are easy to spot. Others prefer to use camel case that smashes together two or more words where the first letter is lowercase but the first letter of each new word is uppercase:

```
#define myConstantName Value
```

For another way to clearly identify constants, some programmers begin every constant name with a lowercase *k*:

```
#define kConstantName Value
```

Since there is no single "best" way to name constants, choose a method that makes sense to you, and use it consistently.

The value you define for a constant can be any number or even a string:

```
#define iLoop 5
#define errorMessage @"Bad memory"
```

To see how you can use constants, modify the program you created in the previous section (named VariableTest) by following these steps:

1. Open the VariableTest project from the previous section.

2. Click the VariableTestAppDelegate.m file stored inside the Classes folder. The code for that file appears in the middle pane of the Xcode window.

3. Modify the code in the VariableTestAppDelegate.m file as follows:

```
#import "VariableTestAppDelegate.h"
#define kLoopCounter 5

@implementation VariableTestAppDelegate

@synthesize window;

- (void)applicationDidFinishLaunching:(NSNotification *)aNotification {
    int counter;
    int myAge = 49;
    float myPaycheck = 5120.75;
    for (counter = 0; counter < kLoopCounter; counter++)
    {
        NSLog (@"This is my age: %i", myAge);
        NSLog (@"This is my paycheck amount: %.2f", myPaycheck);
    }
}

@end
```

4. Choose File ➤ Save or press ⌘S.

5. Click the Build and Run button or choose Build ➤ Build and Run. As long as you didn't mistype anything, you should see a blank window pop up.

6. Quit the program, such as clicking the Stop button or choosing Product ➤ Stop from the Xcode pull-down menus.

7. Choose Run ➤ Console, or press ⇧⌘R. You should see the printed statements created by the NSLog command:

```
2010-08-25 10:44:31.099 VariableTest[1702:a0f] This is my age: 49
2010-08-25 10:44:31.102 VariableTest[1702:a0f] This is my paycheck amount: 5120.75
2010-08-25 10:44:31.103 VariableTest[1702:a0f] This is my age: 49
2010-08-25 10:44:31.103 VariableTest[1702:a0f] This is my paycheck amount: 5120.75
2010-08-25 10:44:31.104 VariableTest[1702:a0f] This is my age: 49
2010-08-25 10:44:31.104 VariableTest[1702:a0f] This is my paycheck amount: 5120.75
2010-08-25 10:44:31.105 VariableTest[1702:a0f] This is my age: 49
2010-08-25 10:44:31.105 VariableTest[1702:a0f] This is my paycheck amount: 5120.75
2010-08-25 10:44:31.106 VariableTest[1702:a0f] This is my age: 49
2010-08-25 10:44:31.106 VariableTest[1702:a0f] This is my paycheck amount: 5120.75
```

In this example, you defined a constant to hold a value of 5. Then you used this constant in a loop to tell the computer to repeat a block of code five times. To modify the number of times your loop runs, you can simply modify the constant value (kLoopCounter) to a new value such as 3 or 300.

This example used a single constant value in a loop just once, but imagine if you needed to use the same constant value in 100 different places in your program. If you just typed a number rather than use a constant value, you would have to change this number in 100 different places, increasing the chance of error.

By using a constant, you need to define the actual number only once, and then you'll automatically change the 100 other places in your program that relies on that constant value. Constants simply help you use a fixed value repetitively throughout your program.

Using Mathematical Operators

Variables can store data, but every program needs to manipulate data somehow. For numbers, the most common way to manipulate data involves mathematical operators, as shown in Table 5–1.

Table 5–1. *Mathematical Operators*

Operator	What It Does	Example
+	Adds	6 + 12 = 18
-	Subtracts	42.25 - 6.7 = 35.55
*	Multiplies	4 * 9 = 36
/	Divides	70 / 10 = 7
%	Modulo (divides two integers and returns the remainder)	72 % 10 = 2

All of these mathematical operators can work with either integer or floating-point numbers, except the modulo operator, which can work only with integers. The simplest way to use mathematical operators is to use one per line:

```
85 + 6 = 91
91 * 7 = 637
```

Of course, you can also cram multiple mathematical operators on a single line, but you have to make sure that the computer calculates numbers in the right order. For example, what happens if you do the following?

```
85 + 6 * 7 = ???
```

Instead of getting 637, the computer would calculate 127. The reason for this is something called *precedence*.

Normally the computer would just calculate results from left to right, but precedence tells the computer which mathematical operators to calculate first. In a line that contains two or more mathematical operators, Objective-C first calculates multiplication (*), division (/), and modulo (%) first. Then it calculates addition (+) and subtraction (-).

In the previous example, the computer would first multiply 6 * 7 to get 42. Then it would add 42 to 85 to get 127. In case you want the computer to add 85 to 6 first, you have to surround those numbers in parentheses like this:

```
(85 + 6) * 7
```

This would cause the computer to add 85 to 6 and get 91, which would make the line look like this:

```
91 * 7 = 637
```

If you have two or more mathematical operators that have equal precedence, the computer simply calculates them from left to right. Consider the following:

```
12 + 9 - 7 + 3 - 45
```

First the computer would calculate 12 + 9 and get 21 like this:

```
21 - 7 + 3 - 45
```

Then it would calculate 21 - 7 and get 14 like this:

```
14 + 3 - 45
```

Adding 14 to 3 would get 17:

```
17 - 45
```

Finally, it would calculate the remaining mathematical operator and get -18.

As a general rule, always use parentheses when using multiple mathematical operators on the same line. Parentheses clarify which mathematical operators the computer calculates first.

Using Strings

Besides numbers, the second most common type of data that programs often need to store and manipulate are strings, which are typically letters but can also include symbols and even numbers. Some examples of a string include the following:

```
"Hello, world!"
"The RX-25 is defective, sir."
"45% of people spend $5.00 or more for lunch 90% of the time."
```

Unlike integer or floating-point numbers that have a built-in data type defined by the Objective-C programming language, strings are treated as an object called NSString.

> **NOTE:** To identify objects that have already been created by Apple, the object names will usually begin with the NS prefix such as NSString. NS stands for NeXTSTEP, which is the operating system that Apple used as a foundation to create Mac OS X.

Declaring a string variable is similar to declaring an integer or floating-point variable. The main difference is that when you declare an NSString variable, you're working with the NSString object, so instead of declaring a variable, you're actually declaring a pointer. So, declaring an NSString variable looks like this:

```
NSString *pointerName;
```

Like all variables, you can assign a value to a variable at the same time you declare it:

```
NSString *myName = @"John Smith";
```

When using strings with NSString variables, you must always put the @ symbol in front of the string, which is enclosed in double quotation marks.

Rather than assign a value to an NSString variable when you declare it, you can just declare the variable and then assign a value to that variable on a different line:

```
NSString *myName;
myName = @"John Smith";
```

One key point to notice is that when you declare an NSString variable, you must use the asterisk (*) symbol since it's a pointer. However, when you assign a value to an NSString variable, you omit the asterisk symbol.

To see how to use NSString variables, modify the VariableTest project by following these steps:

1. Open the VariableTest project from the previous section.

2. Click the VariableTestAppDelegate.m file stored in the Classes folder. The code for that file appears in the middle pane of the Xcode window.

3. Modify the code in the VariableTestAppDelegate.m file as follows:

```
- (void)applicationDidFinishLaunching:(NSNotification *)aNotification {
    NSString *myName;
    myName = @"John Smith";
    int counter;
    int myAge = 49;
    float myPaycheck = 5120.75;
    for (counter = 0; counter < kLoopCounter; counter++)
    {
        NSLog (@"This is my age: %i", myAge);
        NSLog (@"This is my paycheck amount: %.2f", myPaycheck);
    }
    NSLog (@"This is my name: %@", myName);
}
```

4. Click the Build and Run button, or choose Build ➤ Build and Run. As long as you didn't mistype anything, you should see a blank window pop up.

5. Quit the program, such as by clicking the Stop button or choosing Product ➤ Stop from the Xcode pull-down menus.

6. Choose Run ➤ Console or press ⇧⌘R. You should see the printed statements created by the NSLog command:

```
2010-08-25 20:07:05.948 VariableTest[2781:a0f] This is my age: 49
2010-08-25 20:07:05.952 VariableTest[2781:a0f] This is my paycheck amount: 5120.75
2010-08-25 20:07:05.955 VariableTest[2781:a0f] This is my age: 49
2010-08-25 20:07:05.956 VariableTest[2781:a0f] This is my paycheck amount: 5120.75
2010-08-25 20:07:05.956 VariableTest[2781:a0f] This is my age: 49
2010-08-25 20:07:05.957 VariableTest[2781:a0f] This is my paycheck amount: 5120.75
2010-08-25 20:07:05.957 VariableTest[2781:a0f] This is my age: 49
2010-08-25 20:07:05.958 VariableTest[2781:a0f] This is my paycheck amount: 5120.75
2010-08-25 20:07:05.958 VariableTest[2781:a0f] This is my age: 49
2010-08-25 20:07:05.961 VariableTest[2781:a0f] This is my paycheck amount: 5120.75
2010-08-25 20:07:05.962 VariableTest[2781:a0f] This is my name: John Smith
```

Summary

Programming a Mac is similar to programming other types of computers in many ways yet also is different in ways designed to make programming easier. One major difference is that traditional programming forces you to create a single main program and fill it with code. Xcode automatically creates a main program for you, which you'll never need to modify or even look at. Instead of filling your main program with code, Xcode lets you store your code in separate files, which can run when a certain event occurs.

Like all programming languages, Objective-C uses a combination of symbols and commands that look like complete words. To define the end of each line of code, you must use a semicolon. To define a block of code, you use curly brackets. To give special instructions to the Xcode compiler, you need to use the # symbol. For leaving comments directly in your code, you use the // and /* and */ symbols for multiple lines.

Since Objective-C focuses on dividing a large program into objects, you'll need to use square brackets like [and] to identify when you're working with objects. Typically when you're working with objects, you'll need to use pointers, which are identified by the asterisk (*) symbol.

The main purpose of any program is to store and manipulate data. Every program needs to store data in a variable, which can be a number (integer or floating point), Boolean value (YES or NO), or strings (defined by the predefined object NSString). When you need to define a fixed value, you can create a constant using the #define command.

Once you understand the basics to using Xcode to create simple programs that can use constants and different types of variables, you'll be ready to start tackling more complicated programs. Learning to program the Mac involves a combination of learning Objective-C, learning Xcode, and learning the basic principles of object-oriented programming. In the next chapter, you'll learn more about making more complicated types of programs that can make decisions or repeat one or more lines of code, which can give your program more flexibility and versatility.

Chapter **6**

Making Decisions with Branches

The simplest programs consist of one or more instructions or lines of code that the computer follows sequentially, one after another. While such sequential ordering forms the basis for programming, programs need greater flexibility to make decisions depending on the current situation.

A *branch* provides the computer with a choice of two or more different sets of instructions to follow. The simplest type of branch provides two choices, but there's no theoretical limit to the number of branches a program can have. A complicated program may need to make hundreds or even thousands of possible decisions.

Computers decide which choice, or branch, to follow based entirely on a certain condition, known as a *Boolean condition* or *expression*. In real life, people use Boolean expressions all the time to make decisions.

Suppose you want to find something to eat. If you're in a hurry, you might go to a fast-food restaurant. If want a nicer meal, you might look for a sit-down restaurant. In each case, your decision depends on a Boolean condition.

In the first example, the Boolean expression is whether you're in a hurry or not, which can evaluate to either YES or NO. In the second example, the Boolean expression is whether you want a nicer meal. To make decisions, computers need to evaluate a Boolean expression, which determines which branch of instructions to follow.

A typical branch in a video game might ask the user, "Continue playing?" Based on the response (a Boolean expression that evaluates to YES or NO), one branch might run the game over again while the second branch might end the game right away.

Branches and the sequential ordering of code represent two of the three basic building blocks to creating programs. (The third building block is a loop, which you'll learn more about in Chapter 7.) Normally a branch contains one or more instructions arranged sequentially, but a branch can contain other branches, as shown in Figure 6–1.

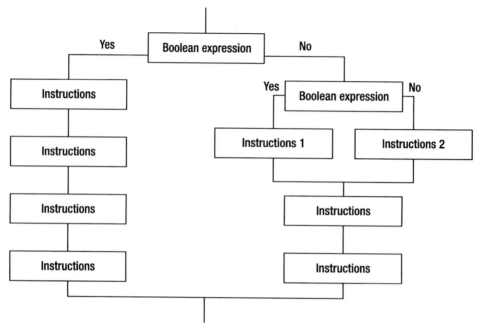

Figure 6–1. *Branches can contain other branches.*

Understanding Boolean Expressions

When making a decision, a person needs to examine a condition. For example, if it's raining, they might take an umbrella or wear a raincoat. In this case, the condition is whether it's raining or not. If so, take an umbrella or raincoat. If not, then don't take either one.

Computers also need to examine conditions to decide which branch of instructions to follow. Such conditions always represent a True or False value, which are called *Boolean conditions*, after Boolean logic.

In the Boolean condition of whether it's raining or not, the Boolean value is either True or False. If it's True, that means it is raining. If it's False, that means it is not raining.

To represent the values of True and False, programming languages treat the value of True as 1 and the value of False as 0. In Objective-C, True values are represented as YES and False values are represented as NO.

The simplest Boolean condition in Objective-C is simply a YES or NO:

```
if (YES)
{
    NSLog (@ "Hello, world!");
}
```

In the preceding example, the code simply prints "Hello, world!" because the condition is always YES. This code is equivalent to the following:

```
NSLog (@ "Hello, world!");
```

A Boolean value of YES or NO is often assigned to a variable:

```
BOOL Flag = YES;
```

This code simply declares a Boolean variable, called `Flag`, and assigns it a value of YES. Rather than assign a value, you could have just declared a Boolean variable and left its value unknown:

```
BOOL Flag;
```

Before you could use such a Boolean variable, you would have to assign it a value of YES or NO. While you can assign a value of YES or NO, it's far more common to evaluate a condition to determine its Boolean value. For example, to determine whether or not to take an umbrella or raincoat, the Boolean condition might be as follows:

```
if (raining outside)
{
   take umbrella or raincoat;
}
```

Depending on whether or not it's raining, this Boolean condition evaluates to either YES or NO. In programming, the Boolean conditions are usually comparisons between two different values. This comparison of values is known as an *expression*, an example of which follows:

```
45 > 10
```

Since 45 is always greater than 10, this Boolean expression always evaluates to YES. Obviously, this is no different from simply replacing the entire 45 > 10 expression with YES. To make such Boolean expressions more useful, it's more common to replace one or more fixed values with a variable. Since the value of a variable can change, this causes the Boolean expression to vary as well.

For example, consider this Boolean expression:

```
X > 10
```

Depending on the actual value of X, this Boolean expression evaluates to either YES or NO. If the value of X is 11 or greater, then this Boolean expression evaluates to YES. If the value of X is 10 or less, it evaluates to NO.

A Boolean expression can even compare two different variables:

```
X > Y
```

This Boolean expression varies depending on the actual values stored in the X and Y variables.

A Boolean expression can even compare mathematical calculations:

```
X + 15 > Y - 47
```

There's actually no limit to the number of variables you can use in a Boolean expression. No matter how many variables are used, the Boolean expression always evaluates to either YES or NO. For example, the following expression would evaluate to YES or NO depending on the values of the four variables:

```
X + 15 + Z > Y - 47 + W
```

Boolean Comparison Operators

A Boolean expression compares two values to determine a YES or NO value. To compare two values, you have to use a Boolean comparison operator. Table 6–1 lists the various Boolean comparison operators.

Table 6–1. *Boolean Comparison Operators*

Boolean Operator	Meaning
==	Equal
!=	Not equal
>	Greater than
>=	Greater than or equal
<	Less than
<=	Less than or equal

NOTE: Unlike some programming languages, to compare whether two values are equal in Objective-C, you have to use double equal signs. If you use a single equal sign, the computer will think you're assigning a value to a variable, such as X = 18. Forgetting this second equal sign is a common error when writing a Boolean expression to compare whether two values are equal.

Assuming that the value of X is 28, Tables 6–2 shows how the computer would evaluate the various Boolean expressions.

Table 6–2. *Evaluating Boolean Expressions*

Boolean Expression	Evaluates To
X == 45	NO
X != 45	YES
X > 45	NO
X >= 45	NO
X < 45	YES
X <= 45	YES

On each side of a Boolean comparison operator, you can have any of the following:

A value, such as 128 > 344

A variable that can represent different values, such as X > 344 or 128 > Y

A mathematical expression with a variable, such as X + 23 > 344

Suppose you had a Boolean expression as follows:

```
X = 36;
if (X < 98)
{
  NSLog (@"Hello, world!");
}
```

The first step that the computer would take is to substitute the value of X into the (X < 98) Boolean expression like this:

```
if (36 < 98)
{
  NSLog (@"Hello, world!");
}
```

The Boolean expression (36 < 98) evaluates to YES, so the next step would look like this:

```
if (YES)
{
  NSLog (@"Hello, world!");
}
```

This code just boils down to this:

```
NSLog (@"Hello, world!");
```

Boolean Logical Operators

Just as mathematical operators let you calculate new values with numbers, Boolean logical operators let you calculate new values using Boolean expressions. Boolean logical operators are useful to evaluate two Boolean expressions.

The following are the four types of Boolean logical operators:

&& (And)

|| (Or)

^ (Xor)

! (Not)

The ! (Not) Operator

The ! (Not) operator is the simplest Boolean logical operator to understand since it simply reverses the value of a Boolean expression. For example:

```
!(YES) = NO
!(NO) = YES
```

Assume the value of X is 57 in the following Boolean expression:

```
!(X == 86)
```

First, the computer would substitute X with 57 in the Boolean expression as follows:

```
!(57 == 86)
```

Now the computer evaluates this Boolean expression to NO:

```
!(NO)
```

The ! operator reverses the Boolean value so that the entire Boolean expression evaluates to the following:

```
!(NO) = YES
```

The ! operator may look puzzling as to its purpose, but consider a program that verifies whether the user typed in a valid password. The loop might look like this:

```
while !(validPassword)
{
  Ask for password;
}
```

This code tells the computer that as long as the password is not valid, it should keep asking for a password.

The && (And) Operator

Sometimes you may need to combine two Boolean expressions to create a single Boolean value. For example, suppose you wanted to decide whether to take an umbrella. First, you might check if it's raining. Then you might check if you need to go out. If both of these Boolean conditions are YES, then you would take an umbrella. Writing this out like code might look like this:

```
if (raining outside) && (need to go outside)
{
  take umbrella;
}
```

If the Boolean expression (raining outside) is NO, then you won't need to take an umbrella regardless of whether you need to go outside or not. Likewise, if the Boolean expression (need to go outside) is NO, then it doesn't matter if it's raining or not since you won't need an umbrella.

The && operator takes two Boolean values and calculates a new result, as shown in Table 6–3.

Table 6–3. *The && (And) Operator Table*

$$	NO	YES
NO	NO && NO = NO	NO && YES = NO
YES	YES && NO = NO	YES && YES = YES

When calculating a new result with the && operator, the Boolean expression represents YES only if both conditions represent YES. If either condition is NO, then the entire Boolean operation is also NO.

The || (Or) Operator

Another way to combine two Boolean expressions to create a single Boolean value is through the || (Or) operator. The || operator takes two Boolean values and calculates a new result, as shown in Table 6–4.

Table 6–4. *The || (Or) Operator Table*

||	NO	YES
NO	NO || NO = NO	NO || YES = YES
YES	YES || NO = YES	YES || YES = YES

When calculating a new result with the || operator, the Boolean expression represents YES if either one (or both) of the conditions also represents YES. If both conditions are NO, then the entire Boolean operation is NO.

For example, suppose you wanted to decide whether to wear boots. First, you might check if it's raining. Second, you might check if it's snowing. If either of these Boolean conditions is YES, then you would wear boots. Writing this out as code might look like this:

```
if (raining outside) || (snowing outside)
{
  wear boots;
}
```

You need to wear boots if (raining outside) is YES or (snowing outside) is YES. The only time the entire Boolean expression does not evaluate to YES is when both Boolean conditions evaluate to NO.

The ^ (Xor) Operator

Yet another way to combine two Boolean expressions to create a single Boolean value is through the ^ (Xor) operator. The ^ operator (also called an exclusive Or) takes two Boolean values and calculates a new result, as shown in Table 6–5.

Table 6–5. *The ^ (Xor) Operator Table*

^	NO	YES
NO	NO ^ NO = NO	NO ^ YES = YES
YES	YES ^ NO = YES	YES ^ YES = NO

With the ^ operator, two Boolean expressions evaluate to NO when both are identical (both NO or both YES). If the two Boolean expressions are different, then they always evaluate to YES.

> **NOTE:** The Xor operator is often used in encryption. One of the simplest encryption algorithms is called the XOR cipher.

Once you understand Boolean expressions, including both comparison and logical operators, you'll be ready to use Boolean expressions in branches and loops when writing your own programs.

Branches

A branch defines two or more possible sets of instructions (code) for the computer to follow, based on a Boolean expression that evaluates to YES or NO. In Objective-C, the two most common types of branches are the if and switch statements.

An if statement lets you choose between two or more alternative sets of instructions to follow. A switch statement behaves exactly like an if statement, but it's simpler to write when you need to provide a large number of alternative sets of instructions.

The Simplest if Statement

The if statement gets its name because it checks a single Boolean expression. If this Boolean expression is YES, then the if statement follows one or more instructions. If this Boolean expression is NO, then it doesn't do anything.

The simplest if statement lets you run exactly one instruction based on a Boolean expression. In Objective-C, this simple if statement looks like this:

```
if (Boolean expression) instruction;
```

To see how to use this simple `if` statement, modify the VariableTest project from Chapter 5 by following these steps:

1. Open the VariableTest project from the previous chapter.

2. Click the `VariableTestAppDelegate.m` file stored inside the Classes folder. The code for that file appears in the middle pane of the Xcode window.

3. Modify the code in the `VariableTestAppDelegate.m` file as follows:

```
- (void)applicationDidFinishLaunching:(NSNotification *)aNotification {
    BOOL Flag = YES;
    if (Flag) NSLog (@"It works!");
}
```

4. Choose File ➤ Save, or press ! S to save your changes.

5. Click the Build and Run button or choose Build ➤ Build and Run. As long as you didn't mistype anything, you should see a blank window pop up.

6. Quit your program by clicking the Stop button or choosing Product ➤ Stop.

7. Choose Run ➤ Console or press " ! R. You should see the printed statements created by the `NSLog` command:

```
2010-08-28 14:51:51.162 VariableTest[9492:a0f] It works!
```

Following Multiple Instructions in an if Statement

The simplest `if` statement lets you run only one instruction if a Boolean expression is YES. In most cases, you'll need to run two or more instructions if a Boolean expression is YES. To do this, you need to use curly brackets around the instructions you want to run:

```
if (Boolean expression) {
    instruction1;
    instruction2;
}
```

To make the curly brackets more visible, you could just place the beginning, left curly bracket on a separate line:

```
if (Boolean expression)
{
    instruction1;
    instruction2;
}
```

In either case, using curly brackets lets you run two or more instructions if a Boolean expression is YES.

The if-else Statement

The `if` statement runs one or more instructions if a Boolean expression is YES. However, if the Boolean expression is NO, then the `if` statement doesn't run any instructions. There may be times when you want the computer to follow one set of instructions if a Boolean expression is YES, but follow another set of instructions if the Boolean expression is NO. In such cases, you have two choices.

First, you can create two separate `if` statements:

```
if (Boolean expression == YES)
{
    instruction1;
    instruction2;
}
if (Boolean expression == NO)
{
    instructionA;
    instructionB;
}
```

No matter what the Boolean expression may be (either YES or NO), the instructions in one of these `if` statements will run. Of course, writing two separate `if` statements can be clumsy, so Objective-C offers an `if-else` statement that lets you define two sets of instructions to follow:

```
if (Boolean expression == YES)
{
    instruction1;
    instruction2;
}
else
{
    instructionA;
    instructionB;
}
```

This single `if-else` statement makes much clearer which set of instructions the computer will follow depending on the value of the Boolean expression. If it's YES, then the computer follows the first set of instructions. If it's NO, then the computer follows the second set of instructions.

The if-else if Statement

The `if-else` statement runs either one set of instructions or a second set of instructions. If the computer does not follow the first set of instructions, it always follows the second set of instructions.

However, you may not want the computer to run a second set of instructions automatically. Instead, you may want to evaluate a second Boolean expression before running the second set of instructions. Such an `if-else if` statement looks like this:

```
if (Boolean expression 1 == YES)
{
```

```
    instruction1;
    instruction2;
}
else if (Boolean expression 2 == YES)
{
    instructionA;
    instructionB;
}
```

Although it's similar to the ordinary `if-else` statement, the `if-else if` statement works a lot differently. If Boolean expression 1 is YES, then the computer runs only the first set of instructions (instruction1 and instruction2). If Boolean expression 1 is NO, then the computer evaluates Boolean expression 2.

If Boolean expression 2 is YES, then the computer follows the second set of instructions (instructionA and instructionB). However, if Boolean expression 2 is NO, then the computer winds up not following any of the instructions.

The preceding `if-else if` statement could be rewritten as follows:

```
if (Boolean expression 1 == YES)
{
    instruction1;
    instruction2;
}

if (Boolean expression 1 == NO) && (Boolean expression 2 == YES)
{
    instructionA;
    instructionB;
}
```

For the computer to follow the second set of instructions (instructionA and instructionB), two conditions must be met. First, Boolean expression 1 must be NO. Second, Boolean expression 2 must be YES.

In addition to letting you evaluate a Boolean expression before running each set of instructions, another advantage of the `if-else if` statement is that it lets you choose from two or more sets of instructions, such as in this example:

```
if (Boolean expression 1 == YES)
{
    instruction1;
    instruction2;
}
else if (Boolean expression 2 == YES)
{
    instructionA;
    instructionB;
}
else if (Boolean expression 3 == YES)
{
    instructions3;
    instructions4;
}
else if (Boolean expression 4 == YES)
{
```

```
    instructionsC;
    instructionsD;
}
```

Unfortunately, the more alternative sets of instructions you include in the `if-else if` statement, the messier your code gets and the harder it is to read. If you need to check a Boolean expression before running multiple alternative instructions, it's simpler to use a `switch` statement.

The switch Statement

The `switch` statement is often used to provide a large number of alternative instructions for the computer to follow. The main difference is that a `switch` statement tries to match a variable to a constant value. For example, consider these two `if` statements:

```
if (X == 45)
{
    instruction1;
    instruction2;
}

if (X == 97)
{
    instructionA;
    instructionB;
}
```

The equivalent `switch` statement might look like this:

```
switch (X)
{
    case 45:
        instruction1;
        instruction2;
        break;

    case 97:
        instructionA;
        instructionB;
        break;
}
```

Rather than just evaluate a YES or NO value, the `switch` statement takes a value and tries to match it. If the value matches to a specific value, then the computer runs that set of instructions:

```
switch (expression)
{
    case match1:
        instruction1;
        instruction2;
        break;

    case match2:
        instruction3;
        instruction4;
```

```
        break;

    case match3:
        instruction5;
        instruction6;
        break;

    default:
        instructionA;
        instructionB;
        break;
}
```

This switch statement is equivalent to the following if statements:

```
if (expression == match1)
{
    instruction1;
    instruction2;
}

if (expression == match2)
{
    instruction3;
    instruction4;
}

if (expression == match3)
{
    instruction5;
    instruction6;
}
else
{
    instructionA;
    instructionB;
}
```

The switch statement is somewhat unusual for two reasons. First, you do not use curly brackets to enclose multiple lines of code inside the switch statement. Second, at the end of each set of instructions, you need to use a break command.

The break command simply tells the computer to stop following instructions. Without this break command, the computer would simply keep following instructions stored in another part of the switch statement. For example, consider the following switch statement where the break command is missing:

```
switch (expression)
{
    case match1:
        instruction1;
        instruction2;

    default:
        instructionA;
        instructionB;
        break;
```

```
}
```

This is actually equivalent to the following, which is probably not what you want:

```
switch (expression)
{
    case match1:
        instruction1;
        instruction2;
        instructionA;
        instructionB;
        break;

  default:
        instructionA;
        instructionB;
        break;
}
```

The case and break commands define the beginning and the end of a group of instructions. If you omit the break command, the computer will get confused and run additional instructions that you didn't intend.

> **NOTE:** Omitting a break command is the number one cause of errors when using the switch statement.

By purposely omitting the break command, you can match multiple values to the same set of instructions:

```
switch (expression)
{
    case match1:
    case match2:
        instruction1;
        instruction2;
        break;

  default:
        instructionA;
        instructionB;
        break;
}
```

The preceding switch statement is equivalent to the following:

```
if (expression == match1)  || (expression == match2)
{
        instruction1;
        instruction2;
}
else
{
        instructionA;
        instructionB;
}
```

To see how to use a simple switch statement, modify the VariableTest project from the section "The Simplest if Statement," earlier in this chapter, by following these steps:

1. Open the VariableTest project.

2. Click the VariableTestAppDelegate.m file stored inside the Classes folder. The code for that file appears in the middle pane of the Xcode window.

3. Modify the code in the VariableTestAppDelegate.m file as follows:

```
- (void)applicationDidFinishLaunching:(NSNotification *)aNotification {
    int X = 2;
    switch (X)
    {
        case 1:
            NSLog (@"X = 1");
            break;
        case 2:
            NSLog (@"X = 2");
            break;
        default:
            NSLog (@"Default code");
            break;
    }
}
```

4. Choose File ➤ Save or press ! S to save your changes.

5. Click the Build and Run button or choose Build ➤ Build and Run. As long as you didn't mistype anything, you should see a blank window pop up.

6. Quit your program by clicking the Stop button or choosing Product ➤ Stop.

7. Choose Run ➤ Console or press " ! R. You should see the printed statements created by the NSLog command:

```
2010-08-28 17:59:32.654 VariableTest[9921:a0f] X = 2
```

Go back and change the first line in the applicationDidFinishLoading method to the following:

```
int X = 1;
```

Now if you run this program and view the log window, you'll see this:

```
2010-08-28 17:59:32.654 VariableTest[9921:a0f] X = 1
```

Go back and change the first line one more time, to the following:

```
int X = 99;
```

Now if you run this program and view the log window, you'll see this:

```
2010-08-28 17:59:32.654 VariableTest[9921:a0f] Default code
```

By examining the `switch` statement, you can see exactly how it behaves based on the value that you give it for X.

Summary

To make decisions, computers rely on Boolean expressions that represent a YES or NO value. The simplest Boolean expressions are YES or NO values, but more complex Boolean expressions rely on comparison operators and logical operators.

Comparison operators compare two values to determine a YES or NO value. The six types of comparison operators include == (equal), != (not equal), > (greater than), >= (greater than or equal to), < (less than), and <= (less than or equal to).

Logical operators change the value of a Boolean expression somehow. The four types of logical operators are ! (Not), && (And), || (Or), and ^ (Xor).

Boolean expressions are always used in branching statements to determine which set of instructions to follow. The simplest type of branching statement is an `if` statement that runs exactly one instruction if a Boolean expression is YES.

Since running a single instruction is limited, most `if` statements can run one or more instructions, enclosed by curly brackets.

For greater flexibility, you can also use an `if-else` statement, which provides two sets of instructions for the branching statement to choose from. For even greater flexibility, there's also an `if-else if` statement, which lets the computer evaluate a Boolean expression before running any set of instructions.

The `if-else if` statement can let you create an unlimited number of alternative sets of instructions to follow, but to make these branches easier to understand, you can often replace the `if-else if` statement with a `switch` statement. The `switch` statement examines a variable and compares that variable to fixed values to determine which set of instructions to follow.

Branching statements give your program the power to react to the user and outside data. As a result, branching statements represent one of the three main building blocks (the other two being loops and the sequential ordering of instructions) for creating any program.

Chapter 7

Repeating Code with Loops

The three basic building blocks for creating programs are the sequential ordering of code, branches (to make decisions), and loops (to run one or more instructions repetitively). Rather than write one long set of instructions to accomplish a task, a loop lets you write a shorter set of instructions that runs multiple times.

Suppose your program needs to ask for a password from the user before granting access. You could write a bunch of code that keeps checking for a valid password, but this gives you no idea ahead of time how many times someone may try to type in a valid password. With a loop, you just need to write one set of instructions for checking the validity of a password and, if it's valid, granting the user access. The loop can run as many times as necessary, depending on how many times the user tries to type in a valid password. By letting your program respond to uncertainty, loops give your program greater versatility in working in the real world.

All loops run one or more instructions repetitively, but there are two types of loops. One type of loop runs a fixed number of times. In Objective-C, this is called a for loop. For example, if you want to give users only three chances to type in a valid password, you could create a loop that runs only three times. The moment the user tries to type in a password a fourth time, your program can stop running and simply deny access altogether.

The second type of loop can run zero or more times, depending on circumstances determined by a Boolean expression. In Objective-C, this is called a while loop. For example, a loop might keep running until the user types in a valid password. That could happen on the first try or the twenty-third try. Since you can't predict ahead of time when a loop should end, you have to let the loop keep running until a certain condition (Boolean expression) is met.

Whereas branches let the computer make decisions, loops let the computer react to uncertainty. When writing Mac programs, you can freely use both types of loops in different parts of your program.

Loops That Run a Fixed Number of Times

The easiest loop to understand is one that runs a fixed number of times, such as 10 or 20 times. By defining exactly how many times you want a loop to run, you can ensure that the loop always ends eventually.

> **NOTE:** If a loop never ends, the program can appear to freeze or hang up. Such never-ending loops are called *endless loops*, and they're the biggest pitfall to avoid when using loops in your program.

To create a loop that runs a fixed number of times, you use a for statement, which looks like this:

```
int countingVariable
for (initialValue; BooleanExpression; incrementExpression)
{
    instructions;
}
```

A for statement consists of four items:

- A counting variable
- An initial value
- A Boolean expression
- An increment expression

The counting variable is defined as an integer before the loop and is used to keep track of how many times the loop has run.

The initial value defines the number that the counting variable is set to when the loop starts. Usually this initial value is 0 or 1, but it can be any value.

The Boolean expression defines when the loop will run. The loop will stop after the counting variable has reached a certain value, such as 4. That means the loop might run four times (depending on its initial value).

The increment expression defines how the counting variable changes. Usually the counting variable changes by 1, but you can define this increment change by any number such as 2, 4, or even a negative number like -3.

To see how to create a loop using the for statement, follow these steps:

1. Open the VariableTest project from the previous chapter.

2. Click the VariableTestAppDelegate.m file stored inside the Classes folder. The code for that file appears in the middle pane of the Xcode window.

3. Modify the code in the VariableTestAppDelegate.m file as follows:

```
- (void)applicationDidFinishLaunching:(NSNotification *)aNotification {
    int i;
    for (i = 0; i < 5; i++)
    {
        NSLog (@"The value of i = %i", i);
    }
}
```

4. Choose File ➤ Save or press ⌘S to save your changes.

5. Click the Build and Run button or choose Build ➤ Build and Run. As long as you didn't mistype anything, you should see a blank window pop up.

6. Quit your program by clicking the Stop button or choosing Product ➤ Stop.

7. Choose Run ➤ Console or press ⇧⌘R. You should see the printed statements created by the NSLog command:

```
2010-08-29 13:23:41.515 VariableTest[11731:a0f] The value of i = 0
2010-08-29 13:23:41.519 VariableTest[11731:a0f] The value of i = 1
2010-08-29 13:23:41.521 VariableTest[11731:a0f] The value of i = 2
2010-08-29 13:23:41.521 VariableTest[11731:a0f] The value of i = 3
2010-08-29 13:23:41.522 VariableTest[11731:a0f] The value of i = 4
```

In this example, the counting variable is i, the initial value is i = 0, and the Boolean expression is i < 5. That means as long as this Boolean expression evaluates to YES (where i is a value less than 5), the loop keeps running. As soon as the Boolean expression i < 5 evaluates to NO (where the value of i equals 5 or greater), then the loop stops.

The increment expression is i++, which is a shortcut for i = i+ 1. The i++ increment expression simply counts by 1. If you wanted to count by a different value, you could replace the i++ expression with something else such as i = i + 4.

The for loop currently runs exactly five times, but you could create a loop that runs five times by using different initial values, Boolean expressions, and increment expressions. For example, this loop also runs five times:

```
int i;
for (i = 105; i > 100; i--)
    {
        NSLog (@"The value of i = %i", i);
    }
```

If you modify the VariableTest program with this loop, the output looks like this:

```
2010-08-29 17:31:56.230 VariableTest[12128:a0f] The value of i = 105
2010-08-29 17:31:56.237 VariableTest[12128:a0f] The value of i = 104
2010-08-29 17:31:56.238 VariableTest[12128:a0f] The value of i = 103
2010-08-29 17:31:56.239 VariableTest[12128:a0f] The value of i = 102
2010-08-29 17:31:56.240 VariableTest[12128:a0f] The value of i = 101
```

In this case, the loop is counting backward from 105 down to 101. The i-- increment expression is equivalent to i = i - 1.

By changing the initial value, the Boolean expression, and the increment expression, you can define how many times you want the loop to run.

> **NOTE:** There's another `for` loop called *fast enumeration*, which you'll learn more about in the chapters about arrays (Chapter 8) and dictionaries (Chapter 9). Essentially, fast enumeration lets you scan through a list of data stored in an array or dictionary without having to count at all.

Quitting a for Loop Prematurely

A `for` loop always runs a fixed number of times. However, you can stop a `for` loop prematurely by using the `break` command along with an `if` statement inside the `for` loop:

```
int i;
for (i = 0; i < 5; i++)
    {
        instructions;
        if (passwordValid)
            {
                break;
            }
    }
```

This `for` loop might give the user five tries to type in a valid password before blocking access altogether. However, if at any time the user types in a valid password, you want to exit the loop that checks for a valid password and grant access to the user.

To see how the `break` command can exit a loop prematurely, follow these steps:

1. Open the VariableTest project from the previous section

2. Click the `VariableTestAppDelegate.m` file stored inside the Classes folder. The code for that file appears in the middle pane of the Xcode window.

3. Modify the code in the `VariableTestAppDelegate.m` file as follows:

```
- (void)applicationDidFinishLaunching:(NSNotification *)aNotification {
    int i;
    for (i = 0; i < 5; i++)
    {
        NSLog (@"The value of i = %i", i);
        if (i == 2)
        {
            break;
        }
    }
}
```

4. Choose File ➤ Save or press ⌘S to save your changes.

5. Click the Build and Run button or choose Build ➤ Build and Run. As long as you didn't mistype anything, you should see a blank window pop up.

6. Quit your program by clicking the Stop button or choosing Product ➤ Stop.

7. Choose Run ➤ Console or press ⇧⌘R. You should see the printed statements created by the NSLog command:

```
2010-08-29 21:07:53.000 VariableTest[12825:a0f] The value of i = 0
2010-08-29 21:07:53.006 VariableTest[12825:a0f] The value of i = 1
2010-08-29 21:07:53.007 VariableTest[12825:a0f] The value of i = 2
```

Notice that instead of running five times, the loop stopped prematurely (as soon as the value of i equals 2) after running only three times.

Skipping in a for Loop

Instead of prematurely exiting a loop, you can force a for loop to skip by using the continue command. Skipping stops the loop from running any remaining instructions in the loop and forces the loop to start over again, but without resetting the counting variable. Like the break command that prematurely exits a loop, the continue command also uses an if statement to determine when to skip or not:

```
int i;
for (i = 0; i < 5; i++)
    {
        if (Boolean expression)
            {
                continue;
            }
        instruction1;
    }
```

If the Boolean expression evaluates to YES, then the computer runs the continue command and immediately jumps back to the top of the loop without running instruction1. If you place instructions ahead of the continue command, those instructions will always run. Any instructions that immediately follow the continue command will get skipped if the continue command runs.

To see how the continue command works to print only even numbers, follow these steps:

1. Open the VariableTest project from the previous section.

2. Click the VariableTestAppDelegate.m file stored inside the Classes folder. The code for that file appears in the middle pane of the Xcode window.

3. Modify the code in the VariableTestAppDelegate.m file as follows:

```
- (void)applicationDidFinishLaunching:(NSNotification *)aNotification {
    int i;
    for (i = 0; i < 5; i++)
    {
        if ((i % 2) != 0)
        {
            continue;
        }
        NSLog (@"The value of i = %i", i);
```

```
        }
    }
```

4. Choose File ➤ Save or press ⌘S to save your changes.

5. Click the Build and Run button or choose Build ➤ Build and Run. As long as you didn't mistype anything, you should see a blank window pop up.

6. Quit your program by clicking the Stop button or choosing Product ➤ Stop.

7. Choose Run ➤ Console or press ⇧⌘R. You should see the printed statements created by the NSLog command:

```
2010-08-29 23:17:25.785 VariableTest[13046:a0f] The value of i = 0
2010-08-29 23:17:25.789 VariableTest[13046:a0f] The value of i = 2
2010-08-29 23:17:25.790 VariableTest[13046:a0f] The value of i = 4
```

Loops That Run Zero or More Times

Sometimes you may need a loop to run based on an outside condition that you can't predict ahead of time. Other times you may not want the loop to run even once depending on outside conditions. In both of these cases, you need to choose a different type of loop, either a while loop or a do-while loop.

The while Loop

The while loop can run zero or more times and looks like this:

```
while (Boolean expression)
    {
        instructions;
        instructions that can change Boolean expression;
    }
```

The while loop repeats one or more instructions and consists of three parts:

- A Boolean expression

- Instructions to repeat

- Instructions that modify the Boolean expression

The Boolean expression determines whether the loop should run. If the Boolean expression evaluates to NO, it's possible that the while loop won't run at all.

The second part of the while loop, the instructions to repeat, can be a single instruction or a group of instructions.

The third, and most important, part of the while loop are instructions that can change the Boolean expression. If you omit instructions that can change the Boolean expression, the Boolean expression can never change from YES to NO, resulting in an endless loop that will hang up or freeze your program, keeping it from working properly.

To see how the while loop works, follow these steps:

1. Open the VariableTest project from the previous section.

2. Click the VariableTestAppDelegate.m file stored inside the Classes folder. The code for that file appears in the middle pane of the Xcode window.

3. Modify the code in the VariableTestAppDelegate.m file as follows:

```
- (void)applicationDidFinishLaunching:(NSNotification *)aNotification {
    int i;
    i = 0;
    while (i < 5)
    {
        NSLog (@"The value of i = %i", i);
        i++;
    }
}
```

4. Choose File ➤ Save or press ⌘S to save your changes.

5. Click the Build and Run button or choose Build ➤ Build and Run. As long as you didn't mistype anything, you should see a blank window pop up.

6. Quit your program by clicking the Stop button or choosing Product ➤ Stop.

7. Choose Run ➤ Console or press ⇧⌘R. You should see the printed statements created by the NSLog command:

```
2010-08-30 19:41:31.559 VariableTest[14914:a0f] The value of i = 0
2010-08-30 19:41:31.562 VariableTest[14914:a0f] The value of i = 1
2010-08-30 19:41:31.564 VariableTest[14914:a0f] The value of i = 2
2010-08-30 19:41:31.564 VariableTest[14914:a0f] The value of i = 3
2010-08-30 19:41:31.565 VariableTest[14914:a0f] The value of i = 4
```

The first two lines create an integer variable (i) and initialize its value to 0. The Boolean expression is (i < 5). Since i contains 0, the Boolean expression (i < 5) evaluates to YES, causing the while loop to run.

Inside the while loop, the NSLog command simply prints the current value of i. The other instruction inside the while loop, i++, changes the value of the i variable. This allows the (i < 5) Boolean expression to evaluate to NO, causing the while loop to stop running eventually.

The do-while Loop

The do-while loop always runs at least once and looks like this:

```
do
    {
        instructions;
        instructions that can change Boolean expression;
    } while (Boolean expression);
```

Like the while loop, the do-while loop also consists of three parts: instructions to repeat, instructions to change the loop's Boolean expression, and the Boolean expression. Since the do-while loop checks its Boolean expression only after it runs through its instructions, the do-while loop always runs at least once.

To see how the do-while loop works, follow these steps:

1. Open the VariableTest project from the previous section.

2. Click the VariableTestAppDelegate.m file stored inside the Classes folder. The code for that file appears in the middle pane of the Xcode window.

3. Modify the code in the VariableTestAppDelegate.m file as follows:

```
- (void)applicationDidFinishLaunching:(NSNotification *)aNotification {
    int i;
    i = 0;
    do
    {
        NSLog (@"The value of i = %i", i);
        i++;
    } while (i < 5);
}
```

4. Choose File ➤ Save or press ⌘S to save your changes.

5. Click the Build and Run button or choose Build ➤ Build and Run. As long as you didn't mistype anything, you should see a blank window pop up.

6. Quit your program by clicking the Stop button or choosing Product ➤ Stop.

7. Choose Run ➤ Console or press ⇧⌘R. You should see the printed statements created by the NSLog command:

```
2010-08-30 19:41:31.559 VariableTest[14914:a0f] The value of i = 0
2010-08-30 19:41:31.562 VariableTest[14914:a0f] The value of i = 1
2010-08-30 19:41:31.564 VariableTest[14914:a0f] The value of i = 2
2010-08-30 19:41:31.564 VariableTest[14914:a0f] The value of i = 3
2010-08-30 19:41:31.565 VariableTest[14914:a0f] The value of i = 4
```

Quitting a while or do-while Loop Prematurely

Just as you can exit a for loop prematurely using the break command, you can exit a while or do-while loop using the break command. Typically, you use an if-then statement to determine when to break:

```
- (void)applicationDidFinishLaunching:(NSNotification *)aNotification {
    int i;
    i = 0;
    do
    {
        NSLog (@"The value of i = %i", i);
        i++;
        if (i == 2)
        {
```

```
        break;
      }
  } while (i < 5);
}
```

This do-while loop runs twice before exiting as soon as the value of i equals 2, printing the following:

```
2010-08-30 20:12:20.535 VariableTest[15016:a0f] The value of i = 0
2010-08-30 20:12:20.537 VariableTest[15016:a0f] The value of i = 1
```

Skipping a while or do-while Loop

You can use the `continue` command to cause the `while` or `do-while` loop to skip over its instructions and return to the beginning. Typically, you use an `if` statement to determine when to skip:

```
- (void)applicationDidFinishLaunching:(NSNotification *)aNotification {
    int i;
    i = 0;
    do
    {
        i++;
        if ((i % 2) != 0)
        {
            continue;
        }
        NSLog (@"The value of i = %i", i);
    } while (i < 5);
}
```

Running this program would print the following:

```
2010-08-30 20:22:51.675 VariableTest[15138:a0f] The value of i = 2
2010-08-30 20:22:51.683 VariableTest[15138:a0f] The value of i = 4
```

Nested Loops

Loops typically contain one or more instructions arranged sequentially. However, it's possible for a loop to contain instructions organized in a branch or even another loop. When one loop appears inside another loop, that's called a *nested loop*, an example of which is shown in Figure 7–1.

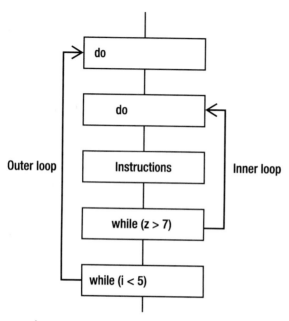

Loops can appear nested within another loop

Figure 7–1. *A nested loop occurs when one loop appears inside of another one.*

When one loop is nested inside another one, the inner loop must always finish running first before the outer loop can finish. The inner loop can even change the Boolean expression that the outer loop depends on, but if you try this, make sure that the outer loop eventually ends or you risk creating an endless loop.

It's possible to nest a while loop inside a for loop, or vice versa. Although there's no limit to the number of loops you can nest within one another, each nested loop makes understanding how the program works more difficult, which could result in unpredictable behavior if you incorrectly modify any code inside any of the nested loops. Use nested loops only when absolutely necessary to make your programs easier to understand.

To see how nested loops work, follow these steps:

1. Open the VariableTest project from the previous chapter.

2. Click the VariableTestAppDelegate.m file stored inside the Classes folder. The code for that file appears in the middle pane of the Xcode window.

3. Modify the code in the VariableTestAppDelegate.m file as follows:

```
- (void)applicationDidFinishLaunching:(NSNotification *)aNotification {
    int i;
    int j;
    i = 0;
    do
    {
        NSLog (@"Outer loop %i", i);
        for (j = 0; j < 3; j++)
```

```
        {
            NSLog (@"     Inner loop number %i", j);
        }
        i++;
    } while (i < 3);
}
```

4. Choose File ➤ Save or press ⌘S to save your changes.

5. Click the Build and Run button or choose Build ➤ Build and Run. As long as you didn't mistype anything, you should see a blank window pop up.

6. Quit your program by clicking the Stop button or choosing Product ➤ Stop.

7. Choose Run ➤ Console or press ⇧⌘R. You should see the printed statements created by the NSLog command:

```
2010-08-30 20:50:53.176 VariableTest[15388:a0f] Outer loop 0
2010-08-30 20:50:53.179 VariableTest[15388:a0f]     Inner loop number 0
2010-08-30 20:50:53.181 VariableTest[15388:a0f]     Inner loop number 1
2010-08-30 20:50:53.182 VariableTest[15388:a0f]     Inner loop number 2
2010-08-30 20:50:53.182 VariableTest[15388:a0f] Outer loop 1
2010-08-30 20:50:53.183 VariableTest[15388:a0f]     Inner loop number 0
2010-08-30 20:50:53.183 VariableTest[15388:a0f]     Inner loop number 1
2010-08-30 20:50:53.184 VariableTest[15388:a0f]     Inner loop number 2
2010-08-30 20:50:53.185 VariableTest[15388:a0f] Outer loop 2
2010-08-30 20:50:53.186 VariableTest[15388:a0f]     Inner loop number 0
2010-08-30 20:50:53.186 VariableTest[15388:a0f]     Inner loop number 1
2010-08-30 20:50:53.187 VariableTest[15388:a0f]     Inner loop number 2
```

Both the inner and outer loops run exactly three times. However, notice that the inner loop repeats multiple times, but the outer loop runs only once.

Summary

Loops represent the third basic building block for creating programs, in addition to sequential instructions and branches. Loops run one or more instructions repetitively. The two types of loops you can create are for and while loops.

Use the for loop when you know exactly how many times you want to run a loop. Use a while loop or do-while loop when you don't know how many times a loop should repeat, so that your program can adapt to outside circumstances.

If you want a loop to run zero or more times, use the while loop. If you need the loop to run at least once, then use the do-while loop. With both the while loop and do-while loop, you must change the Boolean expression inside your loop. If you fail to change the loop's Boolean expression, you risk creating an endless loop.

For greater flexibility, you can nest loops inside one another. Since nested loops can be harder to understand, use nested loops sparingly. Just remember that the inner loop must always runs first before the outer loop can finish.

Loops enable your program to run one or more instructions repetitively. Although loops can eliminate the need to write multiple lines of identical (or nearly identical) instructions, loops do make your programs harder to understand. Combining loops with sequential instructions and branches allows you to create virtually any type of program you wish.

Chapter 8

Understanding the Cocoa Framework

Up until this point in the book, you've been learning the basic principles of programming. First, you learned about the three basic building blocks of programming (sequential instructions, branches, and loops). Next, you learned about Boolean expressions, mathematical operators, variables, and constants.

While it's perfectly possible to create a program using what you've learned so far, programming for the Mac is much harder because you have to write code to create and display your user interface, code to perform common functions, and code to make your program do something unique.

To make Mac programming easier, Apple provides a library of prewritten and tested code, organized in something called the *Cocoa framework*. This library of code uses the features of object-oriented programming (which you'll learn more about in Chapter 9) to store useful code to create your user interface or manipulate or store data. By using these Cocoa framework files (called *classes* in object-oriented programming) provided by Apple, you can reduce the amount of code you need to write so you can create programs faster that are more reliable.

In traditional programming, you would need to write three sets of code to create your user interface, perform common functions, and do something unique to your program. By relying on the Cocoa framework, you can just focus on writing code that makes your program unique, which essentially cuts the amount of code you need to write by one-third, as shown in Figure 8–1.

In a traditional program, you have to write code to create the user interface, perform common tasks, and do something unique to your program.

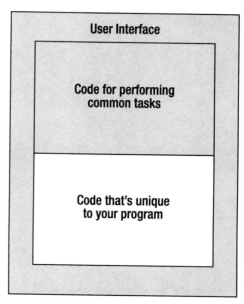

By using objects stored in Apple's Cocoa framework, you can reuse code to create your user interface and perform common functions so you only need to write code unique to your program.

Figure 8–1. *Object-oriented programming can make Mac programming much simpler and faster.*

To use the Cocoa framework, you need to understand how object-oriented programming works, which is the focus of this chapter. Once you understand the basic principles behind object-oriented programming, you'll understand better how to take advantage of Apple's Cocoa framework. As a general rule, always check the Cocoa framework for code before you try to write your own code. In many cases, you'll find that you can reuse the code you need, or at least write less of it yourself, to create a fully functional program.

An Overview of How Object-Oriented Programming Works

Before getting into the details of using object-oriented programming in your own programs, you need to understand how object-oriented programming works in general. Once you understand what you're doing, you'll better understand the actual details of writing Objective-C code using objects.

Starting with a Class

To use an object-oriented programming language like Objective-C, you must first write code that defines a *class*. A class determines what types of data (called *properties*) the class can hold and the subprograms (called *methods*) that the class provides to do something such as manipulate the data stored in its properties.

Although you'll likely need to create your own classes, Apple provides an entire library of classes for you to use, stored in the Cocoa framework. By using the classes of the Cocoa framework, you can write a simple program without ever writing your own classes at all.

A class file by itself simply groups related properties and methods in one location. To actually use a class in your program, you must create (or *instantiate*) an object from that class. Each time you create an object from a class, you can then use that object to store data in its properties and manipulate that object somehow using its methods.

Objects are arbitrary ways to group related data and the subprograms that manipulate that data. Just as there are a million different ways to write a program that works identically, there are also a million different ways to organize data and subprograms into objects.

A single program typically consists of multiple objects that often represent a different physical part of a problem. For example, if you're writing a program to control a train, one object might represent the engine, another object might represent the wheels, and a third object might represent the brakes.

Ideally, when you divide a large program into multiple objects, those objects act like isolated islands. To make a program work, your multiple objects need to cooperate with one another, which they do by passing information (or messages) to each other.

Messages typically tell another object to run one of its methods to do something. For example, an object that represents the brakes of a train might pass a message to the object that represents the train wheels to tell it to stop spinning. By passing messages to each other, objects can work together. Each object knows how to do something useful, and whenever an object needs to do something that's beyond its control, it needs to contact another object and pass it a message to tell that other object what to do.

> **NOTE:** Chapter 12 explains the details of creating classes in Objective-C. Right now, you just need to get a rough understanding of how object-oriented programming works without getting bogged down in the technical details of using a particular programming language.

Objects provide two distinct advantages over traditional programming. First, objects help reduce errors or bugs in a program. Second, objects encourage reusing code to make programming faster and more reliable.

Reducing Bugs

The main idea behind objects is to isolate or encapsulate data and the subprograms that manipulate that data. By grouping in one place all subprograms that manipulate the same data, you can reduce errors.

Traditional programs behave like a single refrigerator in an apartment where five different people store their food. No matter how careful each person might be, chances are good that they'll accidentally move or take something that belongs to someone else. If all five people live in separate apartments with their own refrigerators (like dividing a program into objects), none of these problems could happen.

By isolating data and the subprograms that manipulate that data, objects reduce the chance that errors or bugs in other parts of your program will interfere with important data used by a different part of the program.

Reusing Code

In the past, programmers wrote subprograms and stored them in separate files. If one programmer wanted to modify a subprogram to fix a problem or add a new feature, that programmer had a choice of either creating a duplicate copy of that subprogram and modifying that duplicate, or modifying the original subprogram.

Modifying the original subprogram could cause problems if another part of that program depends on that subprogram. That means any modifications could prevent another part of the program from working.

Duplicating a subprogram and then modifying that duplicate is a safer option, but it creates separate copies of nearly identical subprograms. If you discover a problem with the original subprogram, you have to fix it and fix every modified copy of that subprogram. If you made ten copies of a subprogram, you have to fix ten separate copies of that modified subprogram and hope that your modifications don't accidentally wreck that subprogram and keep it from working.

Objects eliminate this problem by keeping the original subprogram untouched. Instead of making a physical duplicate of a subprogram, you simply create an object based on a class. Your object then has access to the code stored in that class, but you never need to physically copy that code. The result is that your programs can be smaller and easier to understand, and can include a wide variety of features without requiring you to write additional code to make those features work.

Defining Classes

To create an object, you must go through two steps. First, you must create a class using Objective-C code, which defines the properties (data) and methods (subprograms) that manipulate the class's properties. Second, you must declare an arbitrary name that represents an instance of your class, which represents your object.

To create a class, you need to write Objective-C code and store that code in two files that work together, as shown in Figure 8–2. The first file is called a *header file* and ends with the .h file extension. The second file is called an *implementation file* and ends with the .m file extension.

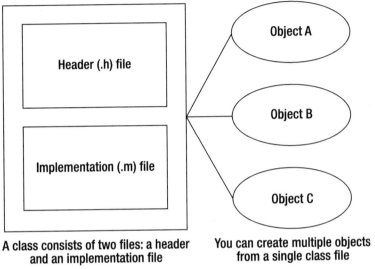

A class consists of two files: a header and an implementation file

You can create multiple objects from a single class file

Figure 8–2. *A class consists of a header file and an implementation file.*

The header (.h) file contains information that other parts of your program may need to know about. For example, if you want other parts of your program to store data in a property, you must specify that property name (a variable) in the header file. Storing any properties or methods in the header file makes those properties or methods visible and accessible to the rest of your program.

The implementation file (.m) contains two types of information. First, the implementation file contains data that you do not want other parts of your program to access. Second, the implementation file contains the actual Objective-C code that makes your methods actually work.

When writing Mac programs, you'll probably write your own classes, but you'll also likely use classes that Apple has already created for you, which make up the Cocoa framework. By using the hundreds of different classes stored in the Cocoa framework, you can add features to your program without ever looking at, or needing to understand, the Objective-C code that actually makes those features work.

Creating an Object

Once you understand how classes work, you need to understand the details of how to create an object using Objective-C. Creating objects is similar to declaring a variable. When declaring variables, you have to specify an arbitrary variable name plus the data type that the variable represents:

```
int myNumber;
```

The first command, `int`, tells the computer that you're creating a variable that can hold only integers. The second command, `myNumber`, is the arbitrary variable name chosen to store an integer.

To create an object, you follow the same convention. Instead of defining a data type, you define a class. Then you define an arbitrary variable name to represent your object:

```
NSString *myName;
```

The `NSString` portion tells the computer that you're creating an `NSString` object. The NS prefix tells you that it's an object from Apple's Cocoa framework that has already been written for you. (When you start defining your own classes in Objective-C code, you can name your classes anything you want, without the NS prefix. Many Apple-created class begins with the NS prefix.)

The second part, *myName, is the arbitrary name chosen that defines your object. Notice that when creating an object, you must use a pointer, which is the asterisk (*) symbol in front of the name.

Just as multiple variables can be of the same data type, you can create multiple objects of the same class:

```
NSString *myName;
NSString *yourName;
```

Again, while you can create your own classes by writing Objective-C code, you'll also be using classes that Apple provides for you in its Cocoa framework. The following are two of the most common types of classes available from the Cocoa framework:

- `NSNumber`: Stores any type of number (integer or floating point)
- `NSString`: Stores text

Storing Data in an Object

After you create an object, you can use that class's methods to store and manipulate its properties that contain data. The simplest way to store data in an `NSString` object is to assign it a string of text:

```
NSString *myName;
myName = @"John Doe";
```

If you want, you can declare and assign a value to an `NSString` object like this:

```
NSString *myName = @"John Doe";
```

> **NOTE:** When assigning a string to an `NSString` type of object, always remember to put the @ symbol in front of the string, such as @"This is a string." Omitting the @ symbol when working with `NSString` object types is a common cause of errors.

Storing data in an NSNumber object isn't as straightforward as storing data in an NSString object. Since you can store both integer and floating-point numbers in an NSNumber object, you need to use special methods that are built into the NSNumber class. When working with most classes, such as NSNumber, you'll use its built-in methods for manipulating its data.

For NSNumber, the two most common methods you'll use are the following:

- numberWithInt: Creates an object that stores an integer value
- numberWithFloat: Creates an object that stores a floating-point number

To store an integer in an NSNumber object, you need to define the object you want to manipulate and the method you want to use. Always use square brackets to define the object and the method to run:

```
[object method];
```

To store a value in an NSNumber object, you must identify the NSNumber class by name followed by the method to run:

```
NSNumber *storeMe;
storeMe = [NSNumber numberWithInt:34];
```

The first line of code defines an object (called storeMe) based on an NSNumber class. The second line assigns a value to the storeMe object using the numberWithInt method. In this case, the numberWithInt method takes the number 34 and stores it in the storeMe object.

You can also declare an object and assign it a value in a single line like this:

```
NSNumber *storeMe = [NSNumber numberWithInt:34];
```

If you replace the numberWithInt method and use another one, such as numberWithFloat, you can store a floating-point number in the NSNumber object:

```
NSNumber *storeMe = [NSNumber numberWithFloat:4.18];
```

To store data in most objects, you often have to use a particular method. To find this method name, you'll need to browse through the class reference for that object in the Developer Documentation available online at the Apple Developer site.

A Sample Program for Manipulating Objects

To see how to declare an object, store data in that object, and print that data, follow these steps:

1. Open the VariableTest project from the previous chapter.

2. Click the VariableTestAppDelegate.m file stored inside the Classes folder. The code for that file appears in the middle pane of the Xcode window.

3. Modify the code in the VariableTestAppDelegate.m file as follows:

```
- (void)applicationDidFinishLaunching:(NSNotification *)aNotification {
    NSNumber *myNumber;
    myNumber = [NSNumber numberWithFloat:3.47];
    NSLog (@"The value in NSNumber = %@", myNumber);
}
```

4. Choose File ➤ Save or press ⌘S to save your changes.

5. Click the Build and Run button or choose Build ➤ Build and Run. As long as you didn't mistype anything, you should see a blank window pop up.

6. Quit your program by clicking the Stop button or choosing Product ➤ Stop.

7. Choose Run ➤ Console or press ⇧⌘R. You should see the printed statements created by the NSLog command:

```
2010-09-01 21:08:33.614 VariableTest[21366:a0f] The value in NSNumber = 3.47
```

The main part of this sample program is that you used the NSNumber class to declare an object named myNumber. Then you stored data into that myNumber object using the numberWithFloat method. Next you used the NSLog command to print the contents of that myNumber object.

Looking Up Method and Property Names for NS Classes

In the example of storing data in an NSNumber object, you may have wondered how anyone could possibly know that you can use the two methods numberWithInt and numberWithFloat for storing data in an NSNumber object, or the stringValue property for retrieving data as a string. The answer is that you have to look up method and property names for classes in the Developer Documentation.

> **NOTE:** Properties hold data, and methods are subprograms that do something useful such as manipulate the properties stored in that object.

Any time you create an object based on one of Apple's existing classes (typically identified by the NS prefix, such as NSString), you can find all the method and property names for that class by browsing through the Developer Documentation within Xcode:

1. From within Xcode, choose Help ➤ Developer Documentation. The window shown in Figure 8–3 appears.

2. Click the Search field in the upper-right corner of the window.

Figure 8-3. *The Search field in the Organizer window*

3. Type a class name such as **NSNumber**. Then press Return. The right pane displays the NSNumber class reference, as shown in Figure 8–4.

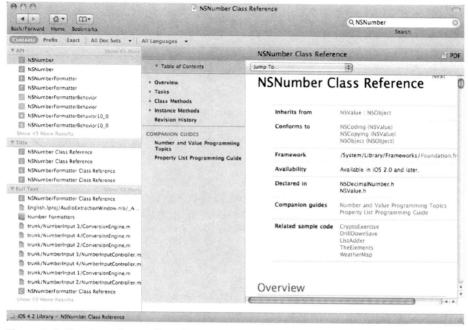

Figure 8–4. *The class reference lists all the available methods.*

4. Scroll down the right pane until you see the list of methods or properties available for your chosen class, as shown in Figure 8–5.

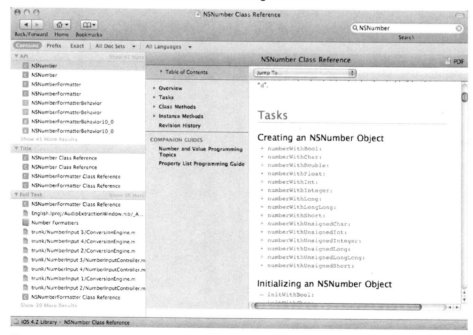

Figure 8–5. *Each class reference lists all its available methods.*

5. Click a method or property name that you want to read about. Detailed information about your chosen method appears as shown in Figure 8–6.

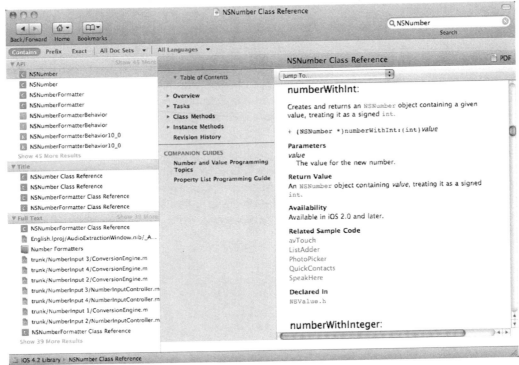

Figure 8–6. *Clicking a method name displays detailed information about that method.*

At any time, you can click the Back (or Forward) button to view a previously viewed screen. When you're done, click the close button in the upper-left corner of the Organizer window to make it go away.

Summary

Objects make Mac programming easier in several ways. The most obvious way is that you can use objects written by Apple in your own programs.. These prewritten classes form Apple's Cocoa framework, which provides tested and reliable code for performing common types of tasks. Using the Cocoa framework saves you time so that you can focus on writing the code that's unique to your particular program.

To create an object, you have to start with a class, which consists of two separate files that work together, a header (.h) file and an implementation (.m) file. Creating an object is much like declaring a variable. First you need to define a class. Then you can use a single class file to create multiple objects.

When you create your own class files, you'll need to write Objective-C code that defines the properties and methods. However, when you use classes stored in Apple's Cocoa framework, you don't have to write any code at all.

To determine what properties and methods are available in an object created from the Cocoa framework, you'll need to search through the Developer Documentation, which you can access through the Xcode Help menu.

Object-oriented programming is nothing more than an arbitrary way to divide a large program into smaller, more manageable parts. Objects help reduce the number of errors or bugs by eliminating the possibility that data can be modified by mistake from another part of your program.

Objects also act as building blocks that you can use to create a program without having to know how they work. All you need to know is how to use them. When creating your own Mac programs, the objects based on Apple's Cocoa framework let you create the user interface and code for performing common tasks without having to write any code yourself. All you need to do is write code for making your program actually do something useful.

Chapter **9**

Manipulating Strings

In previous chapters, you learned how to store integer and floating-point numbers in a variable. However, one of the more common types of data to store is text, otherwise known as a *string*.

There are two parts to a string in Objective-C. First, you must identify a string by using the @ symbol, which identifies the string as a special Objective-C string. Second, you must enclose the string inside double quotation marks, such as @"This is a string" or @"555-1212 is also a string." Strings can contain any characters, including numbers, symbols, and letters.

To store and manipulate strings when creating Mac programs, you use a string class called NSString. One advantage of creating an object from an NSString class is that you can use all of the built-in methods for manipulating strings. In this chapter, you'll learn how to create string variables, how to manipulate strings using methods already created for you by the string class, and how to use two different kinds of string classes called NSString and NSMutableString. If you just need to store a string that will never change while your program runs, you can use the NSString class. If you need to modify a string while your program runs, you can use the NSMutableString class.

Declaring a String Variable

When you create a string variable (either an NSString or NSMutableString), you're working with objects, so you need to create a pointer such as the following:

```
NSString *myName;
NSMutableString *myOtherName;
```

To assign a string to an NSString variable, you simply use the equal sign like this:

```
NSString *myName;
myName = @"John Doe";
```

You can also declare a string and assign a value to it on one line:

```
NSString *myName = @"John Doe";
```

Once you assign a string to an NSString variable, you can never modify that string object again while your program runs. If you want to modify a string object while your program runs, you need to create an NSMutableString variable.

However, assigning a string to an NSMutableString variable is much different. Instead of directly assigning a string, you have to use the stringWithString method:

```
NSMutableString *myString;
myString = [NSMutableString stringWithString: @"This is a string"];
```

If you originally stored a string in an NSString object, you can't modify that string. However, you can modify a copy of that string by storing it in an NSMutableString object:

```
NSString *myName = @"John Doe";
NSMutableString *myString;
myString = [NSMutableString stringWithString: myName];
```

This code simply copies the string stored in the myName variable (NSString type) and stores it in myString (NSMutableString type). Once it is stored in myString, you can then manipulate the string by adding or deleting characters.

Getting the Length of a String

The length of a string includes the number of characters in the string plus any spaces in between. So the string @"Hello, world!" consists of 10 characters, 2 punctuation marks, and 1 space, for a total length of 13. To get the length of a string, you need to use the length method:

```
NSString *myName = @"John Doe";
int counter;
counter = [myName length];
```

To see how the length method works, follow these steps:

1. Open the VariableTest project from the previous chapter.

2. Click the VariableTestAppDelegate.m file stored inside the Classes folder. The code for that file appears in the middle pane of the Xcode window.

3. Modify the code in the VariableTestAppDelegate.m file as follows:

```
- (void)applicationDidFinishLaunching:(NSNotification *)aNotification {
    NSString *myString = @"Hello, world!";
    int counter;
    counter = [myString length];
    NSLog (@"String length = %i", counter);
}
```

4. Choose File ➤ Save or press ⌘S to save your changes.

5. Click the Build and Run button or choose Build ➤ Build and Run. As long as you didn't mistype anything, you should see a blank window pop up.

6. Quit your program by clicking the Stop button or choosing Product ➤ Stop.

7. Choose Run ➤ Console or press ⇧⌘R. You should see the printed statements created by the NSLog command:

```
2010-09-04 17:15:49.929 VariableTest[29949:a0f] String length = 13
```

Comparing Two Strings

To check if two string pointers contain identical text, you have to use the isEqualToString method and list the two strings to compare:

```
[string1 isEqualToString: string2];
```

So if you wanted to compare the memory locations of two string pointers to determine whether they contain identical strings, you could use this code:

```
NSString *myName = @"John Doe";
NSString *hisName = @"John Doe";
if ([myName isEqualToString: hisName])
  {
   NSLog (@"The two strings are equal.");
  }
```

Checking for Prefixes and Suffixes

If you just want to check if a string begins or ends with a certain string such as "The" or a period, you can look for a specific prefix or suffix. To check for certain characters at the beginning of another string, use the hasPrefix method:

```
[string1 hasPrefix: string2];
```

Likewise, if you want to check if a string ends with certain characters, you can use the hasSuffix method:

```
[string1 hasSuffix: string2];
```

In both cases, the hasPrefix or hasSuffix method returns a YES or NO Boolean value. To see how these two methods work, follow these steps:

1. Open the VariableTest project from the previous section.

2. Click the VariableTestAppDelegate.m file stored inside the Classes folder. The code for that file appears in the middle pane of the Xcode window.

3. Modify the code in the VariableTestAppDelegate.m file as follows:

```
- (void)applicationDidFinishLaunching:(NSNotification *)aNotification {
    NSString *myName = @"John Doe";
    NSString *hisName = @"John Doe";
    if ([myName isEqualToString: hisName])
    {
        NSLog (@"The two strings are equal using isEqualToString.");
    }
    BOOL flag;
    flag = [myName hasPrefix: @"John"];
```

```
    if (flag)
    {
        NSLog (@"The hasPrefix method returned YES.");
    }
}
```

4. Choose File ➤ Save or press ⌘S to save your changes.

5. Click the Build and Run button or choose Build ➤ Build and Run. As long as you didn't mistype anything, you should see a blank window pop up.

6. Quit your program by clicking the Stop button or choosing Product ➤ Stop.

7. Choose Run ➤ Console or press ⇧⌘R. You should see the printed statements created by the NSLog command:

```
2010-09-04 19:43:03.883 VariableTest[30388:a0f] The two strings are equal using
isEqualToString.
2010-09-04 19:43:03.886 VariableTest[30388:a0f] The hasPrefix method returned YES.
```

Converting to Uppercase and Lowercase

You can modify the case of a string in three ways:

- capitalizedString: Capitalizes the first letter of each word

- lowercaseString: Converts every character to lowercase

- uppercaseString: Converts every character to uppercase

Uppercase and lowercase only pertain to letters. Any other symbols such as numbers or punctuation marks won't be affected. To use these methods, you must assign the result to a string such as follows:

```
NSString *testString = @"Greetings from another planet.";
NSString *targetString;
targetString = [testString lowercaseString];
```

This would convert the testString text to lowercase and store the result in the targetString variable. To see how all these methods work for changing the case of a string, follow these steps:

1. Open the VariableTest project from the previous section.

2. Click the VariableTestAppDelegate.m file stored inside the Classes folder. The code for that file appears in the middle pane of the Xcode window.

3. Modify the code in the VariableTestAppDelegate.m file as follows:

```
- (void)applicationDidFinishLaunching:(NSNotification *)aNotification {
    NSString *testString = @"Greetings from another planet!";
    NSString *targetString;
    targetString = [testString uppercaseString];
    NSLog (@"All uppercase = %@", targetString);
    NSLog (@"**********");
    targetString = [testString lowercaseString];
```

```
    NSLog (@"All lowercase = %@", targetString);
    NSLog (@"**********");
    targetString = [testString capitalizedString];
    NSLog (@"All capitalized strings = %@", targetString);
    NSLog (@"**********");
    NSLog (@"Original string = %@", testString);
}
```

4. Choose File ➤ Save or press ⌘S to save your changes.

5. Click the Build and Run button or choose Build ➤ Build and Run. As long as you didn't mistype anything, you should see a blank window pop up.

6. Quit your program by clicking the Stop button or choosing Product ➤ Stop.

7. Choose Run ➤ Console or press ⇧⌘R. You should see the printed statements created by the NSLog command:

```
2010-09-04 20:28:07.423 VariableTest[30522:a0f] All uppercase = GREETINGS FROM ANOTHER
PLANET!
2010-09-04 20:28:07.426 VariableTest[30522:a0f] **********
2010-09-04 20:28:07.429 VariableTest[30522:a0f] All lowercase = greetings from another
planet!
2010-09-04 20:28:07.445 VariableTest[30522:a0f] **********
2010-09-04 20:28:07.446 VariableTest[30522:a0f] All capitalized strings = Greetings From
Another Planet!
2010-09-04 20:28:07.447 VariableTest[30522:a0f] **********
2010-09-04 20:28:07.454 VariableTest[30522:a0f] Original string = Greetings from another
planet!
```

Notice that the original string never changes. These methods simply create a new result and store this new result in another string variable.

Converting Strings to Numbers

A string can hold a number, such as @"39.58" or @"43". If a string contains only a number (no letters or symbols), you can convert that string to a number data type such as an integer or a floating-point number using one of the following methods:

- integerValue: Converts a string to an integer

- floatValue: Converts a string to a floating-point value

- doubleValue: Converts a string to a double value, which is a floating-point value that can retain more decimal places

To use one of these methods on a string that contains only a number (they won't work on strings that contain a mix of numbers and characters), use one of the three methods like this:

```
[stringName floatValue];
```

The preceding code would convert a string into an floating point value, which you could store into an floating point variable like this:

```
NSString *floatString = @"52.016";
float myFloat;
myFloat = [floatString floatValue];
```

You can also take a string, holding a floating-point value, and convert it into an integer by using the integerValue method. This cuts off the decimal portion of the number and retains only the integer value, such as turning @"39.78" into just 39.

You can also convert an integer string into a floating-point number using the floatValue method. This simply adds on zeros after the decimal point, such as turning @"58" into 58.000000.

To see these string-to-number conversion methods work, follow these steps:

1. Open the VariableTest project from the previous section.

2. Click the VariableTestAppDelegate.m file stored inside the Classes folder. The code for that file appears in the middle pane of the Xcode window.

3. Modify the code in the VariableTestAppDelegate.m file as follows:

```
- (void)applicationDidFinishLaunching:(NSNotification *)aNotification {
    NSString *integerString = @"47";
    NSString *floatString = @"52.7016";
    int myInteger;
    float myFloat;
    myInteger = [integerString intValue];
    myFloat = [floatString floatValue];
    NSLog (@"Integer value = %i", myInteger);
    NSLog (@"Float value = %f", myFloat);
    NSLog (@"**********");
    myInteger = [floatString integerValue];
    myFloat = [integerString floatValue];
    NSLog (@"Integer value = %i", myInteger);
    NSLog (@"Float value = %f", myFloat);
}
```

4. Choose File ➤ Save or press ⌘S to save your changes.

5. Click the Build and Run button or choose Build ➤ Build and Run. As long as you didn't mistype anything, you should see a blank window pop up.

6. Quit your program by clicking the Stop button or choosing Product ➤ Stop.

7. Choose Run ➤ Console or press ⇧⌘R. You should see the printed statements created by the NSLog command:

```
2010-09-05 09:22:07.334 VariableTest[31785:a0f] Integer value = 47
2010-09-05 09:22:07.343 VariableTest[31785:a0f] Float value = 52.701599
2010-09-05 09:22:07.345 VariableTest[31785:a0f] **********
2010-09-05 09:22:07.347 VariableTest[31785:a0f] Integer value = 52
2010-09-05 09:22:07.351 VariableTest[31785:a0f] Float value = 47.000000
```

Searching for a Substring

If you have a long string, you may need to know whether or not a certain word appears within that longer string. To determine that, you can search a string for a substring using the rangeOfString method.

To search for a substring within another string, you must declare a variable as an NSRange type:

```
NSRange myRange;
```

Then you must use the rangeOfString method to specify the substring to search for within the longer string:

```
[bigString rangeOfString: substring];
```

You next must assign the preceding code to the NSRange variable like this:

```
NSRange myRange;
myRange = [bigString rangeOfString: substring];
```

> **NOTE:** NSRange is a *structure*, which is a special data structure that lets you store multiple variables (called *fields*) inside a single variable name. The complete NSRange structure looks like this:
>
> ```
> typedef struct _NSRange {
>         NSUInteger location;
>         NSUInteger length;
> } NSRange;
> ```

The location Field

The NSRange class includes two fields that you can use to store information about a string: location and length. The location field identifies where the substring appeared in the larger string. If the substring does not appear at all, then the location field contains a value of NSNotFound. If the substring does appear within the larger string, then the location field contains an integer value.

The length Field

If the location field contains an integer value, then the length field contains the length of the substring that was found.

To see how to search for a substring within a larger string, follow these steps:

1. Open the VariableTest project from the previous section.

2. Click the `VariableTestAppDelegate.m` file stored inside the Classes folder. The code for that file appears in the middle pane of the Xcode window.

3. Modify the code in the `VariableTestAppDelegate.m` file as follows:

```
- (void)applicationDidFinishLaunching:(NSNotification *)aNotification {
    NSRange myRange;
    NSString *bigString = @"Learning to program can be fun!";
    myRange = [bigString rangeOfString: @"can be"];
    if (myRange.location == NSNotFound)
    {
        NSLog (@"Substring is not in %@", bigString);
    }
    else
    {
        NSLog (@"Substring found at location = %i", myRange.location);
        NSLog (@"Substring length = %i", myRange.length);
    }
}
```

4. Choose File ➤ Save or press ⌘S to save your changes.

5. Click the Build and Run button or choose Build ➤ Build and Run. As long as you didn't mistype anything, you should see a blank window pop up.

6. Quit your program by clicking the Stop button or choosing Product ➤ Stop.

7. Choose Run ➤ Console or press ⇧⌘R. You should see the printed statements created by the NSLog command:

```
2010-09-05 11:39:03.433 VariableTest[32079:a0f] Substring found at location = 20
2010-09-05 11:39:03.436 VariableTest[32079:a0f] Substring length = 6
```

Searching and Replacing

In addition to searching for a substring within a larger string, you can also search for and replace parts of a string, using either of two techniques. First, you can replace part of a long string starting at a specific location. Second, you can search for a specific substring and replace it with a new substring.

To search for and replace part of a string with a new substring, use the NSMutableString class, which allows the string to change while your program runs.

Replacing Part of a String at a Specific Location

To replace a substring with another substring, you must specify the location and the length of the substring. The location, or index, defines where in the long string you want to start replacing characters.

When working with strings, the first character in a string is at index position 0, the second character is at index position 1, and so on, as shown in Figure 9-1.

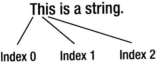

Index 0   Index 1   Index 2

Figure 9–1. *A string is zero-based, so the first character is index 0, the second is index 1, and so on.*

To determine how many characters to replace, you have to specify a numeric value for the substring length. For example, suppose you had this string:

```
@"That is a large string."
```

If you wanted to replace the substring "is" in this string, you would have to specify an index of 5 and a length of 2.

Regardless of the original substring length, you can replace it with a new substring of a different length and the computer will adjust the longer string accordingly. So if you wanted to replace the word "is" with the phrase "was not", the longer string would now read "That was not a large string."

To replace part of a longer string with a substring, you need to use the following:

- replaceCharactersInRange: Swaps out a specific location in a string with a substring

- NSMakeRange(index, length): Defines the index in the string and the number of characters to replace

- withString: Defines the new substring to insert into the longer string

Putting all of these together, you could use the following code:

```
[largeString replaceCharactersInRange: NSMakeRange(5,2) withString: @"was not"];
```

To see how to replace a substring in a specific location of a longer string, follow these steps:

1. Open the VariableTest project from the previous section.

2. Click the VariableTestAppDelegate.m file stored inside the Classes folder. The code for that file appears in the middle pane of the Xcode window.

3. Modify the code in the VariableTestAppDelegate.m file as follows:

```
- (void)applicationDidFinishLaunching:(NSNotification *)aNotification {
    NSMutableString *largeString;
    largeString = [NSMutableString stringWithString: @"That is a string"];
    NSLog (@"Original string = %@", largeString);
    [largeString replaceCharactersInRange: NSMakeRange(5,2) withString: @"was not"];
    NSLog (@"New string = %@", largeString);
}
```

4.   Choose File ➤ Save or press ⌘S to save your changes.

5.   Click the Build and Run button or choose Build ➤ Build and Run. As long as you didn't mistype anything, you should see a blank window pop up.

6.   Quit your program by clicking the Stop button or choosing Product ➤ Stop.

7.   Choose Run ➤ Console or press ⇧⌘R. You should see the printed statements created by the NSLog command:

```
2010-09-05 17:29:04.890 VariableTest[32706:a0f] Original string = That is a string
2010-09-05 17:29:04.893 VariableTest[32706:a0f] New string = That was not a string
```

Searching for and Replacing Part of a String

Suppose you want to search for and replace a substring within another string, but you do not know the exact location of the substring that you want to replace. As an alternative, you can search for a specific substring to replace regardless of its location in the longer string.

To search for and replace part of a longer string with a substring, you need to use the following:

■   replaceOccurrencesOfString: Defines a specific string to replace

■   withString: Defines the string to use and insert in a larger string

■   options: Defines different ways to search such as NSCaseInsensitiveSearch (ignores upper and lower case in a string), NSLiteralSearch (every character must exactly match), NSBackwardsSearch (starts searching from the end), NSAnchoredSearch (only searches from the beginning of the string, or the end if used with NSBackwardsSearch)

■   range: Defines the part of a larger string to search

Putting all of these together, you could use the following code:

```
[newString replaceOccurrencesOfString:@"another"
        withString:@"a modified"
        options:NSCaseInsensitiveSearch
        range:replaceRange];
```

This code would look in the newString variable for the substring "another" and replace it with the string "a modified".

To see how to search for and replace a substring in a longer string, follow these steps:

1. Open the VariableTest project from the previous section.

2. Click the `VariableTestAppDelegate.m` file stored inside the Classes folder. The code for that file appears in the middle pane of the Xcode window.

3. Modify the code in the `VariableTestAppDelegate.m` file as follows:

```
- (void)applicationDidFinishLaunching:(NSNotification *)aNotification {
    NSMutableString *newString;
    newString = [NSMutableString stringWithString: @"This is another string."];
    NSLog (@"Original string = %@", newString);
    NSRange replaceRange = NSMakeRange(0, [newString length]);
    [newString replaceOccurrencesOfString:@"another"
        withString:@"a modified"
        options:NSCaseInsensitiveSearch
        range:replaceRange];
    NSLog (@"New string = %@", newString);
}
```

4. Choose File ➤ Save or press ⌘S to save your changes.

5. Click the Build and Run button or choose Build ➤ Build and Run. As long as you didn't mistype anything, you should see a blank window pop up.

6. Quit your program by clicking the Stop button or choosing Product ➤ Stop.

7. Choose Run ➤ Console or press ⇧⌘R. You should see the printed statements created by the NSLog command:

```
2010-09-05 18:27:54.796 VariableTest[32799:a0f] Original string = This is another
string.
2010-09-05 18:27:54.799 VariableTest[32799:a0f] New string = This is a modified string.
```

Deleting Part of a String

Sometimes you may want to delete part of a string. To do this, you must delete a substring from an `NSMutableString` variable and use the following two methods:

- `deleteCharactersInRange`: Deletes the substring defined by the `rangeOfString` method

- `rangeOfString`: Defines the substring to delete

To use these methods on an `NSMutableString`, you could use code like this:

```
[largeString deleteCharactersInRange: [largeString rangeOfString: @"delete me"]];
```

This code would delete the string `"delete me"` from the string stored in the `largeString` variable. To see how to delete a substring from a longer string, follow these steps:

1. Open the VariableTest project from the previous section.

2. Click the `VariableTestAppDelegate.m` file stored inside the Classes folder. The code for that file appears in the middle pane of the Xcode window.

3. Modify the code in the `VariableTestAppDelegate.m` file as follows:

```
- (void)applicationDidFinishLaunching:(NSNotification *)aNotification {
    NSMutableString *largeString;
    largeString = [NSMutableString stringWithString: @"That is a string"];
    NSLog (@"Original string = %@", largeString);
    [largeString deleteCharactersInRange: [largeString rangeOfString: @"is a "]];
    NSLog (@"New string = %@", largeString);
}
```

4. Choose File ➤ Save or press ⌘S to save your changes.

5. Click the Build and Run button or choose Build ➤ Build and Run. As long as you didn't mistype anything, you should see a blank window pop up.

6. Quit your program by clicking the Stop button or choosing Product ➤ Stop.

7. Choose Run ➤ Console or press ⇧⌘R. You should see the printed statements created by the NSLog command:

```
2010-09-05 18:56:28.351 VariableTest[32877:a0f] Original string = That is a string
2010-09-05 18:56:28.354 VariableTest[32877:a0f] New string = That string
```

When deleting a substring from another string, you may also need to delete the space ahead or after the substring you're deleting. In the preceding example, notice that you must delete the string `"is a "` with a blank space after the letter *a*. If you simply deleted the string `"is a"`, then there would be two spaces left to separate the remaining text, such as `"That   string"`, which may not be what you want.

Extracting a Substring

Deleting a substring just chops that substring out of a longer string and throws that substring away. In case you need to use that substring, you can yank it out and save it in a variable. There are two ways to extract a substring out of a longer string:

■ Specify the location in the longer string and the number of characters to extract

■ Specify the index in the longer string and yank out all characters starting from the defined location to the end of the string

The first method lets you yank out substrings from the middle of a longer string, such as yanking out the word "you" from the longer string `"Hello all you people."`

The second method can extract a substring only from a specific index to the end of the string, making it impossible to extract just a middle portion of a string.

Extracting a Substring with a Location and Length

To extract a substring from a longer string, you need to use the following:

■ `substringWithRange:` Extracts a substring defined by NSMakeRange

- NSMakeRange(index, length): Defines the index and number of characters to extract

When you extract a substring, you're copying part of the original string, so you can extract a substring from either an NSString or NSMutableString like this:

```
[largeString substringWithRange: NSMakeRange(X,Y)];
```

The preceding code returns a string that you can assign to an NSString variable like this:

```
NSString *myString;
myString = [largeString substringWithRange: NSMakeRange(X,Y)];
```

To see how to extract a substring and how it can affect your original string, follow these steps:

1. Open the VariableTest project from the previous section.

2. Click the VariableTestAppDelegate.m file stored inside the Classes folder. The code for that file appears in the middle pane of the Xcode window.

3. Modify the code in the VariableTestAppDelegate.m file as follows:

```
- (void)applicationDidFinishLaunching:(NSNotification *)aNotification {
    NSMutableString *largeString;
    largeString = [NSMutableString stringWithString: @"That is a string"];
    NSLog (@"Original string = %@", largeString);
    NSString *newString;
    newString = [largeString substringWithRange: NSMakeRange(5, 4)];
    NSLog (@"New string = %@", newString);
}
```

4. Choose File ➤ Save or press ⌘S to save your changes.

5. Click the Build and Run button or choose Build ➤ Build and Run. As long as you didn't mistype anything, you should see a blank window pop up.

6. Quit your program by clicking the Stop button or choosing Product ➤ Stop.

7. Choose Run ➤ Console or press ⇧⌘R. You should see the printed statements created by the NSLog command:

```
2010-09-05 20:09:00.058 VariableTest[33337:a0f] Original string = That is a string
2010-09-05 20:09:00.063 VariableTest[33337:a0f] New string = is a
```

Extracting a Substring to the End of a String

A much simpler, but limited, way to extract a substring out of a longer string is to specify a location in the longer string using the substringFromIndex method, which looks like this:

```
[largeString substringFromIndex: X];
```

The preceding code returns a string where the value of X is the index of the first character that you want in your substring. Whatever location you choose (any value, starting with 0), the substringFromIndex method yanks out that substring from that location to the end of the string.

To see how the substringFromIndex method works, follow these steps:

1.   Open the VariableTest project from the previous section.

2.   Click the VariableTestAppDelegate.m file stored inside the Classes folder. The code for that file appears in the middle pane of the Xcode window.

3.   Modify the code in the VariableTestAppDelegate.m file as follows:

```
- (void)applicationDidFinishLaunching:(NSNotification *)aNotification {
    NSMutableString *largeString;
    largeString = [NSMutableString stringWithString: @"That is a string"];
    NSLog (@"Original string = %@", largeString);
    NSString *newString;
    newString = [largeString substringFromIndex: 5];
    NSLog (@"New string = %@", newString);
}
```

4.   Choose File ➤ Save or press ⌘S to save your changes.

5.   Click the Build and Run button or choose Build ➤ Build and Run. As long as you didn't mistype anything, you should see a blank window pop up.

6.   Quit your program by clicking the Stop button or choosing Product ➤ Stop.

7.   Choose Run ➤ Console or press ⇧⌘R. You should see the printed statements created by the NSLog command:

```
2010-09-05 20:20:13.495 VariableTest[33385:a0f] Original string = That is a string
2010-09-05 20:20:13.500 VariableTest[33385:a0f] New string = is a string
```

Appending a Substring

If you have defined a string as an NSMutableString, you can append text to the end of it by using the appendString method like this:

```
[largeString appendString: @" Newly added string"];
```

Whatever text the largeString variable contains, it now includes the string "Newly added string" at the end. When appending text to a string, you may need to put a space ahead of the appended text so that the newly added string doesn't get smashed together with the other string.

To see how to use the appendString method, follow these steps:

1.   Open the VariableTest project from the previous section.

2.   Click the VariableTestAppDelegate.m file stored inside the Classes folder. The code for that file appears in the middle pane of the Xcode window.

3.   Modify the code in the VariableTestAppDelegate.m file as follows:

```
- (void)applicationDidFinishLaunching:(NSNotification *)aNotification {
    NSMutableString *largeString;
    largeString = [NSMutableString stringWithString: @"That is a string"];
    NSLog (@"Original string = %@", largeString);
    [largeString appendString: @" and this is a string too."];
    NSLog (@"New string = %@", largeString);
}
```

4. Choose File ➤ Save or press ⌘S to save your changes.

5. Click the Build and Run button or choose Build ➤ Build and Run. As long as you didn't mistype anything, you should see a blank window pop up.

6. Quit your program by clicking the Stop button or choosing Product ➤ Stop.

7. Choose Run ➤ Console or press ⇧⌘R. You should see the printed statements created by the NSLog command:

```
2010-09-05 20:30:33.054 VariableTest[33424:a0f] Original string = That is a string
2010-09-05 20:30:33.059 VariableTest[33424:a0f] New string = That is a string and this
is a string too.
```

Inserting a String

The appendString method adds a new string to the end of an existing one. If you want to add text in the middle or at the beginning of a string, you have to use the insertString method and specify the index with the atIndex method like this:

```
[largeString insertString: @" Newly added string" atIndex: X];
```

The insertString method defines the string to add, and the atIndex method defines the location in which to insert the string inside another string. When inserting a string inside an existing one, you may need to add an extra space before or after the inserted string so that the text does not appear smashed together.

To see how the insertString method works, follow these steps:

1. Open the VariableTest project from the previous section.

2. Click the VariableTestAppDelegate.m file stored inside the Classes folder. The code for that file appears in the middle pane of the Xcode window.

3. Modify the code in the VariableTestAppDelegate.m file as follows:

```
- (void)applicationDidFinishLaunching:(NSNotification *)aNotification {
    NSMutableString *largeString;
    largeString = [NSMutableString stringWithString: @"That is a string"];
    NSLog (@"Original string = %@", largeString);
    [largeString insertString: @"was and still " atIndex: 5];
    NSLog (@"New string = %@", largeString);
}
```

4. Choose File ➤ Save or press ⌘S to save your changes.

5. Click the Build and Run button or choose Build ➤ Build and Run. As long as you didn't mistype anything, you should see a blank window pop up.

6. Quit your program by clicking the Stop button or choosing Product ➤ Stop.

7. Choose Run ➤ Console or press ⇧⌘R. You should see the printed statements created by the NSLog command:

```
2010-09-05 20:37:54.657 VariableTest[33470:a0f] Original string = That is a string
2010-09-05 20:37:54.661 VariableTest[33470:a0f] New string = That was and still is a
string
```

Summary

After numbers, strings are the second most common type of data for programs to store and manipulate. If you just need to store a string and never modify it, you can declare an NSString variable. If you need to modify a string while your program runs, then you must declare an NSMutableString variable.

The way in which you assign a value to a string variable differs depending on whether you're using an NSString or NSMutableString. With an NSString, you can simply assign a value with the equal sign like this:

```
NSString *myString;
myString = @"My new string contents";
```

To assign a string to an NSMutableString variable, you must use the stringWithString method like this:

```
NSMutableString *myString;
myString = [NSMutableString stringWithString: @"My new string contents"];
```

Strings are any character inside double quotation marks and preceded by a @ symbol. If you store numbers as a string, you can convert those strings into actual integer or floating-point values.

When modifying strings, keep in mind that you may need empty spaces to prevent text from smashing together. Also when manipulating strings, you may need to specify an index position of a string. The first character of a string is considered to be at index 0, the second is at index 1, and so on.

Chapter 10

Arrays

When you store data, such as numbers or strings, in a variable, you can store only one chunk of data at a time. If you need to store five different numbers, you have to create five different variables. If you need to store 100 different numbers, you have to create 100 different variables. Clearly, having to create a new variable to store each new chunk of data is clumsy and inefficient, so programming languages offer a solution called an *array*.

An array essentially acts like a single variable that can store multiple chunks of data. Rather than acting like an individual box that can hold only one chunk of data, such as a single variable, an array acts like a big box divided into sections, where each section can store one chunk of data, as shown in Figure 10–1. Instead of being forced to create and name a new variable for each chunk of data you want to store, you just have to create and name a single array to store multiple chunks of data.

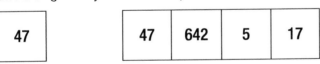

A variable can only hold one chunk of data

An array can hold multiple chunks of data

Figure 10–1. *An array acts like a single variable that can hold multiple data.*

NOTE: Anything used to store data is called a *data structure*. An array is the most common type of data structure, but there are other types of data structures for storing data as well. Each type of data structure has its own advantages and disadvantages.

If you're familiar with another programming language, such as C++, you know that most programming languages provide basic commands for creating and manipulating arrays. However, these basic commands often require you to write a lot of code just to do something as simple as adding or removing data from an array.

Arrays in other programming languages also have the limitation of allowing you to store only one type of data in an array. If you wanted to store integers, you would have to create a separate integer array. If you wanted to store floating-point numbers, or strings, you would have to create another floating-point or string array.

To avoid these limitations, Apple has created a special array class, called NSArray. In addition to providing much simpler commands for manipulating arrays, the NSArray class can store different types of data in the same array.

In Mac programming, there are two types of arrays you can create: NSArray and NSMutableArray. The NSArray is known as a *static array* because you can store data in the array once, but never add, change, or remove data later. The NSMutableArray is known as a *dynamic array* because you can always add data to, change data within, or delete data from the array while your program is running.

In this chapter, you'll learn how to create arrays, how to store data in an array, how to retrieve data in an array, and how to modify an array by adding or deleting data. Arrays are one of the more powerful tools you can use to keep your program's data organized.

Creating an Array

When you create an array (either an NSArray or NSMutableArray), you're working with objects, so you need to create a pointer such as the following:

```
NSArray *myArray;
NSMutableArray *myOtherArray;
```

This simply creates a pointer to an array object. To fill an array with data, you have two options. First, you can declare an array on one line and then fill that array on a second line like this:

```
NSArray *myArray;
myArray = [NSArray arrayWithObjects: object1,  object2, object3, nil];
```

A second way to fill an array with data is to declare and initialize the array on a single line:

```
NSArray *myArray = [NSArray arrayWithObjects: object1,  object2, object3, nil];
```

> **NOTE:** When storing items in an array, make sure you always define the end of the array data with nil. If you omit nil, then the computer won't know when your array ends, which will likely cause your program to run incorrectly, if at all.

Although this example adds only three objects, you can add as many objects to an array as you want. Before you can add an object to an array, you must declare that object ahead of the array:

```
NSString *object1 = @"Hello";
NSString *object2 = @"world!";
NSNumber *object3 = [NSNumber numberWithInt:45];
NSArray *myArray = [NSArray arrayWithObjects: object1,  object2, object3, nil];
```

Before continuing, it's important to know exactly what's happening in this code. First, whenever you see an asterisk used in front of a variable name, your code is probably defining a pointer, and the presence of pointers almost always means you're working with an object. The first three lines of this example create three objects named object1, object2, and object3. The first two objects are string objects (NSString) and the third object is a number object (NSNumber).

> **NOTE:** The value object (NSNumber) is used to hold a value such as an integer (int) or floating-point (float) number. In this case, the NSNumber object holds an NSNumber object that contains the number 45.

Second, the square brackets are almost always used to work with objects as well. The equal sign (=) assigns a value to a variable. In this case, the value inside the square brackets gets assigned to the *myArray pointer.

To see how an array works, follow these steps:

1. Open the VariableTest project from the previous chapter.

2. Click the VariableTestAppDelegate.m file stored inside the Classes folder. The code for that file appears in the middle pane of the Xcode window.

3. Modify the code in the VariableTestAppDelegate.m file as follows:

```
- (void)applicationDidFinishLaunching:(NSNotification *)aNotification {
    NSString *object1 = @"Hello";
    NSString *object2 = @"world!";
    NSNumber *object3 = [NSNumber numberWithInt:45];
    NSArray *myArray;
    myArray= [NSArray arrayWithObjects: object1, object2, object3, nil];
    NSLog(@"Array contents = %@",[myArray componentsJoinedByString:@", "]);
}
```

4. Choose File ➤ Save or press ⌘S to save your changes.

5. Click the Build and Run button or choose Build ➤ Build and Run. As long as you didn't mistype anything, you should see a blank window pop up.

6. Quit your program by clicking the Stop button or choosing Product ➤ Stop.

7. Choose Run ➤ Console or press ⇧⌘R. You should see the printed statements created by the NSLog command:

```
2010-08-31 22:24:10.948 VariableTest[18411:a0f] Array contents = Hello, world!, 45
```

Finding the Right Method to Use

When square brackets work with objects, the object name always appears first. In the previous example, the object is NSArray. The next question is, where did the arrayWithObjects method come from?

To find the answer, you need to remember that Apple has defined plenty of useful classes and stored them in its Cocoa framework for all programmers to use. Any time you see a class that begins with the prefix NS (which stands for NeXTSTEP), that's a clue that you're working with one of Apple's predefined classes.

Since classes almost always include properties (data) and methods (subprograms that manipulate the class's data), you can browse through Apple's Developer Documentation to find a list of all the methods and properties available for any class provided by Apple.

To find this documentation, you need to view the Developer Documentation through the Xcode Help menu. Choose Help ➤ Developer Documentation and search for **NSArray**. This will display a list of different help text about NSArray. Look for and click "NSArrayClass Reference" and you'll see the NSArray class reference, as shown in Figure 10–2.

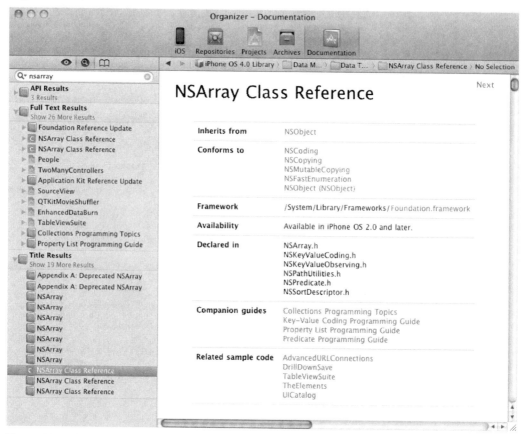

Figure 10–2. *The* NSArray *class reference is available in the Developer Documentation.*

Scroll through this NSArray class reference and look for a method that lets you store data in the NSArray. You may see several methods, but eventually you'll find the arrayWithObjects method listed, along with an explanation of how it works, as shown in Figure 10–3.

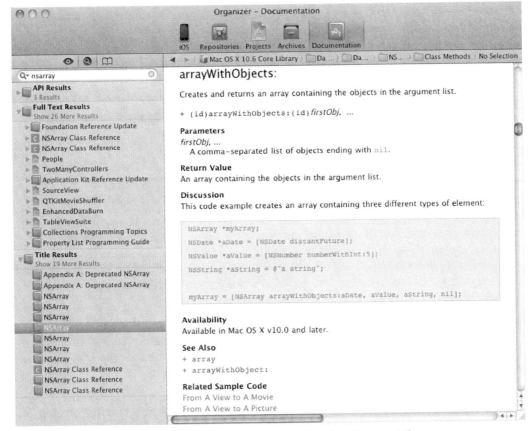

Figure 10–3. *The* `arrayWithObjects` *method explained in the Developer Documentation*

The general rule when working with classes that begin with an NS prefix is to look for the properties and methods you can use to manipulate those objects. Chances are good that Apple already provides the code you need to use, which means that instead of having to write your own code for adding data to an array (which you have to do in other programming languages), Apple lets you choose the method you need, thus reducing the amount of code you need to write and test.

Storing Objects in an Array

Now that you understand where the `arrayWithObjects` method came from, you can use it to store objects in the array. You must separate each object with a comma, and when you're done adding objects to the array, you must use the `nil` value to identify the end of the array. If you don't use `nil` as the last object stored in your array, you could confuse the computer and cause your program to crash.

Just the simple act of adding data to an array showed you quite a bit about the process of writing a Mac program. The biggest trick is simply knowing which methods, in different classes, you can use and how they work, which you can learn by browsing through the Developer Documentation.

Some other ways to learn about different methods available for specific classes include the following:

- Have someone show or tell you

- Find a book or web page that explains that particular method

- Study Objective-C programs written by someone else

Trying to find the right method to use can be like trying to look up a word in a dictionary when you don't know how to spell that word. The first step should be to look up the class reference for the particular object you want to manipulate, such as NSArray.

Suppose you look up a class reference and can't find the method you want. That doesn't necessarily mean that the method you want doesn't exist. Check the class reference for the object to see a list of other classes that the class inherits from. The NSArray class reference (see Figure 10–2) shows that the NSArray class inherits from the NSObject class. So if the method you want isn't available in the NSArray class reference, it might be described in the NSObject class reference.

Remember, every class contains its own methods and properties. When one class inherits from another class, that second class includes all the methods and properties of both classes. Since the NSArray class inherits from the NSObject class, the NSArray class inherits all the methods and properties from the NSObject class.

If you look up the class reference of one class, such as NSArray, in the Developer Documentation, you can view all the methods and properties unique to that particular class. If you then look up the class that the NSArray class inherits from (NSObject), you can see all the methods and properties specific to the NSObject class. However, since NSArray inherits every property and method from NSObject, NSArray winds up containing every property and method available in both NSObject and NSArray, as shown in Figure 10–4.

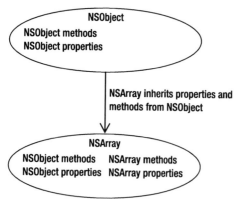

Figure 10–4. *Objects inherit methods and properties from other classes.*

Additional Methods for Filling an Array

When creating and filling an array with data, the most common method you'll use to fill the array with objects is the `arrayWithObjects` method. Of course, there are several other methods for filling an array, such as the following:

- `arrayWithArray`: Fills an array with the contents of an existing array
- `arrayWithContentsOfFile`: Fills an array with data stored in a file
- `arrayWithContentsOfURL`: Fills an array with data retrieved from a URL (web site)

As you can see, every object provides plenty of methods that Apple has already created and tested, so all you have to do is figure out how they work and when to use them in your own program. Using such prewritten and pretested methods helps you build more complicated programs faster and is more reliable than writing and testing your own code.

Counting the Items Stored in an Array

After you have stored data in an array, you can always count the number of items stored in that array by using the `count` command:

```
[arrayName count];
```

The `arrayName` simply represents the name of your array, and the `count` command returns the number of items in that array, so the entire line of code evaluates to a single number. If `arrayName` held six items, the preceding code would return the number 6.

To see how to count items in an array, follow these steps:

1. Open the VariableTest project from the previous section.

2. Click the `VariableTestAppDelegate.m` file stored inside the Classes folder. The code for that file appears in the middle pane of the Xcode window.

3. Modify the code in the `VariableTestAppDelegate.m` file as follows:

```
- (void)applicationDidFinishLaunching:(NSNotification *)aNotification {
    NSString *object1 = @"Hello";
    NSString *object2 = @"world!";
    NSNumber *object3 = [NSNumber numberWithInt:45];
    NSArray *myArray;
    myArray= [NSArray arrayWithObjects: object1, object2, object3, nil];
    NSLog(@"Array contents = %@",[myArray componentsJoinedByString:@", "]);
    NSLog (@"Total number of items in array = %i", [myArray count]);
}
```

4. Choose File ➤ Save or press ⌘S to save your changes.

5. Click the Build and Run button or choose Build ➤ Build and Run. As long as you didn't mistype anything, you should see a blank window pop up.

6. Quit your program by clicking the Stop button or choosing Product ➤ Stop.

7. Choose Run ➤ Console or press ⇧⌘R. You should see the printed statements created by the NSLog command:

```
2010-09-02 11:18:09.034 VariableTest[22851:a0f] Array contents = Hello, world!, 45
2010-09-02 11:18:09.038 VariableTest[22851:a0f] Total number of items in array = 3
```

Accessing an Item in an Array

When you store items in an array, the first item gets stored at one end of the array, the second item gets stored next to the first item, the third item gets stored next to the second item, and so on.

To keep track of all the items stored in an array, the array uses a number called an *array index*. The first item in an array is stored at index 0, the second item in an array is stored at index 1, and so on, as shown in Figure 10–5.

The array index identifies each element by a number.

0   1   2   3

Figure 10–5. *The array index identifies an item's position in an array.*

> **NOTE:** In Objective-C, the first item in an array is at index 0. Such arrays are known as zero-based arrays. In other programming languages, the first item in an array may start at index 1. Such arrays are known as one-based arrays. Most programming languages based on C, such as Objective-C, use zero-based arrays.

To retrieve an item from an array, you need to identify that item's index position in the array. So if you wanted to retrieve the first item in the array, you would retrieve the item stored at index position 0, if you wanted to retrieve the second item in the array, you would retrieve the item stored at index position 1, and so on.

To retrieve a specific item from an array, you have to identify the array, use the objectAtIndex method, and specify the index position:

```
[arrayName objectAtIndex: index];
```

The preceding code would return whatever object was stored in the array at the designated index position. So if you created an array like this,

```
NSArray *myArray = [NSArray arrayWithObjects: @"Hello", @"world", "@Good-bye", nil];
```

you could use the following code to retrieve the second item (index position 1) in the array, which would be "world":

```
[myArray objectAtIndex:1];
```

To see how to retrieve items from an array, follow these steps:

1. Open the VariableTest project from the previous section.

2. Click the `VariableTestAppDelegate.m` file stored inside the Classes folder. The code for that file appears in the middle pane of the Xcode window.

3. Modify the code in the `VariableTestAppDelegate.m` file as follows:

```
- (void)applicationDidFinishLaunching:(NSNotification *)aNotification {
  NSString *object1 = @"Hello";
    NSString *object2 = @"world!";
    NSNumber *object3 = [NSNumber numberWithInt:45];
    NSArray *myArray;
    myArray= [NSArray arrayWithObjects: object1, object2, object3, nil];
    NSLog(@"Array contents = %@",[myArray componentsJoinedByString:@", "]);
    NSLog (@"Index position 1 = %@", [myArray objectAtIndex:1]);
}
```

4. Choose File ➤ Save or press ⌘S to save your changes.

5. Click the Build and Run button or choose Build → Build and Run. As long as you didn't mistype anything, you should see a blank window pop up.

6. Quit your program by clicking the Stop button or choosing Product ➤ Stop.

7. Choose Run ➤ Console or press ⇧⌘R. You should see the printed statements created by the NSLog command:

```
2010-09-03 14:53:37.017 VariableTest[26555:a0f] Array contents = Hello, world!, 45
2010-09-03 14:53:37.021 VariableTest[26555:a0f] Index position 1 = world!
```

Accessing All Items in an Array

Accessing an individual item in an array is fine when you only want that one item. However, if you want to retrieve all the items in an array, and all items stored in the array are of the same data type, you can use something called *fast enumeration*.

Fast enumeration lets you access every item in an array by using a modified `for` loop that looks like this:

```
for (objectType *variable in arrayName)
```

The `objectType` represents the type of objects stored in an array, such as `NSString` or `NSNumber`. The `*variable` is any arbitrarily named variable you want to use. The `arrayName` is the actual array. Suppose you had an array like this:

```
NSString *object1 = @"Hello";
NSString *object2 = @"world!";
NSString *object3 = @"Good-bye";
NSArray *myArray = [NSArray arrayWithObjects: object1, object2, object3, nil];
```

To retrieve every item out of that array using fast enumeration, you could use a `for` loop like this:

```
for (NSString *randomVariable in myArray)
    {
```

```
    NSLog (@"Array element = %@", randomVariable);
    }
```

To see how fast enumeration works, follow these steps:

1. Open the VariableTest project from the previous section.

2. Click on the VariableTestAppDelegate.m file stored inside the Classes folder. The code for that file appears in the middle pane of the Xcode window.

3. Modify the code in the VariableTestAppDelegate.m file as follows:

```
- (void)applicationDidFinishLaunching:(NSNotification *)aNotification {
    NSString *object1 = @"Hello";
    NSString *object2 = @"world!";
    NSString *object3 = @"Good-bye";
    NSArray *myArray;
    myArray= [NSArray arrayWithObjects: object1, object2, object3, nil];
    for (NSString *randomVariable in myArray)
    {
        NSLog (@"Array element = %@", randomVariable);
    }
}
```

4. Choose File ➤ Save or press ⌘S to save your changes.

5. Click the Build and Run button or choose Build ➤ Build and Run. As long as you didn't mistype anything, you should see a blank window pop up.

6. Quit your program by clicking the Stop button or choosing Product ➤ Stop.

7. Choose Run ➤ Console or press ⇧⌘R. You should see the printed statements created by the NSLog command:

```
2010-09-03 15:25:59.460 VariableTest[26668:a0f] Array element = Hello
2010-09-03 15:25:59.461 VariableTest[26668:a0f] Array element = world!
2010-09-03 15:25:59.463 VariableTest[26668:a0f] Array element = Good-bye
```

If you have stored different types of data in an array, then you can access each item in your array using a for loop that starts at 0 and runs for each item stored in the array using the count method:

```
int i;
for (i = 0; i < [arrayName count]; i++)
{
    NSLog (@"Element %i = %@", i, [arrayName objectAtIndex: i]);
}
```

This for loop runs from 0 to the total number of items stored in the array. If you had three items stored in the array, the for loop would run five times (from 0 to 2).

To see how to retrieve data from an array using an ordinary for loop, follow these steps:

1. Open the VariableTest project from the previous section.

2. Click on the VariableTestAppDelegate.m file stored inside the Classes folder. The code for that file appears in the middle pane of the Xcode window.

3. Modify the code in the `VariableTestAppDelegate.m` file as follows:

```
- (void)applicationDidFinishLaunching:(NSNotification *)aNotification {
    NSString *object1 = @"Hello";
    NSString *object2 = @"world!";
    NSNumber *object3 = [NSNumber numberWithInt:45];
    NSArray *myArray;
    myArray= [NSArray arrayWithObjects: object1, object2, object3, nil];
    int i;
    for (i = 0; i < [myArray count]; i++)
    {
        NSLog (@"Element %i = %@", i, [myArray objectAtIndex: i]);
    }
}
```

4. Choose File ➤ Save or press ⌘S to save your changes.

5. Click the Build and Run button or choose Build ➤ Build and Run. As long as you didn't mistype anything, you should see a blank window pop up.

6. Quit your program by clicking the Stop button or choosing Product ➤ Stop.

7. Choose Run ➤ Console or press ⇧⌘R. You should see the printed statements created by the `NSLog` command:

```
2010-09-03 21:13:43.781 VariableTest[27527:a0f] Element 0 = Hello
2010-09-03 21:13:43.784 VariableTest[27527:a0f] Element 1 = world!
2010-09-03 21:13:43.791 VariableTest[27527:a0f] Element 2 = 45
```

Adding Items to an Array

When you declare an array, you have to declare it as either an `NSArray` or `NSMutableArray`. If you declare an array as an `NSArray`, you can store data in it once, but never again. If you want your program to be able to store and change data in an array while your program runs, you need to declare your array as an `NSMutableArray` like this:

```
NSMutableArray *arrayName;
```

To add data to an `NSMutableArray`, you need to define the `NSMutableArray` to use, use the `addObject` method, and specify the data to add:

```
[arrayName addObject: newObject];
```

Suppose you had the following `NSMutableArray` and filled it with data like this:

```
NSString *object1 = @"Hello";
NSString *object2 = @"world!";
NSString *object3 = @"Good-bye";
NSMutableArray *myArray;
myArray= [NSMutableArray arrayWithObjects: object1, object2, object3, nil];
```

You could add data to this array by using code like this:

```
[myArray addObject: @"New item"];
```

This would add the object @"New item" at the end of the array named myArray. To see how the addObject method works, follow these steps:

1. Open the VariableTest project from the previous section.

2. Click the VariableTestAppDelegate.m file stored inside the Classes folder. The code for that file appears in the middle pane of the Xcode window.

3. Modify the code in the VariableTestAppDelegate.m file as follows:

```
- (void)applicationDidFinishLaunching:(NSNotification *)aNotification {
    NSString *object1 = @"Hello";
    NSString *object2 = @"world!";
    NSString *object3 = @"Good-bye";
    NSMutableArray *myArray;
    myArray= [NSMutableArray arrayWithObjects: object1, object2, object3, nil];
    for (NSString *randomVariable in myArray)
    {
        NSLog (@"Array element = %@", randomVariable);
    }
    [myArray addObject: @"New item"];
    NSLog (@"**********");
    for (NSString *randomVariable in myArray)
    {
        NSLog (@"Array element = %@", randomVariable);
    }
}
```

4. Choose File ➤ Save or press ⌘S to save your changes.

5. Click the Build and Run button or choose Build ➤ Build and Run. As long as you didn't mistype anything, you should see a blank window pop up.

6. Quit your program by clicking the Stop button or choosing Product ➤ Stop.

7. Choose Run ➤ Console or press ⇧⌘R. You should see the printed statements created by the NSLog command:

```
2010-09-03 16:14:56.614 VariableTest[26819:a0f] Array element = Hello
2010-09-03 16:14:56.614 VariableTest[26819:a0f] Array element = world!
2010-09-03 16:14:56.615 VariableTest[26819:a0f] Array element = Good-bye
2010-09-03 16:14:56.616 VariableTest[26819:a0f] **********
2010-09-03 16:14:56.617 VariableTest[26819:a0f] Array element = Hello
2010-09-03 16:14:56.619 VariableTest[26819:a0f] Array element = world!
2010-09-03 16:14:56.620 VariableTest[26819:a0f] Array element = Good-bye
2010-09-03 16:14:56.633 VariableTest[26819:a0f] Array element = New item
```

The first time the for loop runs, it prints all three items in the array (Hello, world!, and Good-bye). The second time the for loops runs, it prints four items stored in the array (Hello, world!, Good-bye, and New item). The addObject method always adds the new item at the end of the array.

Inserting Items into an Array

The addObject method is fine when you just want to store an item at the end of the array. However, what if you want to store an item in a specific part of an array, such as the beginning or somewhere in the middle? In that case, you have to use the insertObject method, which looks like this:

```
[arrayName insertObject: newObject atIndex: index];
```

The main difference between the addObject method and the insertObject method is that when you use the insertObject method, you must also specify the index position where you want to add the new item. If you wanted to insert a new item as the second item in the array, which would be index position 1, you would do so like this:

```
[arrayName insertObject: newObject atIndex: 1];
[myArray addObject: @"New item"];
```

This would add the object @"New item" at the end of the array named myArray. To see how the addObject method works, follow these steps:

1. Open the VariableTest project from the previous section.

2. Click on the VariableTestAppDelegate.m file stored inside the Classes folder. The code for that file appears in the middle pane of the Xcode window.

3. Modify the code in the VariableTestAppDelegate.m file as follows:

```
- (void)applicationDidFinishLaunching:(NSNotification *)aNotification {
    NSString *object1 = @"Hello";
    NSString *object2 = @"world!";
    NSString *object3 = @"Good-bye";//[NSNumber numberWithInt:45];
    NSMutableArray *myArray;
    myArray= [NSMutableArray arrayWithObjects: object1, object2, object3, nil];
    for (NSString *randomVariable in myArray)
    {
        NSLog (@"Array element = %@", randomVariable);
    }
    [myArray insertObject: @"New item" atIndex: 1];
    NSLog (@"*********");
    for (NSString *randomVariable in myArray)
    {
        NSLog (@"Array element = %@", randomVariable);
    }
}
```

4. Choose File ➤ Save or press ⌘S to save your changes.

5. Click the Build and Run button or choose Build ➤ Build and Run. As long as you didn't mistype anything, you should see a blank window pop up.

6. Quit your program by clicking the Stop button or choosing Product ➤ Stop.

7. Choose Run ➤ Console or press ⇧⌘R. You should see the printed statements created by the NSLog command:

```
2010-09-03 19:00:06.133 VariableTest[27100:a0f] Array element = Hello
```

```
2010-09-03 19:00:06.136 VariableTest[27100:a0f] Array element = world!
2010-09-03 19:00:06.137 VariableTest[27100:a0f] Array element = Good-bye
2010-09-03 19:00:06.139 VariableTest[27100:a0f] **********
2010-09-03 19:00:06.144 VariableTest[27100:a0f] Array element = Hello
2010-09-03 19:00:06.144 VariableTest[27100:a0f] Array element = New item
2010-09-03 19:00:06.145 VariableTest[27100:a0f] Array element = world!
2010-09-03 19:00:06.146 VariableTest[27100:a0f] Array element = Good-bye
```

Just remember that when you specify an index position for inserting an item into an array, that index position must be available. So, for example, if you have an array that consists of three items, which would correspond to index positions 0, 1, and 2, and you try to insert a new item at any index position that's 3 or higher, your program won't work.

Deleting Items from an Array

Just as you can add and insert new items into an array, you can delete items from an array. When you delete an item, you must specify the index position of the item that you want to delete.

There are actually several methods you can use to delete an item from an array:

- removeLastObject: Deletes the last item in the array

- removeObjectAtIndex: Deletes an item at a specific index position

- removeAllObjects: Deletes everything from an array

- removeObject: Deletes all instances of an item stored in an array

Deleting the Last Item in an Array

When you just want to delete the last item in an array, you need to specify the array name and use the removeLastObject method like this:

```
[arrayName removeLastObject];
```

Deleting an Item from a Specific Index Position

Another way to delete an item from an array is to specify the index position of the item that you want to delete using this code:

```
[arrayName removeObjectAtIndex: index];
```

So if you wanted to delete the second item in an array, you would specify index position 1:

```
[arrayName removeObjectAtIndex: 1];
```

Deleting Every Item from an Array

If you need to clear out an entire array, you could delete items one at a time, but it's much faster to wipe out everything at once using the `removeAllObjects` method like this:

```
[arrayName removeAllObjects];
```

Deleting All Instances of an Item from an Array

It's possible to store identical data in different parts of an array. For example, you might store the string @"Hello" in the first index position of an array and also in the sixth index position of that same array.

If you want to delete all @"Hello" strings in an array, you can use the `removeObject` method and specify the data that you want to delete:

```
[arrayName removeObject: object];
```

So if you wanted to delete the @"Hello" string from an array, you would use this code:

```
[arrayName removeObject: @"Hello"];
```

To see all the different ways to delete items from an array, follow these steps:

1. Open the VariableTest project from the previous section.

2. Click the VariableTestAppDelegate.m file stored inside the Classes folder. The code for that file appears in the middle pane of the Xcode window.

3. Modify the code in the VariableTestAppDelegate.m file as follows:

```
- (void)applicationDidFinishLaunching:(NSNotification *)aNotification {
    NSString *object1 = @"Hello";
    NSString *object2 = @"world!";
    NSString *object3 = @"Good-bye";
    NSString *object4 = @"Hello";
    NSString *object5 = @"More data";
    NSString *object6 = @"Hello";
    NSString *object7 = @"Last data";
    NSMutableArray *myArray;
    myArray= [NSMutableArray arrayWithObjects: object1, object2, object3, object4,
object5, object6, object7, nil];
    NSLog (@"***** Original array *****");
    for (NSString *randomVariable in myArray)
    {
        NSLog (@"Array element = %@", randomVariable);
    }

    NSLog (@" ");
    NSLog (@"***** Deleting last array item *****");
    [myArray removeLastObject];
    for (NSString *randomVariable in myArray)
    {
        NSLog (@"Array element = %@", randomVariable);
    }
```

```
NSLog (@" ");
NSLog (@"***** Deleting item at index position 2 *****");
[myArray removeObjectAtIndex: 2];
for (NSString *randomVariable in myArray)
{
    NSLog (@"Array element = %@", randomVariable);
}

NSLog (@" ");
NSLog (@"***** Deleting all instances of Hello *****");
[myArray removeObject: @"Hello"];
for (NSString *randomVariable in myArray)
{
    NSLog (@"Array element = %@", randomVariable);
}
}
```

4.   Choose File ➤ Save or press ⌘S to save your changes.

5.   Click the Build and Run button or choose Build ➤ Build and Run. As long as you didn't mistype anything, you should see a blank window pop up.

6.   Quit your program by clicking the Stop button or choosing Product ➤ Stop.

7.   Choose Run ➤ Console or press ⇧⌘R. You should see the printed statements created by the NSLog command:

```
2010-09-03 20:48:16.715 VariableTest[27435:a0f] ***** Original array *****
2010-09-03 20:48:16.725 VariableTest[27435:a0f] Array element = Hello
2010-09-03 20:48:16.726 VariableTest[27435:a0f] Array element = world!
2010-09-03 20:48:16.726 VariableTest[27435:a0f] Array element = Good-bye
2010-09-03 20:48:16.727 VariableTest[27435:a0f] Array element = Hello
2010-09-03 20:48:16.729 VariableTest[27435:a0f] Array element = More data
2010-09-03 20:48:16.730 VariableTest[27435:a0f] Array element = Hello
2010-09-03 20:48:16.731 VariableTest[27435:a0f] Array element = Last data
2010-09-03 20:48:16.732 VariableTest[27435:a0f]
2010-09-03 20:48:16.738 VariableTest[27435:a0f] ***** Deleting last array item *****
2010-09-03 20:48:16.740 VariableTest[27435:a0f] Array element = Hello
2010-09-03 20:48:16.741 VariableTest[27435:a0f] Array element = world!
2010-09-03 20:48:16.742 VariableTest[27435:a0f] Array element = Good-bye
2010-09-03 20:48:16.742 VariableTest[27435:a0f] Array element = Hello
2010-09-03 20:48:16.743 VariableTest[27435:a0f] Array element = More data
2010-09-03 20:48:16.744 VariableTest[27435:a0f] Array element = Hello
2010-09-03 20:48:16.758 VariableTest[27435:a0f]
2010-09-03 20:48:16.759 VariableTest[27435:a0f] ***** Deleting item at index position 2
*****
2010-09-03 20:48:16.760 VariableTest[27435:a0f] Array element = Hello
2010-09-03 20:48:16.761 VariableTest[27435:a0f] Array element = world!
2010-09-03 20:48:16.762 VariableTest[27435:a0f] Array element = Hello
2010-09-03 20:48:16.763 VariableTest[27435:a0f] Array element = More data
2010-09-03 20:48:16.764 VariableTest[27435:a0f] Array element = Hello
2010-09-03 20:48:16.764 VariableTest[27435:a0f]
2010-09-03 20:48:16.765 VariableTest[27435:a0f] ***** Deleting all instances of Hello
*****
2010-09-03 20:48:16.766 VariableTest[27435:a0f] Array element = world!
2010-09-03 20:48:16.766 VariableTest[27435:a0f] Array element = More data
```

Summary

Arrays let you store multiple chunks of data in a single variable. To create an array, you have to create a pointer to an array based on the NSArray or NSMutableArray class. If you just want to store data in an array, use the NSArray class. If you want your program to be able to add data to or delete data from an array while your program is running, use the NSMutableArray class.

Arrays can store different types of data or the same type of data. If you store the same type of data in an array, you can use fast enumeration to access every item in your array. If you store different types of data in an array, you need to use a traditional for loop to retrieve each item in the array.

You can add an item to an NSMutableArray at the end of that array or at a specific index position. You can also delete data from an array in several ways: delete data from a specific position in the array (either from the end of the array or at a specific index position), delete one or more instances of data stored in the array, or delete all items from an array. Arrays are just one way to store multiple, related chunks of data in a single variable.

Chapter 11

Dictionaries and Sets

When you store data in an array, you can retrieve it by searching for that specific data or by keeping track of the index position of that data. Since searching for data or storing index positions of data can be cumbersome, there are two other data structures you can use called a *dictionary* and a *set*.

Dictionaries act like arrays, but they contain a paired key for each stored value, allowing you to search for a stored value just by knowing its key. Sets make it easy to compare lists and are useful for grouping items and determining whether one set is a subset or intersection of another set.

In this chapter, we explore the ins and outs of both of these data structures.

Dictionary Basics

A dictionary stores two chunks of data. First, there's the actual data or value itself that you want to store. Second, there's a key associated with that value. This key can be any short word or phrase that helps identify your actual data. Now instead of trying to search for your data, you just search for this key. Once you find the key, the key will point to your value, as shown in Figure 11–1.

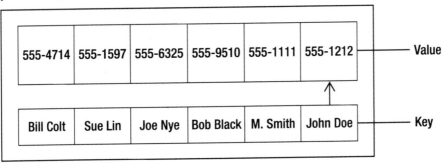

A Dictionary data structure contains a
value and a key that points to the data

Figure 11–1. *A dictionary stores values and keys associated with that value.*

For example, you could store a list of phone numbers in an array, but how would you know how to find the one phone number you wanted? Trying to remember which index position each phone number is stored in would prove difficult, and trying to search for a specific phone number is equally clumsy.

However, if you stored each phone number with a key, where each key contained a person's name, you could use the keys to find a desired phone number. Instead of searching for the phone number, you could search for the name John Doe or M. Smith, and that key would show you John Doe's or M. Smith's phone number.

To create a dictionary for storing data, you can create an NSDictionary or an NSMutableDictionary. The NSDictionary can store data but will not let you add, change, or remove data later. The NSMutableDictionary can store, add, change, or delete data from the dictionary while your program is running.

Creating and Putting Data in a Dictionary

When you create a dictionary, you have to decide whether you want to create a static dictionary (NSDictionary) that can only store data but not let you modify it or create a dynamic dictionary (NSMutableDictionary) that can store, add, or remove data while your program runs.

To create and initialize an NSDictionary, you need to use the dictionaryWithObjectsAndKeys method:

```
NSDictionary *myDictionary = [NSDictionary dictionaryWithObjectsAndKeys: @"Data1",
@"Key1", @"Data2", @"Key2", nil];
```

When filling a dictionary with data using the dictionaryWithObjectsAndKeys method, you must make sure each chunk of data is immediately followed by its associated key. When you're done adding data, you must end the list with nil.

You can also use the dictionaryWithObjectsAndKeys method to create and initialize an NSMutableDictionary too. This can be convenient when storing one or two key-value pairs. However, if you need to store large amounts of data, you may find it easier to use the setObject and forKey methods to add a single key-value pair at a time.

To use the setObject and forKey methods, you must first declare an NSMutableDictionary with a pointer:

```
NSMutableDictionary *myOtherDictionary = [NSMutableDictionary dictionary];
```

This creates a pointer to an empty dictionary object. After you have created a dictionary, you can fill it with data. Data in a dictionary consists of a key-value pair where you store the data (value) along with its key.

For each chunk of data (a key-value pair) that you want to store in a dictionary, you have to use the setObject and forKey methods on a separate line like this:

```
[dictionaryName setObject: @"Data" forKey: @"Key"];
```

In the previous code, you would use the actual dictionary name and substitute your actual data and key in between the double quotation marks. If your dictionary was named phonebook and you wanted to store the data 555-1478 with a key John Doe, you could use the following:

```
[phoneBook setObject: @"555-1478" forKey: @"John Doe"];
```

Counting the Items Stored in a Dictionary

After you have stored data in a dictionary, you can always count the number of items stored in that dictionary by using the count command:

```
[dictionaryName count];
```

The dictionaryName simply represents the name of your dictionary, and the count command returns the number of items in that dictionary, so the entire line of previous code evaluates to a single number. If dictionaryName held six key-value pairs of data, the previous code would return the number 6.

To see how to count items in a dictionary, follow these steps:

1. Open the VariableTest project from the previous section.

2. Click the VariableTestAppDelegate.m file stored in the Classes folder. The code for that file appears in the middle pane of the Xcode window.

3. Modify the code in the VariableTestAppDelegate.m file as follows:

```
- (void)applicationDidFinishLaunching:(NSNotification *)aNotification {
    NSMutableDictionary *myDictionary = [NSMutableDictionary dictionary];
    [myDictionary setObject: @"555-1212" forKey: @"John Doe"];
    [myDictionary setObject: @"555-9999" forKey: @"Al Jones"];
    [myDictionary setObject: @"555-5555" forKey: @"Mary Smith"];

    int counter;
    counter = [myDictionary count];
    NSLog (@"Number of items = %i", counter);
}
```

4. Choose File ➤ Save or press ⌘S to save your changes.

5. Click the Build and Run button, or choose Build ➤ Build and Run. As long as you didn't mistype anything, you should see a blank window pop up.

6. Quit the program, such as by clicking the Stop button or choosing Product ➤ Stop from the Xcode pull-down menus.

7. Choose Run ➤ Console, or press ⇧⌘R. You should see the printed statements created by the NSLog command:

```
2010-09-06 14:39:48.536 VariableTest[656:a0f] Number of items = 3
```

Retrieving an Item from a Dictionary

To retrieve an item from a dictionary, you only need to know the *key* associated with that data, using the objectForKey method like this:

```
[dictionaryName objectForKey: @"Key"];
```

The previous code returns the data associated with the key, so you may need to create a variable to hold this data:

```
NSString *myString;
myString = [myDictionary objectForKey: @"Key"];
```

To see how to retrieve data from a dictionary by using a key, follow these steps:

1. Open the VariableTest project from the previous section.

2. Click the VariableTestAppDelegate.m file stored in the Classes folder. The code for that file appears in the middle pane of the Xcode window.

3. Modify the code in the VariableTestAppDelegate.m file as follows:

```
- (void)applicationDidFinishLaunching:(NSNotification *)aNotification {
    NSMutableDictionary *myDictionary = [NSMutableDictionary dictionary];
    [myDictionary setObject: @"555-1212" forKey: @"John Doe"];
    [myDictionary setObject: @"555-9999" forKey: @"Al Jones"];
    [myDictionary setObject: @"555-5555" forKey: @"Mary Smith"];

    int counter;
    counter = [myDictionary count];
    NSLog (@"Number of items = %i", counter);

    NSString *myString;
    myString = [myDictionary objectForKey: @"Al Jones"];
    NSLog (@"Al Jones is associated with %@", myString);
}
```

4. Choose File ➤ Save or press ⌘S to save your changes.

5. Click the Build and Run button, or choose Build ➤ Build and Run. As long as you didn't mistype anything, you should see a blank window pop up.

6. Quit the program, such as by clicking the Stop button or choosing Product ➤ Stop from the Xcode pull-down menus.

7. Choose Run ➤ Console, or press ⇧⌘R. You should see the printed statements created by the NSLog command:

```
2010-09-06 16:15:53.608 VariableTest[1041:a0f] Number of items = 3
2010-09-06 16:15:53.611 VariableTest[1041:a0f] Al Jones is associated with 555-9999
```

Deleting Data from a Dictionary

If you have an NSMutableDictionary, you may want to remove data from it. To do this, you need to identify the key associated with that data and then use the removeObjectForKey method like this:

```
[dictionaryName removeObjectForKey: @"Key"];
```

In case you want to remove all data from a dictionary, you can use the removeAllObjects method:

```
[dictioinaryName removeAllObjects];
```

To see how the removeObjectForKey and removeAllObjects methods, follow these steps:

1. Open the VariableTest project from the previous section.

2. Click the VariableTestAppDelegate.m file stored in the Classes folder. The code for that file appears in the middle pane of the Xcode window.

3. Modify the code in the VariableTestAppDelegate.m file as follows:

```
- (void)applicationDidFinishLaunching:(NSNotification *)aNotification {
    NSMutableDictionary *myDictionary = [NSMutableDictionary dictionary];
    [myDictionary setObject: @"555-1212" forKey: @"John Doe"];
    [myDictionary setObject: @"555-9999" forKey: @"Al Jones"];
    [myDictionary setObject: @"555-5555" forKey: @"Mary Smith"];

    int counter;
    counter = [myDictionary count];
    NSLog (@"Number of items = %i", counter);

    NSString *myString;
    myString = [myDictionary objectForKey: @"Al Jones"];
    NSLog (@"Al Jones is associated with %@", myString);

    [myDictionary removeObjectForKey: @"John Doe"];
    NSLog (@"Number of items = %i", [myDictionary count]);

    [myDictionary removeAllObjects];
    NSLog (@"Number of items = %i", [myDictionary count]);
}
```

4. Choose File ➤ Save or press ⌘S to save your changes.

5. Click the Build and Run button, or choose Build ➤ Build and Run. As long as you didn't mistype anything, you should see a blank window pop up.

6. Quit the program, such as by clicking the Stop button or choosing Product ➤ Stop from the Xcode pull-down menus.

7. Choose Run ➤ Console, or press ⇧⌘R. You should see the printed statements created by the NSLog command:

```
2010-09-06 16:46:21.010 VariableTest[1160:a0f] Number of items = 3
2010-09-06 16:46:21.023 VariableTest[1160:a0f] Al Jones is associated with 555-9999
```

```
2010-09-06 16:46:21.025 VariableTest[1160:a0f] Number of items = 2
2010-09-06 16:46:21.025 VariableTest[1160:a0f] Number of items = 0
```

Copying a Dictionary

When you create an NSDictionary, you can add data to it only once. If you later want to add or delete data, you can't. The simplest solution is to create and use an NSMutableDictionary right from the start.

A second solution is to copy the contents of an NSDictionary into an NSMutableDictionary. Then you can manipulate the contents in the NSMutableDictionary. This might be handy when you want only one part of your program to modify the data in a dictionary but you don't want to risk giving your entire program the ability to modify the contents of a dictionary.

To copy the contents of a dictionary into another dictionary, you can use the addEntriesFromDictionary method like this:

```
[newDictionary addEntriesFromDictionary: oldDictionary];
```

This code copies the data from the oldDictionary and puts it into the newDictionary.

To see how the addEntriesFromDictionary method works, follow these steps:

1. Open the VariableTest project from the previous section.

2. Click the VariableTestAppDelegate.m file stored in the Classes folder. The code for that file appears in the middle pane of the Xcode window.

3. Modify the code in the VariableTestAppDelegate.m file as follows:

```
- (void)applicationDidFinishLaunching:(NSNotification *)aNotification {
    NSDictionary *staticDictionary = [NSDictionary dictionaryWithObjectsAndKeys:
@"Data1", @"Key1", @"Data2", @"Key2", nil];
    NSLog (@"Number of items in NSDictionary = %i", [staticDictionary count]);

    NSMutableDictionary *newDict = [NSMutableDictionary dictionary];
    [newDict addEntriesFromDictionary: staticDictionary];
    NSLog (@"Count in new Dictionary = %i", [newDict count]);
}
```

4. Choose File ➤ Save or press ⌘S to save your changes.

5. Click the Build and Run button, or choose Build ➤ Build and Run. As long as you didn't mistype anything, you should see a blank window pop up.

6. Quit the program, such as by clicking the Stop button or choosing Product ➤ Stop from the Xcode pull-down menus.

7. Choose Run ➤ Console, or press ⇧⌘R. You should see the printed statements created by the NSLog command:

```
2010-09-06 17:48:38.577 VariableTest[1374:a0f] Number of items in NSDictionary = 2
2010-09-06 17:48:38.578 VariableTest[1374:a0f] Count  in new Dictionary = 2
```

Copying Dictionary Data Into an Array

After you've stored data in a dictionary, you'll essentially have two lists of data: the keys and the associated values. If you need to use this information separately, you can selectively copy all the keys or all the values from a dictionary and store them in an array. To retrieve all the keys or values stored in a dictionary, you need to use the allKeys or allValues method:

```
[dictionaryName allKeys];
```

or

```
[dictionaryName allValues];
```

Both the allKeys and allValues methods return an array, so you'll need to assign the previous code to an array:

```
NSArray *myArray = [myDictionary allKeys];
```

To see how to retrieve keys and values from a dictionary and store them in an array, follow these steps:

1. Open the VariableTest project from the previous section.

2. Click the VariableTestAppDelegate.m file stored in the Classes folder. The code for that file appears in the middle pane of the Xcode window.

3. Modify the code in the VariableTestAppDelegate.m file as follows:

```
- (void)applicationDidFinishLaunching:(NSNotification *)aNotification {
    NSMutableDictionary *myDictionary = [NSMutableDictionary dictionary];
    [myDictionary setObject: @"555-1212" forKey: @"John Doe"];
    [myDictionary setObject: @"555-5555" forKey: @"Mary Smith"];
    [myDictionary setObject: @"555-9999" forKey: @"Al Jones"];
    NSArray *myArray = [myDictionary allKeys];
    int i;
    for (i = 0; i < [myDictionary count]; i++)
    {
        NSLog (@"Key %i = %@", i, [myArray objectAtIndex:i]);
    }

    NSArray *secondArray = [myDictionary allValues];
    for (i = 0; i < [myDictionary count]; i++)
    {
        NSLog (@"Value %i = %@", i, [secondArray objectAtIndex:i]);
    }
}
```

4. Choose File ➤ Save or press ⌘S to save your changes.

5. Click the Build and Run button, or choose Build ➤ Build and Run. As long as you didn't mistype anything, you should see a blank window pop up.

6. Quit the program, such as by clicking the Stop button or choosing Product ➤ Stop from the Xcode pull-down menus.

7. Choose Run ➤ Console, or press ⇧⌘R. You should see the printed statements created by the NSLog command:

```
2010-09-07 15:10:19.045 VariableTest[3579:a0f] Key 0 = John Doe
2010-09-07 15:10:19.048 VariableTest[3579:a0f] Key 1 = Mary Smith
2010-09-07 15:10:19.050 VariableTest[3579:a0f] Key 2 = Al Jones
2010-09-07 15:10:19.058 VariableTest[3579:a0f] Value 0 = 555-1212
2010-09-07 15:10:19.059 VariableTest[3579:a0f] Value 1 = 555-5555
2010-09-07 15:10:19.060 VariableTest[3579:a0f] Value 2 = 555-9999
```

Sorting Keys

You can store data in a dictionary in any order. If you later need to sort this data, you can use the values stored in your dictionary to sort the keys by using the keysSortedByValueUsingSelector method. This method returns your sorted list of keys as an array.

To see how to sort a dictionary by its values, follow these steps:

1. Open the VariableTest project from the previous section.

2. Click the VariableTestAppDelegate.m file stored in the Classes folder. The code for that file appears in the middle pane of the Xcode window.

3. Modify the code in the VariableTestAppDelegate.m file as follows:

```
- (void)applicationDidFinishLaunching:(NSNotification *)aNotification {
    NSMutableDictionary *myDictionary = [NSMutableDictionary dictionary];
    [myDictionary setObject: @"75" forKey: @"John Doe"];
    [myDictionary setObject: @"42" forKey: @"Mary Smith"];
    [myDictionary setObject: @"09" forKey: @"Al Jones"];

    NSArray *sortedKeysArray = [myDictionary
keysSortedByValueUsingSelector:@selector(compare:)];
    int i;
    for (i = 0; i < [sortedKeysArray count]; i++)
    {
        NSLog (@"Array element %i = %@", i, [sortedKeysArray objectAtIndex:i]);
    }
}
```

4. Choose File ➤ Save or press ⌘S to save your changes.

5. Click the Build and Run button, or choose Build ➤ Build and Run. As long as you didn't mistype anything, you should see a blank window pop up.

6. Quit the program, such as by clicking the Stop button or choosing Product ➤ Stop from the Xcode pull-down menus.

7. Choose Run ➤ Console, or press ⇧⌘R. You should see the printed statements created by the NSLog command:

```
2010-09-07 16:19:47.672 VariableTest[3829:a0f] Array element 0 = Al Jones
2010-09-07 16:19:47.677 VariableTest[3829:a0f] Array element 1 = Mary Smith
```

```
2010-09-07 16:19:47.677 VariableTest[3829:a0f] Array element 2 = John Doe
```

Because the value 09 is associated with the key Al Jones, this value is the lowest so Al Jones gets stored first. The next highest value is 42, which means Mary Smith gets stored second. Finally, the highest value is 75, so John Doe gets stored last in the array.

Access All Items in a Dictionary

A dictionary can store dozens, hundreds, or thousands of key-value pairs of data. To access all items stored in a dictionary, you can use the `for-in` statement:

```
id myObject;
for (myObject in myDictionary)
```

The first line of this code declares an object variable using the `id` keyword. The second line of code tells the computer to access each key in the dictionary where each key gets stored in the `myObject` variable.

The `for-in` statement repeat for each key-value pair stored in the dictionary, so if you have 23 key-value pairs stored in a dictionary, the `for-in` loop will repeat 23 times.

To see how the `for-in` statement can access each item in a dictionary, follow these steps:

1. Open the VariableTest project from the previous section.

2. Click the `VariableTestAppDelegate.m` file stored in the Classes folder. The code for that file appears in the middle pane of the Xcode window.

3. Modify the code in the `VariableTestAppDelegate.m` file as follows:

```
- (void)applicationDidFinishLaunching:(NSNotification *)aNotification {
    NSMutableDictionary *myDictionary = [NSMutableDictionary dictionary];
    [myDictionary setObject: @"75" forKey: @"John Doe"];
    [myDictionary setObject: @"42" forKey: @"Mary Smith"];
    [myDictionary setObject: @"09" forKey: @"Al Jones"];

    id myObject;
    for (myObject in myDictionary)
    {
        NSLog (@"Key = %@", myObject);
        NSLog (@"Value = %@", [myDictionary objectForKey: myObject]);
        NSLog (@"*****");
    }
}
```

4. Choose File ➤ Save or press ⌘S to save your changes.

5. Click the Build and Run button, or choose Build ➤ Build and Run. As long as you didn't mistype anything, you should see a blank window pop up.

6. Quit the program, such as by clicking the Stop button or choosing Product ➤ Stop from the Xcode pull-down menus.

7. Choose Run ➤ Console, or press ⇧⌘R. You should see the printed statements created by the NSLog command:

```
2010-09-07 17:27:37.196 VariableTest[4190:a0f] Key = John Doe
2010-09-07 17:27:37.199 VariableTest[4190:a0f] Value = 75
2010-09-07 17:27:37.199 VariableTest[4190:a0f] *****
2010-09-07 17:27:37.200 VariableTest[4190:a0f] Key = Mary Smith
2010-09-07 17:27:37.201 VariableTest[4190:a0f] Value = 42
2010-09-07 17:27:37.202 VariableTest[4190:a0f] *****
2010-09-07 17:27:37.202 VariableTest[4190:a0f] Key = Al Jones
2010-09-07 17:27:37.202 VariableTest[4190:a0f] Value = 09
2010-09-07 17:27:37.203 VariableTest[4190:a0f] *****
```

Using Sets

Besides arrays (see Chapter 8) and dictionaries, a third type of data structure available is a set. A *set* is a group of related data such as the numbers 5, 38, and 7, or the letters A, M, Y, and T. What makes sets useful, as data structures, are the three types of operations you can perform on a set: membership, union, and intersection.

The membership operation lets you quickly verify whether an item is a member of a set. This can be handy when you need to check whether something belongs in a larger group, such as a list of names that are allowed access to a computer. When a user types in a name, the computer could simply check whether this name is a member of the set of valid usernames.

If you stored a list of valid usernames in an array or dictionary, you would have to exhaustively check each item in the array or dictionary with the user's name. If your array or dictionary contained 1,000 valid usernames, then you would have to compare the user's name with each of these 1,000 valid usernames before determining whether it matched. With a set, you could determine whether the name was a member of that valid username set in a single operation.

The union operation lets you combine two sets into a single set. The intersection operation lets you identify the common items shared by two sets.

Creating and Putting Data in a Set

You can create two types of sets: an NSSet, which can only store data but won't let you modify it, or an NSMutableSet, which lets you store, add, or remove data while your program runs.

> **NOTE:** If you want to modify data in an NSSet, you can copy it into an NSMutableSet using the setWithSet method.

To create and initialize an NSSet or NSMutableSet, you need to create a pointer like this:

```
NSSet *mySet;
```

```
NSMutableSet *myOtherSet;
```

Then you can use the setWithObjects method to define a list of data to store in a set like this:

```
NSSet *mySet;
mySet = [NSSet setWithObjects: @"Joe", @"Mary", @"Sue", @"Olly", nil];
```

When using the setWithObjects method, make sure you end your list with nil, or else the computer won't know that it's reached the end of the data list that you want to add into the set.

If you have data already stored in an array, you can store this array data into a set by using the setWithArray method.

Counting the Number of Items in a Set

No matter how you fill a set, you can always count how many items are in that set by using the count method:

```
NSSet *mySet;
mySet = [NSSet setWithObjects: @"Joe", @"Mary", @"Sue", @"Olly", nil];
NSLog (@"Count = %i", [mySet count]);
```

This code would simply print the following:

```
Count = 4
```

Checking Whether Data Is in a Set

After you store data in a set, you can later check whether that set contains a specific chunk of data by using the containsObject method:

```
[setName containsObject: object];
```

This line of code returns a Boolean value of either YES (if the object is already in the set) or NO (if the object is not already stored in the set). To see how to use the containsObject method with a set, follow these steps:

1. Open the VariableTest project from the previous section.

2. Click the VariableTestAppDelegate.m file stored in the Classes folder. The code for that file appears in the middle pane of the Xcode window.

3. Modify the code in the VariableTestAppDelegate.m file as follows:

```
- (void)applicationDidFinishLaunching:(NSNotification *)aNotification {
    NSSet *mySet;
    mySet = [NSSet setWithObjects: @"Joe", @"Mary", @"Sue", @"Olly", nil];
    NSLog (@"Set members = %i", [mySet count]);
    if ([mySet containsObject:@"Joe"])
        {
            NSLog (@"Found member in set");
        }
```

```
        else
        {
            NSLog (@"No member found in set");
        }
    }
```

4. Choose File ➤ Save or press ⌘S to save your changes.

5. Click the Build and Run button, or choose Build ➤ Build and Run. As long as you didn't mistype anything, you should see a blank window pop up.

6. Quit the program, such as by clicking the Stop button or choosing Product ➤ Stop from the Xcode pull-down menus.

7. Choose Run ➤ Console, or press ⇧⌘R. You should see the printed statements created by the NSLog command:

```
2010-09-08 09:30:02.714 VariableTest[2090:a0f] Set members = 4
2010-09-08 09:30:02.720 VariableTest[2090:a0f] Found member in set
```

Adding and Removing Data in a Set

If you create an NSMutableSet, you can add and remove data from that set while your program runs. To add an item to an NSMutableSet, you just need to use the addObject method and specify the item to add like this:

```
[mySet addObject: @"Bo"];
```

If you have data already stored in an array, you can add that entire array to a set using the addObjectsFromArray method like this:

```
NSArray *myArray = [NSArray arrayWithObjects: @"Hello",  @"world", @"Good-bye", nil];
[mySet addObjectsFromArray: myArray];
```

Just as you can add a single item or an group of items to a set, so can you also remove a single item or all items from a set. To remove an item from a set, you need to use the removeObject method and specify the exact item you want to remove from the set:

```
[mySet removeObject:@"Joe"];
```

If you just want to remove everything in a set, you can use the removeAllObjects method:

```
[mySet removeAllObjects];
```

To see how to add and remove items with sets, follow these steps:

1. Open the VariableTest project from the previous section.

2. Click the VariableTestAppDelegate.m file stored in the Classes folder. The code for that file appears in the middle pane of the Xcode window.

3. Modify the code in the VariableTestAppDelegate.m file as follows:

```
- (void)applicationDidFinishLaunching:(NSNotification *)aNotification {
NSMutableSet *mySet;
```

```
    mySet = [NSMutableSet setWithObjects: @"Joe", @"Mary", @"Sue", @"Olly", nil];
    NSLog (@"Set members = %i", [mySet count]);

    [mySet addObject: @"Bo"];
    NSLog (@"Set members = %i", [mySet count]);

    NSString *object1 = @"Hello";
    NSString *object2 = @"world!";
    NSNumber *object3 = [NSNumber numberWithInt:45];
    NSArray *myArray = [NSArray arrayWithObjects: object1,  object2, object3, nil];

    [mySet addObjectsFromArray: myArray];
    NSLog (@"Set members = %i", [mySet count]);

    [mySet removeObject:@"Joe"];
    NSLog (@"Set members = %i", [mySet count]);

    [mySet removeAllObjects];
    NSLog (@"Set members = %i", [mySet count]);
}
```

4. Choose File ➤ Save or press ⌘S to save your changes.

5. Click the Build and Run button, or choose Build ➤ Build and Run. As long as you didn't mistype anything, you should see a blank window pop up.

6. Quit the program, such as by clicking the Stop button or choosing Product ➤ Stop from the Xcode pull-down menus.

7. Choose Run ➤ Console, or press ⇧⌘R. You should see the printed statements created by the NSLog command:

```
2010-09-29 22:13:05.779 VariableTest[5949:a0f] Set members = 4
2010-09-29 22:13:05.782 VariableTest[5949:a0f] Set members = 5
2010-09-29 22:13:05.783 VariableTest[5949:a0f] Set members = 8
2010-09-29 22:13:05.784 VariableTest[5949:a0f] Set members = 7
2010-09-29 22:13:05.785 VariableTest[5949:a0f] Set members = 0
```

Accessing All Items in a Set

When you store data in a set, you may later want to know how to access each item. One way to do this is through a for-in statement:

```
id myObject;
for (myObject in mySet)
```

The first line of this code declares an object variable using the id keyword. The second line of code tells the computer to access each item in a set. If you have 30 chunks of data stored in a set, the for-in loop will repeat 30 times.

To see how the for-in statement can access each item in a set, follow these steps:

1. Open the VariableTest project from the previous section.

2. Click the `VariableTestAppDelegate.m` file stored in the Classes folder. The code for that file appears in the middle pane of the Xcode window.

3. Modify the code in the `VariableTestAppDelegate.m` file as follows:

```
- (void)applicationDidFinishLaunching:(NSNotification *)aNotification {
    NSSet *mySet;
    mySet = [NSSet setWithObjects: @"Joe", @"Mary", @"Sue", @"Olly", nil];
    NSLog (@"Set members = %i", [mySet count]);

    id testObject;
    for (testObject in mySet)
        {
            NSLog (@"Member = %@", testObject);
        }
}
```

4. Choose File ➤ Save or press ⌘S to save your changes.

5. Click the Build and Run button, or choose Build ➤ Build and Run. As long as you didn't mistype anything, you should see a blank window pop up.

6. Quit the program, such as by clicking the Stop button or choosing Product ➤ Stop from the Xcode pull-down menus.

7. Choose Run ➤ Console, or press ⇧⌘R. You should see the printed statements created by the NSLog command:

```
2010-09-08 09:58:36.571 VariableTest[2177:a0f] Set members = 4
2010-09-08 09:58:36.577 VariableTest[2177:a0f] Member = Sue
2010-09-08 09:58:36.578 VariableTest[2177:a0f] Member = Joe
2010-09-08 09:58:36.582 VariableTest[2177:a0f] Member = Mary
2010-09-08 09:58:36.583 VariableTest[2177:a0f] Member = Olly
```

Getting the Intersection of Two Sets

If you have two sets, you can check whether a common item appears in both sets by using the `intersectsSet` method like this:

```
[firstSet intersectsSet: secondSet]
```

If a common item appears in both sets, then the `intersectsSet` method returns a YES Boolean value. Otherwise, it returns a NO Boolean value.

Identifying a Subset of a Set

If all the members of one set are contained within another set, that first set is considered a subset. For example, suppose you defined a set like this:

```
mySet = [NSSet setWithObjects: @"Joe", @"Mary", @"Sue", @"Olly", nil];
```

If you defined another set like this:

```
otherSet = [NSSet setWithObjects: @"Joe", @"Mary", nil];
```

then the otherSet is considered to be a subset of mySet since every item in otherSet (Joe and Mary) is also contained in mySet. To identify a subset, you need to use the isSubsetOfSet method like this:

[otherSet isSubsetOfSet: mySet]

This code will return a YES Boolean value if otherSet is a subset of mySet. Otherwise, it returns a NO Boolean value. Note that if you reverse the position of the two sets, you can completely change the outcome:

[mySet isSubsetOfSet: otherSet]

In this case, the code asks whether mySet is a subset of otherSet. Since it is not, it returns a NO Boolean value.

To see how to check for the intersection and subset of a set, follow these steps:

1. Open the VariableTest project from the previous section.

2. Click the VariableTestAppDelegate.m file stored in the Classes folder. The code for that file appears in the middle pane of the Xcode window.

3. Modify the code in the VariableTestAppDelegate.m file as follows:

```
- (void)applicationDidFinishLaunching:(NSNotification *)aNotification {
    NSSet *mySet;
    mySet = [NSSet setWithObjects: @"Joe", @"Mary", @"Sue", @"Olly", nil];
    NSLog (@"Set members = %i", [mySet count]);

    NSSet *newSet;
    newSet = [NSSet setWithObjects: @"Bill", @"Mary", nil];

    if ([mySet intersectsSet: newSet])
    {
        NSLog (@"Found a match");
    }
    else
    {
        NSLog (@"No match");
    }

    NSSet *thirdSet;
    thirdSet = [NSSet setWithObjects: @"Joe", @"Mary", nil];

    if ([mySet isSubsetOfSet: newSet])
    {
        NSLog (@"Subset found");
    }
    else
    {
        NSLog (@"No subset");
    }

    if ([thirdSet isSubsetOfSet: mySet])
    {
        NSLog (@"Subset");
    }
```

```
    else
    {
        NSLog (@"No subset");
    }
}
```

4. Choose File ➤ Save or press ⌘S to save your changes.

5. Click the Build and Run button, or choose Build ➤ Build and Run. As long as you didn't mistype anything, you should see a blank window pop up.

6. Quit the program, such as by clicking the Stop button or choosing Product ➤ Stop from the Xcode pull-down menus.

7. Choose Run ➤ Console, or press ⇧⌘R. You should see the printed statements created by the NSLog command:

```
2010-09-29 22:37:32.985 VariableTest[6103:a0f] Set members = 4
2010-09-29 22:37:32.988 VariableTest[6103:a0f] Found a match
2010-09-29 22:37:32.989 VariableTest[6103:a0f] No subset
2010-09-29 22:37:32.992 VariableTest[6103:a0f] Subset
```

Summary

Two other ways of storing data are dictionaries and sets. Dictionaries act like arrays that contain a paired key for each stored value, allowing you to search for a stored value just by knowing its key. Sets are useful for grouping items together and determining whether one set is a subset or intersection of another set. Sets make it easy to compare lists.

With both dictionaries and sets, you can add (and remove) one item at a time or add a bunch of data stored in an array. You can completely empty both a dictionary and a set.

Dictionaries and sets are advanced data structures that you may never need to use, but if you find yourself using arrays and finding that arrays are too clumsy, then consider using a dictionary or a set. By choosing the right data structure, you can save yourself time by not having to write a lot of code.

For example, if you stored data in two different arrays, trying to see whether one array contained all the elements of a second array would involve a lot of code to compare each item in the array. However, if you stored both arrays in two different sets, you could use the isSubsetOfSet method and determine whether one set is a subset of another using a single line of code.

Pick the right data structure, and your program can be easier to write and more reliable. Pick the wrong data structure, and your program could be harder to write and less reliable. The more you know about different types of data structures, the more likely you'll know how to choose the best one for your particular program.

Chapter 12

Creating Classes and Objects

In the previous chapters when you were working with strings (NSString), arrays (NSArray), dictionaries (NSDictionary), and sets (NSSet), you were working with predefined classes that Apple's programmers have already created. Although it's entirely possible to write fairly sophisticated programs using the predefined classes stored in the Cocoa framework, chances are good you'll need to create custom classes for your own programs, which means you need to know how to create your own classes.

A class defines the properties (data) and subprograms (methods) that work together in isolation from the rest of your program. The basic idea behind a class is to act as a modular building block to create a larger program. Ideally, each class should be completely self-contained, so you can easily yank it out and replace it with a new class without affecting the rest of your program.

Classes can be specific to a program that you're working on, or they can be more general, allowing you to reuse those classes in other programs. For example, you might create a special mathematical class that performs scientific or financial calculations. Once you create a class that works, you can plug it into another program, allowing you to create other programs faster than writing each program from scratch every time.

To create your own classes, you'll need to write Objective-C code. After you define a class, you can use that class file to create multiple objects within your program. Ideally, your class should be general enough so you can create multiple objects from it, but it's perfectly possible to create a class and just create a single object from it.

The two main features of every class are its properties and its methods. Properties let your objects store data. Methods let your objects manipulate data or perform a specific action. Although a class can exist without properties or methods, most classes include one or more properties and one or more methods.

Creating properties and methods involves writing Objective-C code, so this chapter will show you how to define properties and methods and where to define them in your class files.

Creating a Class

Every class gets stored as a separate pair of files called the *header* (.h) and *implementation* (.m). For convenience's sake, you can store your class files inside the Classes folder, or you can create and name your own folders to store your classes. Xcode ignores the names of your folders since these folder names are for your convenience in organizing all the files that make up your project.

When you create a class, your new class will be based on an existing class, so it automatically inherits the properties and methods of that existing class. Although there are different types of classes you can base your class on, you'll most likely use the NSObject class to create custom classes for your own program.

> **NOTE:** Some other common types of classes include specialized features for representing data in a window (NSDocument), controlling the basic drawing and printing functions of a program (NSView), controlling a user interface (NSViewController), or controlling a single window in a user interface (NSWindowController).

To create a class file, follow these steps:

1. Choose File ➤ New File. A template dialog box appears, as shown in Figure 12–1.

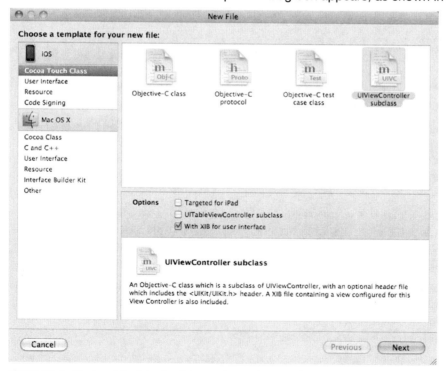

Figure 12–1. *The template dialog box lets you choose the type of file to create.*

NOTE: You can also right-click a folder, in the left pane of the Xcode window, where you want to add a file. When a pop-up menu appears, choose New File to display the templates dialog box (see Figure 12–1).

2. Click Cocoa Class under the Mac OS X category in the left pane of the template dialog box.

3. Click the Objective-C class icon.

4. (Optional) Click the Subclass of pop-up menu, and choose the type of class you want to base your class on, such as NSDocument. In most cases, you'll use the default class of NSObject.

5. Click the Next button. A Save As dialog box appears, letting you choose a name for your class.

6. Type a descriptive name for your class. Names must not use spaces or special characters. In general, use descriptive names for your classes, and capitalize the first letter of words such as a class named MyClass or RobotMovementUnit.

7. Click the Finish button. Your new class files appear in the Classes folder, as shown in Figure 12–2.

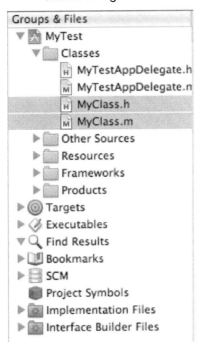

Figure 12–2. *Your new class files appear in your selected folder.*

> **NOTE:** You can always drag a file to move it to a new folder or create a new folder to hold your class files.

Understanding the Code in a Class

When you create a class, Xcode creates a header (.h) and an implementation (.m) file. The header file contains the following basic code:

```
#import <Cocoa/Cocoa.h>

@interface Class : NSObject {
@private

}

@end
```

The basic idea behind the header file is to list all the properties and methods that other parts of your program can use. Here's what each line in the header file does:

- #import <Cocoa/Cocoa.h>: Includes all the Cocoa framework interfaces for creating a basic Macintosh program. Without this, you would have to write a lot of additional code yourself to handle basic chores such as displaying windows and pull-down menus.

- @interface Class: NSObject {: Identifies your class name (which is Class in this example) and shows which class it's based on, which is NSObject.

- @private: Identifies any variables that are used in the class but not accessible to other parts of the program. You can also replace or add @public to identify variables that are accessible to other parts of the program.

- @end: Defines the end of the interface for your class file.

The header file typically defines the properties and methods available in a class. The implementation file is where you'll write most of your Objective-C code. Initially, the implementation file of a class file looks like this:

```
#import "MyClass.h"

@implementation Class

- (id)init {
    if ((self = [super init])) {
        // Initialization code here.
    }

    return self;
}
```

```
- (void)dealloc {
    // Clean-up code here.

    [super dealloc];
}
```

@end

Here's what each part of the implementation file does:

- **#import "Class.h"**: Includes the class's header file.

- **@implementation Class**: Defines the beginning of your implementation file and identifies the name of your class (in this example it's simply Class).

- **-(id)init**: This block of code defines the initialization method, which is where you'll write Objective-C that needs to run first.

- **-(void)dealloc {**: This block of code defines the dealloc method, which is the last method to run when your object is no longer needed. This is where you'll write Objective-C code to handle any cleanup issues with your class.

Deleting Class Files

If you've created class files, you can always delete them at any time. When you delete class files, you'll have two options. One is to physically delete the class files and remove them from your project. The second is to remove the references to those class files from your project but keep them physically on your hard disk. That way, if you no longer need a class in your program but think you might use that class in another project, you can keep it for future use.

To delete class files, follow these steps:

1. Click the header file you want to delete.

2. Hold down the ⌘ key, and click the accompanying implementation file that you want to delete. Xcode highlights your two class files.

3. Choose Edit ➤ Delete. A dialog box appears, asking whether you want to delete the files or just remove the references to those files, as shown in Figure 12–3.

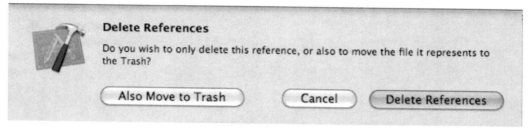

Figure 12–3. *You can physically delete class files or just remove the references to them.*

4. Click the Also Move to Trash button (to physically delete your class files), or click the Delete References button (to keep the class files but remove them from your project).

> **NOTE:** When you delete class files, you can't undo this action, so make sure you really want to delete any selected class files.

A Program Example of a Class

Working with classes involves several steps. First, you must create a class. Second, you must make that class accessible to another part of your program using the #import directive. Third, you must create an instance of that class using an object. Fourth, you can finally use the object to access the methods and properties defined by the class.

If this sounds long and complicated, it's not, but it will become clearer as you go through the basic steps for creating and using a class:

1. Open the VariableTest project from the previous chapter.

2. Follow steps 1–8 in the "Creating a Class" section. In step 6 of these steps, name your class MyClass.

3. Click the MyClass.m file stored in the Classes folder. The code for that file appears in the middle pane of the Xcode window.

4. Modify the init method code in the MyClass.m file by adding the bold line as follows:

```
- (id)init {
    if ((self = [super init])) {
        // Initialization code here.
        NSLog (@"Hello, world!");
    }

    return self;
}
```

At this point, all you've done is added an NSLog command inside the MyClass init method. This init method will always run as soon as you create an instance of your class. If you ran your program now, you wouldn't see this "Hello, world!" message because nowhere in your code have you created an instance of MyClass.

In the next steps, you'll create an instance of MyClass within the VariableTestAppDelegate.m file as follows:

5. Click the VariableTestAppDelegate.m file in the Classes folder. The middle pane of the Xcode window displays your VariableTestAppDelegate.m code.

6. Add the line #import "MyClass.h" underneath the #import "VariableTestAppDelegate.h" line like this:

```
#import "VariableTestAppDelegate.h"
#import "MyClass.h"
```

This #import "MyClass.h" file tells the computer to make all the code in the MyClass files accessible inside this VariableTestAppDelegate.m file.

7. Modify the applicationDidFinishLaunching method as follows:

```
- (void)applicationDidFinishLaunching:(NSNotification *)aNotification {
    MyClass *testObject = [[MyClass alloc] init];
    [testObject release];
}
```

The applicationDidFinishLaunching method runs as soon as your program starts running. The first line inside this method creates an instance of MyClass by creating a pointer called *testObject. When creating an instance of a class that you've created, you also need to allocate memory for this object (using the alloc method) and run the init method of the MyClass object (using the init method).

The second line inside the applicationDidFinishLaunching method runs the release method. When you allocate memory for an object (using the alloc method), you should eventually release that memory for that object when you no longer need that object any more.

> **NOTE:** Keeping track of your program's memory usage is one of the biggest nuisances of writing Objective-C programs and also the cause of the most common types of errors. If your program keeps allocating memory without ever releasing it, you could run into a problem called a *memory leak*, which can cause your program to crash or interfere with other running programs. When writing Mac OS X programs, Xcode can use something called *garbage collection*, which means the computer takes care of its memory to eliminate or reduce problems that involve memory usage by your program.

8. Choose File ➤ Save or press ⌘S to save your changes.

9. Click the Build and Run button, or choose Build ➤ Build and Run. As long as you didn't mistype anything, you should see a blank window pop up.

10. Quit the program by clicking the Stop button or choosing Product ➤ Stop from the Xcode pull-down menus.

11. Choose Run ➤ Console, or press ⇧⌘R. You should see the printed statements created by the NSLog command:

```
2010-09-09 18:26:48.345 VariableTest[5059:a0f] Hello, world!
```

When you ran your program, these are the basic steps that occurred:

1. Your program ran and immediately launched the applicationDidFinishLaunching method inside the VariableTestAppDelegate.m file.

2. The first line inside the applicationDidFinishLaunching method created an instance of MyClass, allocated memory for that instance (testObject), and ran the init method of MyClass.

3. The init method inside MyClass ran the NSLog command that printed "Hello, world!" in the log window.

4. The second line inside the applicationDidFinishLaunching method releases the memory allocated for testObject.

When you quit the program, you could peek inside the Log window and see the "Hello, world!" message that the NSLog command, inside the init method, printed out.

Creating Methods

In the previous example, you simply added an NSLog command inside the existing init method of MyClass. In most cases when you're creating your own classes, you'll need to create additional methods and make them run from another part of your program.

The basic steps to creating a method are as follows:

1. Declare the method name in your class's header (.h) file.

2. Write the actual code for the method in the class's implementation (.m) file.

3. Call the method from another part of your program.

A typical method declaration looks like this:

```
-(data type)methodName: parameters;
```

The data type determines the type of value the method calculates, such as an integer or floating-point number. If you wanted your method to calculate an integer, your method declaration would look like this:

```
-(int)methodName: parameters;
```

In many cases, you simply want the method to run its code and not return a value at all. When a method does not return any value, its data type is declared as void like this:

```
-(void)methodName: parameters;
```

The method name can be any descriptive name that you want. Typically, a method name uses camel case where the first letter appears lowercase, but the first letter of subsequent words appear in uppercase:

```
-(void) shootRockets: parameters;
-(float) predictStockPrice: parameters;
-(BOOL) trustMeBecauseYouLikeMe: parameters;
```

The parameters represent data that the method may need to work. If your method doesn't require any outside data to work, you can drop the parameter altogether:

```
-(void)methodName;
```

If your method requires an integer value, the method declaration might look like this with an integer parameter:

```
-(void)methodName: (int)inputData;
```

To see how create a method in a class, follow these steps:

1. Open the VariableTest project from the previous section.

2. Click the MyClass.h file inside the Classes folder, and modify the code by adding the bold text as follows:

```
#import <Cocoa/Cocoa.h>

@interface MyClass : NSObject {

@private

}

-(void)displayMessage;

@end
```

> **NOTE:** A method declaration in a header (.h) file always ends with a semicolon.

3. Click the MyClass.m file inside the Classes folder, and add the displayMessage method as follows:

```
#import "MyClass.h"

@implementation MyClass

- (id)init {
    if ((self = [super init])) {
        // Initialization code here.
        NSLog (@"Hello, world!");
    }

    return self;
}
- (void)dealloc {
```

```
    // Clean-up code here.

    [super dealloc];
}

-(void)displayMessage
{
    NSLog (@"Good-bye!");
}

@end
```

> **NOTE:** When writing the implementation of your method, be sure that no semicolon appears at the end of your method's name.

4. Click the VariableTestAppDelegate.m file stored in the Classes folder, and modify the code in the VariableTestAppDelegate.m file as follows:

```
#import "VariableTestAppDelegate.h"
#import "MyClass.h"

@implementation VariableTestAppDelegate

@synthesize window;

- (void)applicationDidFinishLaunching:(NSNotification *)aNotification {
    MyClass *testObject = [[MyClass alloc] init];
    [testObject displayMessage];
    [testObject release];
}

@end
```

5. Choose File ➤ Save or press ⌘S to save your changes.

6. Click the Build and Run button, or choose Build ➤ Build and Run. As long as you didn't mistype anything, you should see a blank window pop up.

7. Quit the program by clicking the Stop button or choosing Product ➤ Stop from the Xcode pull-down menus.

8. Choose Run ➤ Console, or press ⇧⌘R. You should see the printed statements created by the NSLog command:

```
2010-09-09 21:55:52.492 VariableTest[5314:a0f] Hello, world!
2010-09-09 21:55:52.494 VariableTest[5314:a0f] Good-bye!
```

The "Good-bye!" message comes from this line:

```
[testObject displayMessage];
```

This line tells the computer to run the displayMessage method stored in testObject. Since testObject is an instance of the class MyClass, you have to peek inside the

MyClass implementation (.m) file to see the actual displayMessage method, which contains the NSLog command that prints "Good-bye!"

Passing Parameters

A method can simply run its code in the same way every time it's called from another part of a program. However, a more flexible method might accept outside data and modify its behavior based on that outside data. To accept data, a method needs to accept to define a parameter list. The parameter list defines a data type and variable name for each chunk of outside data it accepts:

```
-(void)methodName: (data type) variable name;
```

If you wanted a method to accept an integer value, your parameter list might look like this:

```
-(void)methodName: (int) myAge;
```

To call this method and make it run, you would use code like this:

```
[objectName methodName: value];
```

Notice that if a method defines a parameter, then calling that method must also include a value to pass as a parameter to the function. To see how parameters work with methods, follow these steps:

1. Open the VariableTest project from the previous section.

2. Click the MyClass.h file inside the Classes folder, and modify the code as follows:

```
#import <Cocoa/Cocoa.h>

@interface MyClass : NSObject {

@private

}

-(void)displayMessage: (int)myLoop;

@end
```

3. Choose File ➤ Save or press ⌘S to save your changes.

4. Click the MyClass.m file inside the Classes folder, and add the displayMessage method as follows:

```
#import "MyClass.h"

@implementation MyClass

- (id)init {
    if ((self = [super init])) {
        // Initialization code here.
        NSLog (@"Hello, world!");
    }
```

```
        return self;
    }

- (void)dealloc {
    // Clean-up code here.

    [super dealloc];
    }

-(void)displayMessage: (int)myLoop
{
    NSLog (@"The loop will repeat %i times", myLoop);
    int i;
    for (i = 0; i < myLoop; i++)
    {
        NSLog (@"The value of i = %i", i);
    }
}

@end
```

5. Click the VariableTestAppDelegate.m file stored in the Classes folder, and modify the code in the VariableTestAppDelegate.m file as follows:

```
#import "VariableTestAppDelegate.h"
#import "MyClass.h"

@implementation VariableTestAppDelegate

@synthesize window;

- (void)applicationDidFinishLaunching:(NSNotification *)aNotification {
    MyClass *testObject = [[MyClass alloc] init];
    [testObject displayMessage:5];
    [testObject release];
}

@end
```

6. Choose File ➤ Save or press ⌘S to save your changes.

7. Click the Build and Run button, or choose Build ➤ Build and Run. As long as you didn't mistype anything, you should see a blank window pop up.

8. Quit the program by clicking the Stop button or choosing Product ➤ Stop from the Xcode pull-down menus.

9. Choose Run ➤ Console, or press ⇧⌘R. You should see the printed statements created by the NSLog command:

```
2010-09-10 13:18:06.994 VariableTest[622:a0f] Hello, world!
2010-09-10 13:18:06.997 VariableTest[622:a0f] The loop will repeat 5 times
2010-09-10 13:18:06.998 VariableTest[622:a0f] The value of i = 0
2010-09-10 13:18:06.999 VariableTest[622:a0f] The value of i = 1
2010-09-10 13:18:07.000 VariableTest[622:a0f] The value of i = 2
```

```
2010-09-10 13:18:07.000 VariableTest[622:a0f] The value of i = 3
2010-09-10 13:18:07.004 VariableTest[622:a0f] The value of i = 4
```

When the `[testObject displayMessage:5];` line runs, it passes the value of 5, which gets stored in the `myLoop` variable. The `displayMessage` method uses this `myLoop` variable to determine how many times to run a loop. In this example, you're passing the value of 5 to the `displayMessage` method, but if you change this value to another number, such as 12, you would make the `displayMessage` run its loop 12 times.

Passing Multiple Parameters

In the previous example, you created a method that accepted a single parameter, an integer value named `myLoop`. A method can actually accept multiple parameters if you want. For each parameter that you want a function to accept, you just need to separate them with a colon (:) like this:

```
-(void)methodName;     // Zero parameters
-(void)methodName: (data type) variable1;     // One parameter
-(void)methodName: (data type) variable1 name: (data type) variable2;     // Two
parameters
```

To call and run a method, you must make sure you supply the method with the proper type and number of parameters it expects:

```
[objectName methodName];     // Zero parameters
[objectName methodName: value];     // One parameter
[objectName methodName: value1 name: value2];     // Two parameters
```

Suppose you created a method that expects two parameters:

```
-(void)methodName: (int) aNumber  name: (BOOL) aFlag;
```

To call and run this method, you must make sure you include an integer and a Boolean value with the function name. First, you must list the integer value, and second you must list the Boolean value:

```
[objectType methodName: 4 name: YES;     // Valid
[objectType methodName: YES name: 4;     // Invalid!!!
[objectType methodName: 4;     // Invalid!!!
```

The second line is invalid because the method expects an integer first and a Boolean value second. The third line is invalid because the method expects two parameters, but the third line passes it only one parameter, a single integer.

Passing Objects as Parameters

When you pass data types such as numbers (`int` or `float`) or Boolean (`BOOL`) values as a parameter, you need to create a variable to hold that data:

```
-(void)displayMessage: (int)myLoop;
```

However, many times you may need to pass an object, such as an `NSString` string. When working with objects, you need a pointer, which you can identify using the asterisk symbol:

```
-(void)displayMessage: (NSString *) myName;
```

This parameter tells the computer that the method expects an NSString object and to use the myName variable as a pointer to that object.

To see how to use both multiple parameters and objects as parameters passed to a method, follow these steps:

1. Open the VariableTest project from the previous section.

2. Click the MyClass.h file inside the Classes folder, and modify the code as follows:

```
#import <Cocoa/Cocoa.h>

@interface MyClass : NSObject {

@private

}

-(void)displayMessage: (NSString *) myName count:(int)myLoop;

@end
```

> **NOTE:** If you have multiple parameters, you may not want to list them on a single line. Instead, you can use a separate line for each parameter to make it more readable like this:
>
> ```
> -(void)displayMessage: (NSString *) myName
>          count:(int)myLoop;
> ```

3. Choose File ➤ Save or press ⌘S to save your changes.

4. Click the MyClass.m file inside the Classes folder, and add the displayMessage method as follows:

```
#import "MyClass.h"

@implementation MyClass

- (id)init {
    if ((self = [super init])) {
        // Initialization code here.
        NSLog (@"Hello, world!");
    }

    return self;
}

- (void)dealloc {
    // Clean-up code here.

    [super dealloc];
}
```

```
-(void)displayMessage: (NSString *) myName count:(int)myLoop;
{
    NSLog (@"Hello, %@", myName);
    NSLog (@"The loop will repeat %i times", myLoop);
    int i;
    for (i = 0; i < myLoop; i++)
    {
        NSLog (@"The value of i = %i", i);
    }
}

@end
```

5. Choose File ➤ Save or press ⌘S to save your changes.

6. Click the VariableTestAppDelegate.m file stored in the Classes folder, and modify the code in the VariableTestAppDelegate.m file as follows:

```
#import "VariableTestAppDelegate.h"
#import "MyClass.h"

@implementation VariableTestAppDelegate

@synthesize window;

- (void)applicationDidFinishLaunching:(NSNotification *)aNotification {
    MyClass *testObject = [[MyClass alloc] init];
    [testObject displayMessage: @"John Doe" count:5];
    [testObject release];
}

@end
```

7. Choose File ➤ Save or press ⌘S to save your changes.

8. Click the Build and Run button, or choose Build ➤ Build and Run. As long as you didn't mistype anything, you should see a blank window pop up.

9. Quit the program by clicking the Stop button or choosing Product ➤ Stop from the Xcode pull-down menus.

10. Choose Run ➤ Console, or press ⇧⌘R. You should see the printed statements created by the NSLog command:

```
2010-09-10 13:30:17.648 VariableTest[707:a0f] Hello, world!
2010-09-10 13:30:17.656 VariableTest[707:a0f] Hello, John Doe
2010-09-10 13:30:17.664 VariableTest[707:a0f] The loop will repeat 5 times
2010-09-10 13:30:17.665 VariableTest[707:a0f] The value of i = 0
2010-09-10 13:30:17.665 VariableTest[707:a0f] The value of i = 1
2010-09-10 13:30:17.666 VariableTest[707:a0f] The value of i = 2
2010-09-10 13:30:17.667 VariableTest[707:a0f] The value of i = 3
2010-09-10 13:30:17.668 VariableTest[707:a0f] The value of i = 4
```

Practice changing the number (5) and string (@"John Doe") passed as a parameter to the displayMessage method to see how to change the displayMessage's output.

Returning Values from a Method

A method can accept zero or more parameters to do something useful. In many cases, the method simply runs its code, but sometimes you may need a method to calculate and return a single value. When a method does not return a value, its data type is void:

```
-(void)displayMessage;
```

When that method returns a value, you need to identify the data type of that value:

```
-(int)displayMessage;
-(float)displayMessage;
-(NSString *)displayMessage;
```

A typical method that returns a value looks like this:

```
-(data type)methodName
{
    return value;
}
```

The data type defines what type of data the method returns, and the return command specifies the exact value to return. When using a method that returns a value, your code can simply treat that method as a value like this:

```
int myCounter;
myCounter = 2 + [objectName methodName];
```

To see how to create a simple method that returns a value, follow these steps:

1. Open the VariableTest project from the previous section.

2. Click the MyClass.h file inside the Classes folder, and modify the code as follows:

```
#import <Cocoa/Cocoa.h>

@interface MyClass : NSObject {

@private

}

-(void)displayMessage: (NSString *) myName count:(int)myLoop;
-(int)calculateValue;

@end
```

3. Click the MyClass.m file inside the Classes folder, and add the displayMessage method as follows:

```
#import "MyClass.h"

@implementation MyClass

- (id)init {
    if ((self = [super init])) {
        // Initialization code here.
        NSLog (@"Hello, world!");
```

```
    }

    return self;
}

- (void)dealloc {
    // Clean-up code here.

    [super dealloc];
}

-(void)displayMessage: (NSString *) myName count:(int)myLoop
{
    NSLog (@"Hello, %@", myName);
    NSLog (@"The loop will repeat %i times", myLoop);
    int i;
    for (i = 0; i < myLoop; i++)
    {
        NSLog (@"The value of i = %i", i);
    }
}

-(int)calculateValue
{
    return 4;
}

@end
```

4. Choose File ➤ Save or press ⌘S to save your changes.

5. Click the VariableTestAppDelegate.m file stored in the Classes folder, and modify the code in the VariableTestAppDelegate.m file as follows:

```
#import "VariableTestAppDelegate.h"
#import "MyClass.h"

@implementation VariableTestAppDelegate

@synthesize window;

- (void)applicationDidFinishLaunching:(NSNotification *)aNotification {
    MyClass *testObject = [[MyClass alloc] init];
    int tempVar;
    tempVar = [testObject calculateValue];
    [testObject displayMessage:@"John Doe" count: tempVar];
    [testObject release];
}

@end
```

6. Choose File ➤ Save or press ⌘S to save your changes.

7. Click the Build and Run button, or choose Build ➤ Build and Run. As long as you didn't mistype anything, you should see a blank window pop up.

8. Quit the program by clicking the Stop button or choosing Product ➤ Stop from the Xcode pull-down menus.

9. Choose Run ➤ Console or press ⇧⌘R. You should see the printed statements created by the NSLog command:

```
2010-09-10 17:44:55.769 VariableTest[1167:a0f] Hello, world!
2010-09-10 17:44:55.774 VariableTest[1167:a0f] Hello, John Doe
2010-09-10 17:44:55.775 VariableTest[1167:a0f] The loop will repeat 4 times
2010-09-10 17:44:55.775 VariableTest[1167:a0f] The value of i = 0
2010-09-10 17:44:55.777 VariableTest[1167:a0f] The value of i = 1
2010-09-10 17:44:55.778 VariableTest[1167:a0f] The value of i = 2
2010-09-10 17:44:55.787 VariableTest[1167:a0f] The value of i = 3
```

The applicationDidFinishLaunching method declares an integer variable called tempVar. Then it calls the calculateValue method inside testObject.

Peeking into the calculateValue method stored in the MyClass.m file, you can see that the calculateValue method is declared as an integer data type, and inside its curly brackets it uses the return command to return a value. In this case, the value is simply 4.

The value 4 replaces the code [testObject calculateValue] and gets assigned to the tempVar variable. This tempVar variable now gets inserted into the [testObject displayMessage:@"John Doe" count: tempVar]; line. Since tempVar represents the number 4, this 4 gets passed to the displayMessage method, which uses it to run its loop four times.

The calculateValue method always returns 4. To avoid returning the same value every time, most methods will accept outside data to calculate a different value to return. To see how to create a method that accepts a parameter and uses it to return a different value, follow these steps:

1. Open the VariableTest project.

2. Click the MyClass.h file inside the Classes folder, and modify the code as follows:

```
#import <Cocoa/Cocoa.h>

@interface MyClass : NSObject {

@private

}

-(void)displayMessage: (NSString *) myName count:(int)myLoop;
-(int)calculateValue: (int)outsideData;
@end
```

3. Choose File ➤ Save or press ⌘S to save your changes.

4. Click the MyClass.m file inside the Classes folder, and add the displayMessage method as follows:

```
#import "MyClass.h"
```

```objc
@implementation MyClass

- (id)init {
    if ((self = [super init])) {
        // Initialization code here.
        NSLog (@"Hello, world!");
    }

    return self;
}
- (void)dealloc {
    // Clean-up code here.

    [super dealloc];
}
-(void)displayMessage: (NSString *) myName count:(int)myLoop
{
    NSLog (@"Hello, %@", myName);
    NSLog (@"The loop will repeat %i times", myLoop);
    int i;
    for (i = 0; i < myLoop; i++)
    {
        NSLog (@"The value of i = %i", i);
    }
}

-(int)calculateValue: (int)outsideData
{
    int hold;
    hold = outsideData + outsideData;
    return hold;
}

@end
```

5. Choose File ➤ Save or press ⌘S to save your changes.

6. Click the VariableTestAppDelegate.m file stored in the Classes folder, and modify the code in the VariableTestAppDelegate.m file as follows:

```objc
#import "VariableTestAppDelegate.h"
#import "MyClass.h"

@implementation VariableTestAppDelegate

@synthesize window;

- (void)applicationDidFinishLaunching:(NSNotification *)aNotification {
    MyClass *testObject = [[MyClass alloc] init];
    int tempVar;
    tempVar = [testObject calculateValue:1];
    [testObject displayMessage:@"John Doe" count: tempVar];
    [testObject release];
}
```

@end

7. Choose File ➤ Save or press ⌘S to save your changes.

8. Click the Build and Run button, or choose Build ➤ Build and Run. As long as you didn't mistype anything, you should see a blank window pop up.

9. Quit the program by clicking the Stop button or choosing Product ➤ Stop from the Xcode pull-down menus.

10. Choose Run ➤ Console, or press ⇧⌘R7. You should see the printed statements created by the NSLog command:

```
2010-09-10 19:45:23.746 VariableTest[1405:a0f] Hello, world!
2010-09-10 19:45:23.749 VariableTest[1405:a0f] Hello, John Doe
2010-09-10 19:45:23.750 VariableTest[1405:a0f] The loop will repeat 2 times
2010-09-10 19:45:23.751 VariableTest[1405:a0f] The value of i = 0
2010-09-10 19:45:23.751 VariableTest[1405:a0f] The value of i = 1
```

The applicationDidFinishLaunching method now calls the calculateValue method by passing it 1 as a parameter.

The calculateValue method in the MyClass.m file stores this number in a variable called outsideData. Then it creates an integer variable called hold, adds the value of outsideData to itself, and stores this value into the hold variable. Finally, it returns the hold variable to the [testObject calculateValue:1] line inside the applicationDidFinishLaunching method.

The tempVar variable now contains the value returned by the calculateValue method (which is now 2) and passes that value to the displayMessage method, which runs its loop two times.

Passing by Reference

Normally when you pass data to a method, that method can't change the value of that passed data. This is called *passing by value*, which essentially makes a separate copy of data and then lets the method manipulate that copy of the data, leaving the original data untouched. If you want a method to change and return more than one value, you have to pass data to a method through something called *passing by reference*.

Passing by reference relies on pointers. A pointer simply points or identifies a memory address that contains data. When you send data to a method through passing by reference, you're sending the method the pointer to data. This means that when the method alters that data, it's altering the only copy of that data. The end result is that the method can change the value of data that other parts of the program can then use.

To pass data by reference, you must use the asterisk symbol to identify a pointer in your method:

```
-(data type)methodName: (data type *) pointerName;
```

In the implementation (.m) file, you must always use the asterisk symbol to identify the parameter as a pointer:

```
-(data type)methodName: (data type *) pointerName
{
    return *pointerName + *pointerName;
}
```

When calling a method that passes data by reference, place the ampersand (&) symbol in front of the passed data:

```
[testObject methodName: &passedData];
```

> **NOTE:** You only need to use the ampersand (&) symbol when passing data such as a number. You can omit the ampersand (&) symbol if you're passing a pointer.

To see how to pass data by reference and how that allows a method to change a value used by other parts of the program, follow these steps:

1. Open the VariableTest project.

2. Click the MyClass.h file inside the Classes folder, and modify the code as follows:

```
#import <Cocoa/Cocoa.h>

@interface MyClass : NSObject {

@private

}
-(void)displayMessage: (NSString *) myName count:(int)myLoop;
-(int)calculateValue: (int *)outsideData;
@end
```

3. Choose File ➤ Save or press ⌘S to save your changes.

4. Click the MyClass.m file inside the Classes folder, and add the displayMessage method as follows:

```
#import "MyClass.h"

@implementation MyClass

- (id)init {
    if ((self = [super init])) {
        // Initialization code here.
        NSLog (@"Hello, world!");
    }

    return self;
}

- (void)dealloc {
    // Clean-up code here.
```

```
        [super dealloc];
    }

    -(void)displayMessage: (NSString *) myName count:(int)myLoop
    {
        NSLog (@"Hello, %@", myName);
        NSLog (@"The loop will repeat %i times", myLoop);
        int i;
        for (i = 0; i < myLoop; i++)
        {
            NSLog (@"The value of i = %i", i);
        }
    }

    -(int)calculateValue: (int *)outsideData
    {
        int hold;
        hold = *outsideData + *outsideData;
        *outsideData = 99;
        return hold;
    }

@end
```

5. Choose File ➤ Save or press ⌘S to save your changes.

6. Click the VariableTestAppDelegate.m file stored in the Classes folder, and modify the code in the VariableTestAppDelegate.m file as follows:

```
#import "VariableTestAppDelegate.h"
#import "MyClass.h"

@implementation VariableTestAppDelegate

@synthesize window;

- (void)applicationDidFinishLaunching:(NSNotification *)aNotification {
    MyClass *testObject = [[MyClass alloc] init];
    int counter = 1;
    NSLog (@"The value of counter = %i", counter);
    int tempVar;
    tempVar = [testObject calculateValue:&counter];
    NSLog (@"Now the value of counter = %i", counter);
    [testObject displayMessage:@"John Doe" count: tempVar];
    [testObject release];
}

@end
```

7. Choose File ➤ Save or press ⌘S to save your changes.

8. Click the Build and Run button, or choose Build ➤ Build and Run. As long as you didn't mistype anything, you should see a blank window pop up.

9. Quit the program by clicking the Stop button or choosing Product ➤ Stop from the Xcode pull-down menus.

10. Choose Run ➤ Console, or press ⇧⌘R. You should see the printed statements created by the NSLog command:

```
2010-09-10 21:33:44.345 VariableTest[1690:a0f] Hello, world!
2010-09-10 21:33:44.371 VariableTest[1690:a0f] The value of counter = 1
2010-09-10 21:33:44.385 VariableTest[1690:a0f] Now the value of counter = 99
2010-09-10 21:33:44.386 VariableTest[1690:a0f] Hello, John Doe
2010-09-10 21:33:44.388 VariableTest[1690:a0f] The loop will repeat 2 times
2010-09-10 21:33:44.389 VariableTest[1690:a0f] The value of i = 0
2010-09-10 21:33:44.390 VariableTest[1690:a0f] The value of i = 1
```

In the applicationDidFinishLaunching method, the counter variable gets passed by reference to the calculateValue method, which reassigns the value of its parameter (called *outsideData) to the value 99. Now when the applicationDidFinishLaunching method prints the value of the counter variable again, its value has changed from 1 to 99.

Creating Class Properties

A class represents a self-contained arbitrary object. If you were writing a program to control an airplane, you might divide that program into objects where one object represents the wings, another object represents the tail, and a third object represents the engines. To do something useful, objects need methods. To store important data, objects also need properties.

A property is nothing more than a variable that an object uses to hold information sent to it (from another object) or that it can send to other objects. For example, an object representing an airplane's engine might need to receive data from the pilot, telling it to increase or decrease thrust. Likewise, this engine object might also need to send fuel information to the pilot. Properties simply give objects the ability to accept and store information sent to it and create and send information, as shown in Figure 12–4.

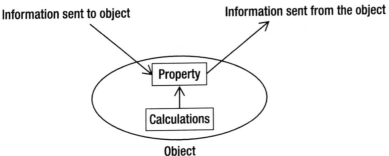

Figure 12–4. *Properties allow an object to send and receive information.*

To define a property in a class, you need to do the following:

1. Declare a variable in the header (.h) file.

2. Create a property from the declared variable in the header (*.h) file.

3. Create accessor methods for that property in the implementation (.m) file, which allows the property to store data.

Defining Properties

The header file of a class is where you declare variable and make it a property. Declaring a variable is straightforward. Underneath the @private heading in the header file, just declare your variable normally:

```
@private
    datatype variableName;
    classType *pointerName;
```

Next, you need to define your declared variables as properties, which other parts of your program can access. To do this, you simply use the @property (assign) or @property (retain) command such as:

```
@property (assign) datatype variableName;
@property (retain) classType *pointerName;
```

When working with data types such as numbers (int or float) or Boolean values (BOOL), you use the @property (assign) command. When declaring an instance of a class to create an object, you use @property (retain). The retain command tells the computer to retain the object in memory, which you don't need to do when declaring integer or Boolean variables.

> **NOTE:** In addition to the @property (retain) command, you can also use the @property (assign) or @property (copy) commands with objects. The @property (assign) command is used with objects when you need to keep track of memory, such as when writing iPhone/iPad apps. The @property (copy) command is used when working with objects that are mutable, such as NSMutableString.

Next, you need to create accessor methods in the implementation (.m) file for each property you declare. The accessor methods simply let other objects store or retrieve information in your defined property.

In other object-oriented programming languages, you must physically write these accessor methods yourself. In Objective-C, you can create these accessor methods automatically by simply using the @synthesize command for each property like this:

```
@synthesize variableName
@synthesize pointerName;
```

> **NOTE:** When using the @synthesize command, you do not need to use the asterisk (*) symbol to identify pointers.

Accessing and Getting Values in Properties

After you've created a property in a class file, you can create an instance of that class (an object) like this:

```
classType *objectName;
```

To assign a value to an object's property, there are two methods. First, you can use the traditional Objective-C technique that uses square brackets like this:

```
[objectName setPropertyName: value];
```

A second way to assign a value to an object's property uses something called *dot syntax*, which is what many other object-oriented programming languages use. The dot syntax version of assigning a value to a property looks like this:

```
objectName.propertyName = value;
```

Both methods are equivalent, so use whichever method you prefer. Dot syntax is simpler, and most of Apple's sample code and documentation uses dot syntax.

> **NOTE:** One key difference between the two methods is that when using the first method with square brackets, the first letter of the property name is uppercase, while in the dot syntax method, the first letter of the property name is lowercase.

To retrieve a value from an object's property, you also have two methods. The first method looks like this:

```
variable = [objectName propertyName];
```

The dot syntax method looks similar:

```
variable = objectName.propertyName;
```

To see how to create and use properties, follow these steps:

1. Open the VariableTest project from the previous section.

2. Click the MyClass.h file inside the Classes folder, and modify the code as follows:

```
#import <Cocoa/Cocoa.h>

@interface MyClass : NSObject {

@private
    NSString *personName;
    int loopVar;
```

```
}

@property (retain) NSString *personName;
@property (assign) int loopVar;

-(void)displayMessage: (NSString *) myName count:(int)myLoop;
-(int)calculateValue: (int *)outsideData;

@end
```

3. Choose File ➤ Save or press ⌘S to save your changes.

4. Click the MyClass.m file inside the Classes folder, and add the displayMessage method as follows:

```
#import "MyClass.h"

@implementation MyClass

@synthesize personName;
@synthesize loopVar;

- (id)init {
    if ((self = [super init])) {
        // Initialization code here.
        NSLog (@"Hello, world!");
    }

    return self;
}

- (void)dealloc {
    // Clean-up code here.

    [super dealloc];
}

-(void)displayMessage: (NSString *) myName count:(int)myLoop;
{
    NSLog (@"Hello, %@", myName);
    NSLog (@"The loop will repeat %i times", myLoop);
    int i;
    for (i = 0; i < myLoop; i++)
    {
        NSLog (@"The value of i = %i", i);
    }
}

-(int)calculateValue: (int *)outsideData
{
    int hold;
    hold = *outsideData + *outsideData;
    *outsideData = 99;
    return hold;
}

@end
```

5. Choose File ➤ Save or press ⌘S to save your changes.

6. Click the VariableTestAppDelegate.m file stored in the Classes folder, and modify the code in the VariableTestAppDelegate.m file as follows:

```
#import "VariableTestAppDelegate.h"
#import "MyClass.h"

@implementation VariableTestAppDelegate

@synthesize window;


- (void)applicationDidFinishLaunching:(NSNotification *)aNotification {
    MyClass *testObject = [[MyClass alloc] init];
    testObject.personName = @"John Smith";
    testObject.loopVar = 2;
    //[testObject setPersonName: @"John Smith"];
    //[testObject setLoopVar: 2];
    int repeatLoop;
    repeatLoop = testObject.loopVar;
    [testObject displayMessage:testObject.personName count: repeatLoop];
    [testObject release];
}

@end
```

The previous code lists the two methods for assigning values to a property. The dot syntax version is used, while the square bracket version is commented out. If you want, you can comment out the dot syntax version and remove the comment symbols (//) from the square bracket version to see that they work identically.

7. Choose File ➤ Save or press ⌘S to save your changes.

8. Click the Build and Run button, or choose Build ➤ Build and Run. As long as you didn't mistype anything, you should see a blank window pop up.

9. Quit the program by clicking the Stop button or choosing Product ➤ Stop from the Xcode pull-down menus.

10. Choose Run ➤ Console, or press ⇧⌘R. You should see the printed statements created by the NSLog command:

```
2010-09-11 11:39:24.448 VariableTest[2858:a0f] Hello, world!
2010-09-11 11:39:24.455 VariableTest[2858:a0f] Hello, John Smith
2010-09-11 11:39:24.458 VariableTest[2858:a0f] The loop will repeat 2 times
2010-09-11 11:39:24.460 VariableTest[2858:a0f] The value of i = 0
2010-09-11 11:39:24.462 VariableTest[2858:a0f] The value of i = 1
```

In the applicationDidFinishLaunching method, the code declares an integer variable called repeatLoop. Then it assigns the value of testObject.loopVar to this repeatLoop variable, which is then passed as a parameter to the displayMessage method. Another way to assign a value to the repeat Loop variable would be like this:

```
repeatLoop = [testObject loopVar];
```

Summary

You use Objective-C to create a class, which is divided into two files: the header (.h) file and the implementation (.m) file. After you've created a class, you can create an instance of that class, which is an object.

Classes need to define methods and properties. A method consists of a data type, method name, and parameter list. The data type of a method determines what type of data the method returns. If a method doesn't return any data, its data type is void:

```
-(void) methodName;
```

If the method returns a data type, just list that data type in the parentheses like this:

```
-(float) methodName;
```

If the method returns an object type, you must use the asterisk symbol to define a pointer like this:

```
-(NSString *) methodName;
```

If you need to pass data to a method, the method declaration needs to define the data type for that data and a variable name to hold that data. Separate multiple parameters with a colon like this:

```
-(void) methodName: (datatype) variableName1: name (datatype) variableName2;
```

To pass data to a method, you must send the correct data type and the correct number of values defined by the parameter list. So if the method expects two integer values, you can call that method like this:

```
[objectName methodName: 4 name: 98];
```

Methods can also change the values of their parameters through passing by reference. When you want to change a value of a parameter, you must define the method with the asterisk symbol to define a pointer like this:

```
-(void) methodName: (datatype *) variableName;
```

When you call that method and pass it a parameter, you must identify that parameter with the ampersand (&) symbol like this:

```
[objectName methodName: &variable];
```

If you pass a pointer as a parameter, you can omit the ampersand (&) symbol.

To create properties, you must declare a variable and define it as a property in the header (.h) file of the class. When creating properties from data types like integer or Boolean, you use the @property (assign) command. When creating properties from classes like NSString, you use the @property (retain) command.

After declaring your properties in the header (.h) file, the final step is to use the @synthesize command in the implementation (.m) file so you can save and retrieve data from that property.

To assign or retrieve values from properties, you can use the square bracket technique or the dot syntax technique. Storing a value in a property through both techniques looks like this:

```
[objectName setPropertyName: value];
objectName.propertyName = value;
```

To retrieve data from a property, you can use the square bracket or dot syntax technique like this:

```
Variable = [objectName propertyName];
Variable = objectName.propertyName;
```

An object's properties let it accept data from other parts of the program or create data that other parts of the program may need. Methods make the object do something useful. By understanding how to create objects from class files and how to create and use properties and methods, you'll be able to create your own objects and understand how to use Apple's prewritten and tested classes stored in the Cocoa framework.

Chapter 13

Inheritance, Method Overriding, and Events

In the previous chapter, you learned how to create classes and use them to create objects. By using encapsulation to define a class with its own properties and methods, objects can isolate the details of their code from the rest of a program.

Although encapsulation helps improve program reliability, both inheritance and method overriding allow you to reuse existing objects to create more sophisticated programs faster and easier than before. When creating a Mac program, you'll be using the classes stored in the Cocoa framework to give your program the typical functionality of a Mac program without requiring you to write any code at all.

Inheritance lets you reuse an existing object and modify it. Method overriding lets you reuse the same method name but just alter the code that makes the method actually work. Together with encapsulation, inheritance and method overriding let you create more reliable software with less work.

Object Inheritance

The entire Cocoa framework is based on classes that inherit methods and properties from other classes. When you create your own classes, you can base your new class on an existing class to gain the functionality you want without writing the code to get it.

Over time, there's a good chance you'll create a particularly useful class that you'll want to reuse in another program. Rather than copying it and then modifying the copy of the class, it's better just to inherit the properties and methods from that class.

You've actually been using inheritance every time you create a new class. If you look carefully, the @interface portion of the class header (.h) file defines the class that you're inheriting from, such as NSObject like this:

```
@interface MyClass : NSObject
```

This line simply says that MyClass inherits from NSObject, which is the basic class that every class is based on. If you want a class to inherit from a class that you created, you need to do the following:

```
#import "OldClass.h"

@interface MyClass : OldClass
```

This first line tells the computer to import and make accessible all the code stored in the OldClass.h file. The second line tells the computer that MyClass inherits all the properties and methods stored in the OldClass files (OldClass.h and OldClass.m).

To see how inheritance can work, follow these steps:

1. Open the VariableTest project from the previous chapter.

2. Click the MyClass.h file inside the Classes folder, and modify the code as follows:

```
#import <Cocoa/Cocoa.h>

@interface MyClass : NSObject {

@private
    int position;
    NSString *name;

}

@property (assign) int position;
@property (retain) NSString *name;

-(int)changePosition: (int)myPosition;

@end
```

3. Choose File ➤ Save or press ⌘S to save your changes.

4. Click the MyClass.m file inside the Classes folder, and modify the code as follows:

```
#import "MyClass.h"

@implementation MyClass

@synthesize position;
@synthesize name;

- (id)init {
    if ((self = [super init])) {
        // Initialization code here.

    }

    return self;
}

- (void)dealloc {
    // Clean-up code here.
    [name release];
```

```
        [super dealloc];
}

-(int)changePosition: (int)myPosition
{
    int newPosition;
    newPosition = self.position + myPosition;
    return newPosition;
}

@end
```

The changePosition method takes its own property (position) and adds it to the myPosition variable. Normally when you need to use an object's property, you must state the object's name, but since the object is manipulating its own property, you can just replace its name with self instead.

5.   Choose File ➤ Save or press ⌘S to save your changes.

6.   Click the VariableTestAppDelegate.m file stored inside the Classes folder, and modify the code in the VariableTestAppDelegate.m file as follows:

```
#import "VariableTestAppDelegate.h"
#import "MyClass.h"

@implementation VariableTestAppDelegate

@synthesize window;

- (void)applicationDidFinishLaunching:(NSNotification *)aNotification {
    MyClass *testObject = [[MyClass alloc] init];
    testObject.position = 45;
    NSLog (@"The object's current position = %i", testObject.position);
    testObject.position = [testObject changePosition:10];
    NSLog (@"The new object position = %i", testObject.position);
    [testObject release];
}

@end
```

The applicationDidFinishLoading method creates an object called testObject, sets its property (position) to 45, prints out this position property, calls the changePosition method, and assigns the changePosition method's result to the position property, which gets printed again so you can see the result.

7.   Choose File ➤ Save or press ⌘S to save your changes.

8.   Click the Build and Run button, or choose Build ➤ Build and Run. As long as you didn't mistype anything, you should see a blank window pop up.

9.   Quit the program by clicking the Stop button or choosing Product ➤ Stop from the Xcode pull-down menus.

10. Choose Run ➤ Console, or press ⇧⌘R. You should see the printed statements created by the NSLog command:

```
2010-09-11 21:30:26.157 VariableTest[4567:a0f] The object's current position = 45
2010-09-11 21:30:26.160 VariableTest[4567:a0f] The new object position = 55
```

The output to the Log window verifies that the testObject's property (position) and method (changePosition) is working. The changePosition method simply accepts a value, adds 10 to it, and returns this sum.

Once you've tested to make sure your object is working correctly, the next step is to create a new object, inherit properties and methods from MyClass, and use the new, inherited class to verify that it works, which you can do by following these steps:

1. Open the VariableTest project from the previous section.

2. Choose File ➤ New File. A template dialog box appears.

3. Click Cocoa under Mac OS X in the left pane of the template dialog box.

4. Click the Objective-C class icon, and click the Next button. A Save As dialog box appears.

5. Choose the Classes folder in the Group pop-up menu, and type **NewClass** for your class name. Then click the Save button. The NewClass.h and NewClass.m files appear in your Classes folder.

6. Click the NewClass.h file, and modify the code as follows:

```
#import <Cocoa/Cocoa.h>
#import "MyClass.h"

@interface NewClass : MyClass {
@private

}

@end
```

The two main changes you need to make in the NewClass.h file are to add the #import "MyClass.h" line and define NewClass to inherit from MyClass through the @interface NewClass : MyClass line.

7. Choose File ➤ Save or press ⌘S to save your changes.

8. Click the VariableTestAppDelegate.m file, and modify the code as follows:

```
#import "VariableTestAppDelegate.h"
#import "MyClass.h"
#import "NewClass.h"

@implementation VariableTestAppDelegate

@synthesize window;

- (void)applicationDidFinishLaunching:(NSNotification *)aNotification {
    MyClass *testObject = [[MyClass alloc] init];
    testObject.position = 45;
    NSLog (@"The object's current position = %i", testObject.position);
```

```
    testObject.position = [testObject changePosition:10];
    NSLog (@"The new object position = %i", testObject.position);
    [testObject release];
    NewClass *newObject = [[NewClass alloc] init];
    newObject.position = 32;
    NSLog (@"The object's current position = %i", newObject.position);
    newObject.position = [newObject changePosition:10];
    NSLog (@"The new object position = %i", newObject.position);
    [newObject release];
}

@end
```

To make the `VariableTestAppDelegate.m` file capable of accessing the code stored in the `NewClass.h` file, you must import it using the `#import "NewClass.h"` line. The last five lines in the `applicationDidFinishLaunching` method create a `newObject`, based on `NewClass`. At this point, the `NewClass` file does not contain any code since it inherits all its code from the `MyClass` file.

To verify that `NewClass` really does inherit its code from the `MyClass` file, this code then assigns the value 32 into the position property of `newObject`, which it then prints out. Next, it runs the `moveMe` method using a value of 10. The result of this `moveMe` method gets stored in the position property of `newObject`, which then gets printed again to show how it changed.

9. Choose File ➤ Save or press ⌘S to save your changes.

10. Click the Build and Run button, or choose Build ➤ Build and Run. As long as you didn't mistype anything, you should see a blank window pop up.

11. Quit the program by clicking the Stop button or choosing Product ➤ Stop from the Xcode pull-down menus.

12. Choose Run ➤ Console, or press ⇧⌘R. You should see the printed statements created by the NSLog command:

```
2010-09-11 23:03:18.721 VariableTest[4776:a0f] The object's current position = 45
2010-09-11 23:03:18.724 VariableTest[4776:a0f] The new object position = 55
2010-09-11 23:03:18.721 VariableTest[4776:a0f] The object's current position = 32
2010-09-11 23:03:18.724 VariableTest[4776:a0f] The new object position = 42
```

Even though the `NewsClass` file does not contain the position property or the `changePosition` method, the property and method still work because they're defined in the `MyClass` file, which is where the `NewClass` file inherited it.

Method Overriding

When you create a class with its own properties and methods, you took advantage of encapsulation, which is one of the main features of object-oriented programming. The second main feature is inheritance, where one object can inherit the properties and methods of another object without physically duplicating its code.

The third feature of object-oriented programming is method overriding, where two objects can have identically named methods that can work differently from one another.

To use method overriding, you simply create a new class that inherits from an existing class. In this new class, you create a method that's identically named as a method in the other class.

To see how method overriding works, follow these steps:

1. Open the VariableTest project from the previous section.

2. Click the NewClass.h file, and modify the code as follows:

```
#import <Cocoa/Cocoa.h>
#import "MyClass.h"

@interface NewClass : MyClass {
@private

}

-(int)changePosition: (int)myPosition;

@end
```

All you're doing in this code is declaring a moveMe method that's identical to the moveMe method stored in the MyClass file.

3. Choose File ➤ Save or press ⌘S to save your changes.

4. Click the NewClass.m file, and modify the code as follows:

```
#import "NewClass.h"

@implementation NewClass

- (id)init {
    if ((self = [super init])) {
        // Initialization code here.
    }

    return self;
}

- (void)dealloc {
    // Clean-up code here.

    [super dealloc];
}

-(int)changePosition: (int)myPosition
{
    int newPosition;
    newPosition = self.position * myPosition;
    return newPosition;
}

@end
```

This code redefines how the changePosition method works. In the MyClass file, the changePosition method adds self.position + myPosition. In this moveMe method, it multiples self.position * myPosition.

5. Choose File ➤ Save or press ⌘S to save your changes.

6. Click the Build and Run button, or choose Build ➤ Build and Run. As long as you didn't mistype anything, you should see a blank window pop up.

7. Quit the program by clicking the Stop button or choosing Product ➤ Stop from the Xcode pull-down menus.

8. Choose Run ➤ Console, or press ⇧⌘R. You should see the printed statements created by the NSLog command:

```
2010-09-11 23:03:18.721 VariableTest[4776:a0f] The object's current position = 45
2010-09-11 23:03:18.724 VariableTest[4776:a0f] The new object position = 55
2010-09-11 23:03:18.726 VariableTest[4776:a0f] The object's current position = 32
2010-09-11 23:03:18.727 VariableTest[4776:a0f] The new object position = 320
```

Even though both the testObject (based on MyClass) and newObject (based on NewClass) use identical method names, method overriding lets you use the same method name in multiple objects.

Responding to Events

Without writing a single line of code, you can create a Mac program that knows how to display pull-down menus and windows. If you move or resize the window, it behaves exactly like a typical Mac program. However, most parts of your user interface also have a list of predefined events that they can recognize.

In most cases, you can ignore all or most of these events and just let your program behave in its default mode. However, sometimes you may want to respond to certain types of events. To do this, you can create a method to respond to that specific event and store that method in another object. One common type of object that handles different events is called a *delegate*.

For example, the sample program you've been modifying throughout this book has a method called applicationDidFinishLaunching, which runs every time your program successfully starts. This applicationDidFinishLaunching method is automatically included in a file called AppDelegate. (The name of your project gets added to the front of this file name, so if you named your project MyTest, the complete name of the file would be MyTestAppDelegate.)

A delegate is simply a class (consisting of a header and an implementation file) that contains methods for handling a list of predefined events for a specific part of your program. Every time you create a basic Mac program, Xcode automatically creates an AppDelegate file, which is a delegate object for handling events related to your entire application, which is why it's called AppDelegate.

Understanding the Application Delegate

Every program is based on a class called NSApplication. This class contains all the code needed to make your program behave like a typical Mac program without you having to write a single line of code.

To respond to different events related to your application, your application relies on a file called AppDelegate. This AppDelegate file is where you'll create and store your methods for responding to different events related to the application.

To find the different types of events that an application can recognize, follow these steps:

1. Choose Help ➤ Developer Documentation. A window appears.

2. Click in the Search field in the upper-right corner, type **NSApplicationDelegate**, and press Return. A list of help topics related to your search query appears in the left pane of the Organizer window.

3. Click the NSApplicationDelegate Protocol topic. A help screen for the NSApplicationDelegate Protocol Reference appears, as shown in Figure 13–1.

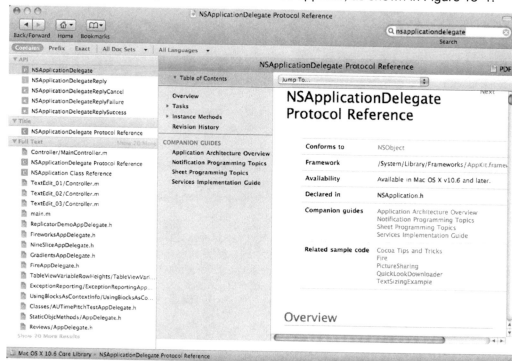

Figure 13–1. *The NSApplicationDelegate Protocol Reference help screen*

4. Scroll down this NSApplicationDelegate Protocol Reference screen until you find the list of events, under the Tasks category heading, that your application can respond to, as shown in Figure 13–2.

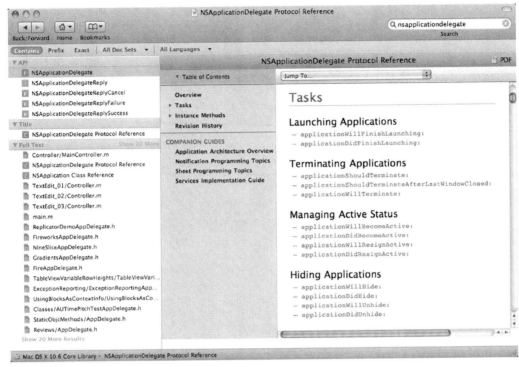

Figure 13–2. *Your new class files appear in your selected folder.*

By identifying a particular class, you can find the list of events that the object can recognize. For the NSApplication class, which forms the basis for every Mac program you create, the following are the different events that the application can recognize:

Launching Applications

```
- applicationWillFinishLaunching:
- applicationDidFinishLaunching:
```

Terminating Applications

```
- applicationShouldTerminate:
- applicationShouldTerminateAfterLastWindowClosed:
- applicationWillTerminate:
```

Managing Active Status

```
- applicationWillBecomeActive:
- applicationDidBecomeActive:
- applicationWillResignActive:
- applicationDidResignActive:
```

Hiding Applications

```
- applicationWillHide:
- applicationDidHide:
- applicationWillUnhide:
- applicationDidUnhide:
```

Managing Windows

```
- applicationWillUpdate:
- applicationDidUpdate:
- applicationShouldHandleReopen:hasVisibleWindows:
```

Managing the Dock Menu

```
- applicationDockMenu:
```

Displaying Errors

```
- application:willPresentError:
```

Managing the Screen

```
- applicationDidChangeScreenParameters:
```

Opening Files

```
- application:openFile:
- application:openFileWithoutUI:
- application:openTempFile:
- application:openFiles:
- applicationOpenUntitledFile:
- applicationShouldOpenUntitledFile:
```

Printing

```
- application:printFile:
- application:printFiles:withSettings:showPrintPanels:
```

You'll never need to recognize all of these possible events, but you may need to recognize some of them for your particular program. If you study these different types of events, you'll notice that they are in three categories: events that will happen, events that did happen, or events that are happening right now.

- If you respond to an event that includes will in its name, then your code will run before the event actually occurs.

- If you respond to an event that includes did in its name, then your code will run after the event actually occurs.

- If you respond to an event that does not include the words did or will, then your code runs as the particular event occurs.

To see how some of these events can work, follow these steps:

1. Open the VariableTest project from the previous chapter.

2. Click the VariableTestAppDelegate.m file in the Classes folder. The middle pane of the Xcode window displays your VariableTestAppDelegate.m code.

3. Modify the VariableTestAppDelegate.m file as follows:

```
#import "VariableTestAppDelegate.h"
#import "MyClass.h"

@implementation VariableTestAppDelegate

@synthesize window;

- (void)applicationDidFinishLaunching:(NSNotification *)aNotification {
    NSLog(@"applicationDidFinishLaunching");
}

-(void)applicationDidBecomeActive:(NSNotification *)aNotification {
    NSLog (@"applicationDidBecomeActive");
}

-(void)applicationWillTerminate:(NSNotification *)aNotification {
    NSLog (@"applicationWillTerminate");
}

@end
```

4. Choose File ➤ Save or press ⌘S to save your changes.

5. Click the Run button, or choose Product ➤ Run. As long as you didn't mistype anything, you should see a blank window pop up.

6. Click another program that's running, or click the desktop to make your program inactive.

7. Quit the program by choosing the VariableTest ➤ Quit command or pressing ⌘Q.

8. Choose Run ➤ Console, or press ⇧⌘R. You should see the printed statements created by the NSLog command:

```
2010-09-11 18:04:18.424 VariableTest[3850:a0f] applicationDidFinishLaunching
2010-09-11 18:04:18.434 VariableTest[3850:a0f] applicationDidBecomeActive
2010-09-11 18:04:25.574 VariableTest[3850:a0f] applicationDidBecomeActive
2010-09-11 18:04:29.344 VariableTest[3850:a0f] applicationWillTerminate
```

When you ran your program, this what happened:

1. Your program ran and immediately launched the applicationDidFinishLaunching method inside the VariableTestAppDelegate.m file.

2. Your program's window appeared on the screen, which triggered the applicationDidBecomeActive method.

3. When you made another program active and then switched back to your program, the applicationDidBecomeActive method ran a second time.

4. When you quit your program, the applicationWillTerminate method ran.

As you can see, your application can respond to a variety of different events, but it's up to you to create methods to respond to those events by writing Objective-C code in the AppDelegate file.

Summary

Object-oriented programming allows encapsulation, inheritance, and method overriding. Encapsulation isolates code from the rest of your program, making it easier to build a large program out of smaller parts. Inheritance lets you reuse code without physically copying it. Method overriding lets you write different code for identically named methods stored in different objects.

By using classes from the Cocoa framework, you're already using classes that inherit from other classes. If you create a class and want to inherit code from that class, you need to follow two steps. First, you need to use the #import command to import all the code from the class that you want to inherit from. Second, you need to define your new class as being based on another class like this:

```
#import "OldClass.h"

@interface NewClass : OldClass
```

To override a method, you just need to define an identically named method in a different class. When you call that message, you must also identify the object name so the computer knows which method to use and where that method is stored.

Finally, as you develop your programs, you'll find that parts of your user interface already know how to respond to different types of events that can occur. Normally you can ignore these events, but if you want to respond to them for a particular reason, you need to write a method with code that tells your program how to react when that specific event occurs.

By understanding how to use encapsulation, inheritance, and method overriding to create objects, you'll better understand how objects can make up your user interface, which you'll learn about in the next part of this book.

Every user interface object, such as a button or text field, can also respond to different types of events, which you may need to respond to through methods stored in a delegate file for that user interface object.

In this first part of the book, you've gone from learning the basics to using Xcode and Objective-C to learning how to write simple Objective-C programs that take advantage of object-oriented features. In the next part of this book, you'll learn how to tie your Objective-C code to your user interface to make your programs truly look and act like real Mac programs.

Chapter 14

Creating a User Interface

Up until now, the sample programs you've created have simply printed data to the Log window using the NSLog command. Although this can be fine for testing your program, it's definitely not how you want users to interact with your program.

If you're creating a Mac program, users expect your program to behave just like a regular Mac program by displaying pull-down menus at the top of the screen with familiar menu titles such as File, Edit, View, and Help. Users also expect to interact with your program through windows and dialog boxes that you can move, resize, and shrink from the middle of the screen.

Within each window and dialog box, users expect to see buttons, check boxes, text fields, sliders, and radio buttons that allow them to input data to your program and display some sort of output in return.

In this chapter, you'll learn about the basics behind a user interface and how to use the various tools to create your own user interface.

Getting to Know Interface Builder

The portion of Xcode that lets you visually design your user interface is called Interface Builder. In the old days, you had to write code to make your program work and then write additional code to create your user interface. You can still do that if you want, but it's far simpler and more reliable to use Interface Builder to create your user interface.

When you write Objective-C code, you store it in class files that have the .h and .m file extensions, which are usually stored in the Classes folder. When you create a user interface, you store it in a file that has the .xib file extension, often called *nib* files because they were once called NeXTSTEP Interface Builder files. Xcode typically stores your user interface .xib files in the Resources folder, as shown in Figure 14–1.

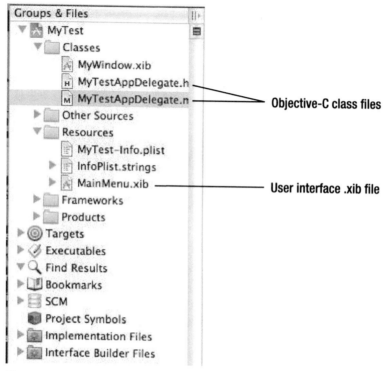

Figure 14-1. *The Resources folder contains your user interface* `.xib` *files.*

Simple programs may have only one user interface, typically stored in the Resources folder as the `MainMenu.xib` file. If your program needs to display different types of interfaces, such as a video game that may need to display an actual game along with various control panels for customizing the game, your program may need two or more `.xib` files.

The basic idea behind using Interface Builder is to create and design your user interface, which includes a window along with common user interface items such as buttons, check boxes, and sliders.

Creating a New User Interface .xib File

When you create a new project, your project will likely create a `MainMenu.xib` file automatically. If you created a project where this file doesn't exist or if you need to add additional user interface `.xib` files, follow these steps:

1. Choose File ➤ New File. A template dialog box appears.

2. Click User Interface under the Mac OS X category in the left pane. Different types of user interface files appear in the right pane, as shown in Figure 14-2.

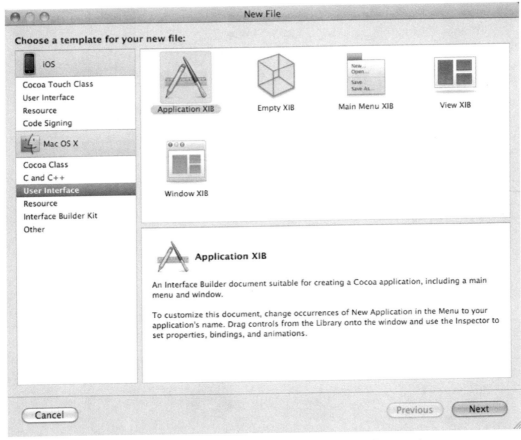

Figure 14–2. *The template dialog box lets you choose the type of user interface file to create.*

3. Click an icon that represents the type of user interface file you want to create. The five choices are as follows:

    ■ *Application*: Creates a complete user interface that provides pull-down menus and a window

    ■ *Main Menu XIB*: Creates a new pull-down menu bar

    ■ *Window XIB*: Creates a new window

    ■ *View XIB*: Creates a custom window for displaying items

    ■ *Empty XIB*: Creates a bare-bones user interface

4. Click the Next button. A Save As dialog box appears, letting you choose a name for your user interface file.

5. Type a descriptive name for your user interface `.xib` file.

6. Click the Finish button. Your new user interface files appears. You may want to drag and drop this .xib file to another folder.

Understanding the Parts of a .XIB File

When you create a typical Mac program, Xcode automatically creates a MainMenu.xib file that contains the bulk of your program's user interface, which is represented as icons that appear in the Interface Builder window, as shown in Figure 14–3.

Figure 14–3. *Icons represent different parts of your* .xib *user interface file.*

In Figure 14–3, a horizontal line divides the icons into two groups. The icons above the horizontal line are known as *placeholder objects*. The icons underneath the vertical line are known as *interface objects*.

Placeholder Objects

Placeholder objects represent items stored outside your user interface .xib file, which work as a link between your Objective-C code and your user interface. The three common placeholder objects include the following:

- *File's Owner*: The File's Owner icon defines which class file links to the .xib user interface file. You can pair up only one class file at a time to each .xib user interface file.

- *First Responder*: The First Responder icon defines how to handle any actions that the user takes upon viewing the user interface displayed by the .xib file.

- *Application*: The Application icon defines how your program behaves. If you don't customize the Application icon, your program will behave by default like a regular Mac program.

When you're learning to program using Xcode, you'll probably never need to change the options available in the File Owner's, First Responder, or Application icon.

Interface Objects

Interface objects represent the different parts of the user interface stored in a specific .xib file. The four common interface objects include the following:

- *Main Menu*: The Main Menu icon represents the pull-down menu that appears at the top of the screen.

- *Window*: The Window icon represents the window that appears on the screen.

- *App Delegate*: The App Delegate icon defines the class file that contains the Objective-C code to respond to different types of events. The App Delegate icon normally defines the `ProgramNameAppDelegate` file, where `ProgramName` is your actual program name.

- *Font Manager*: The Font Manager icon defines the class that controls the displayed fonts on the user interface. By default, this class is the `NSFontManager` class.

In most cases, you'll need only one Main Menu, App Delegate, and Font Manager icon. However, you might have more than one Window icon. In addition, you can define additional objects to interact with your user interface.

The Main Menu icon will let you edit the pull-down menus of your user interface. The Window icon displays the window of your user interface, which is where you'll drag and drop different user interface objects such as buttons, text fields, and check boxes.

Out of all the placeholder and interface object icons displayed, you'll spend most of your time only using the Main Menu and Window icons and accepting the default values of the rest of the other icons.

Toggling the View of Placeholder and Interface Objects

By default, your placeholder and interface object icons appear as icons (see Figure 14–3). However, you can switch to a different view (List, Icons, or Columns) by choosing the View menu or by clicking the View Mode icon, as shown in Figure 14–4.

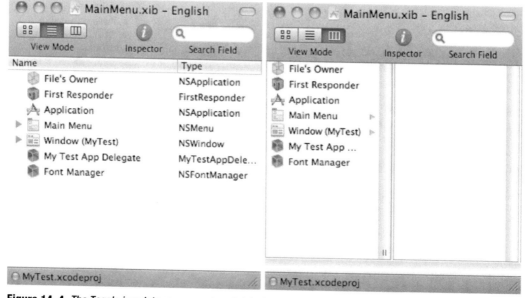

Figure 14–4. *The Toggle icon lets you expand or shrink the appearance of placeholder and interface objects.*

Besides displaying each icon with its descriptive name, the List and Columns view lets you view the parts that make up each icon, such as the individual menus that make up the Main Menu icon. Just click the gray disclosure triangle that appears to the left of an icon to view its additional parts, as shown in Figure 14–5.

Figure 14–5. *The expanded view lets you see the parts that make up each icon.*

Designing a User Interface

The design of your user interface typically appears through the Window icon, which displays the actual window where you can place various user interface objects such as buttons, text fields, and pictures.

The basic idea behind designing a user interface is to pick a user interface object and drag it on the window of your .xib file. Then you may need to customize this object, such as changing its position or size. Finally, you'll need to link or connect some (but not all) of your user interface objects to your Objective-C code, so that way your user interface can respond to certain actions, such as the user clicking a button, and display information on the screen.

To see how create a simple user interface, follow these steps:

1. Choose File ➤ Close Project to shut down any currently displayed projects on the screen.

2. Choose File ➤ New Project. A template dialog box appears.

3. Click Application under Mac OS X in the left pane.

4. Click the Cocoa Application icon in the right pane, and click the Next button. Another dialog box appears, asking for the name of your project.

5. Type any name, such as **MyTest**, and click the Next button. A Save As dialog box appears.

6. Choose a folder to store your project, and click the Save button.

7. Click the disclosure triangle to the left of the Resources folder. The `MainMenu.xib` file appears.

8. Click the `MainMenu.xib` file. The Interface Builder window appears.

9. Click the Window icon. Your user interface's window appears on the screen, as shown in Figure 14–6.

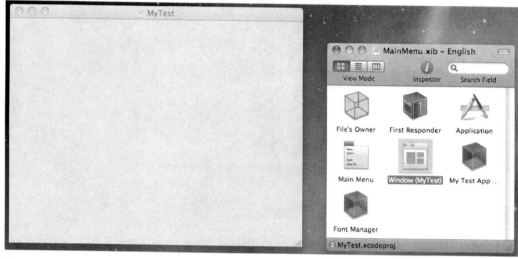

Figure 14–6. *Clicking the Windows icon displays the window of your user interface.*

10. Choose Tools ➤ Library. The Library window appears.

11. Click the Objects tab near the top of the Library window, as shown in Figure 14–7.

Figure 14–7. *The Object Library window displays different user interface objects you can use.*

12. Scroll down through the Object Library until you find the Push Button icon.

13. Drag and drop the Push Button object anywhere over your open window, as shown in Figure 14–8.

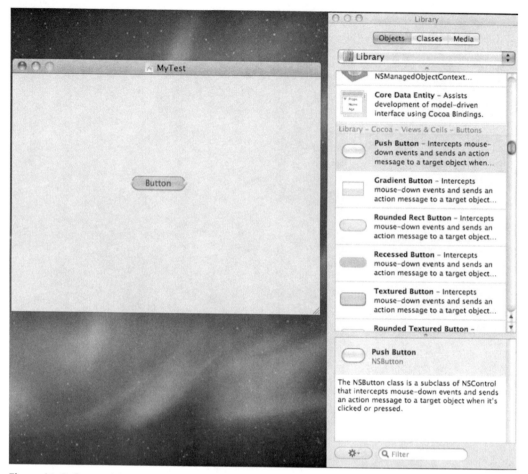

Figure 14–8. *Drag and drop user interface objects over the window to design a user interface.*

14. Scroll through the Object Library until you find a Wrapping Text Field icon.

15. Drag and drop the Wrapping Text Field object on the window, as shown in Figure 14–9.

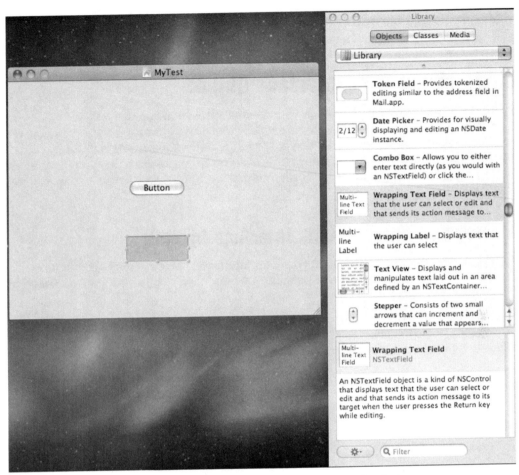

Figure 14–9. *The Wrapping Text Field object displays a field where users can type text.*

16. Choose File ➤ Save or press ⌘S to save your changes.

17. Switch to Xcode; click the Build and Run button, or choose Build ➤ Build and Run. A blank window appears on the screen with the button you placed on the window. Although you can click the button, it won't do anything because you haven't written any Objective-C code to make it work yet.

18. Click in the Wrapping Text Field, and type **bbrown** (deliberately misspelling *brown*.

19. Right-click the misspelled word to display a pop-up menu, and choose Spelling and Grammar ➤ Show Spelling and Grammar. A dialog box appears, highlighting your misspelled word and offering a possible correct spelling. Without writing a single line of code, your program already includes a built-in spell-checker, courtesy of Apple's Cocoa framework.

20. Quit the program by clicking the Stop button or choosing Product ➤ Stop from the Xcode pull-down menus.

Customizing User Interface Objects

By dragging and dropping objects on your user interface, you can design your program's appearance without writing a single line of code. However, placing objects on your user interface is just a start since you'll need to further customize each user interface object to give it a descriptive name or to resize or precisely position objects. Customizing the appearance of your user interface can make your program look nice for your user.

Moving and Resizing User Interface Objects

When you drag and drop objects on your user interface, chances are good that those objects won't be the exact size and position you need them. To fix this, you may need to move objects or resize them.

The simplest way to move an object is to drag it on the screen, and the simplest way to resize an object is to click it to display handles around its edges and then drag one of its handles. Although this can be fast and easy, it can also be imprecise.

To help you position an object in relation to any existing objects on the user interface, Interface Builder displays guidelines that show you when objects appear aligned, as shown in Figure 14–10.

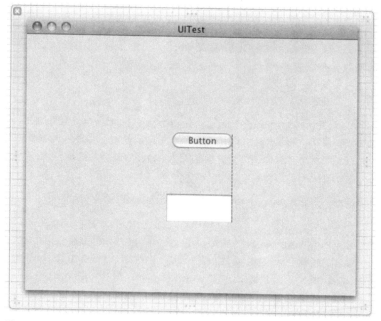

Figure 14–10. *Interface Builder displays guidelines to help you align objects on your user interface.*

If you need to precisely align objects, you can specify the object's position in relation to the bottom-left corner of the user interface window. You can also precisely define an object's width and height.

To see how to move and resize an object, follow these steps:

1. Click the object you want to move or resize.

2. Choose Tools ➤ Size Inspector, or press ⌘3. The Size window appears where you can type in numbers to define the object's position (relative to the bottom-left corner of the user interface window, which is defined as the origin) and size, as shown in Figure 14–11.

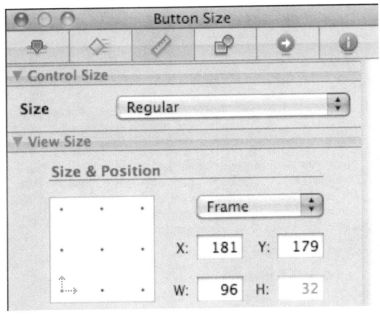

Figure 14–11. *The Size window lets you define the position and size of an object.*

Autosizing and Anchoring User Interface Objects

When you place an object on a user interface, it may look perfect—until the user actually runs your program and resizes the window. Suddenly buttons and text fields can get skewered out of proportion to one another or appear cut off, as shown in Figure 14–12.

Figure 14–12. *Resizing a window can wreck the appearance of a user interface.*

One option is to prevent the user from resizing the user interface window. However, a better solution is to anchor and autosize your user interface objects so they adjust no matter how the user resizes the user interface window.

Autosizing means that the object shrinks or grows in height and/or width as the window shrinks or grows. Anchoring means that an edge of the object remains a fixed distance from the side of the user interface window no matter how much the user may resize that window. The combination of anchoring and autoresizing can make your user interface adjust to any size that the user makes the user interface window.

To anchor and autosize an object, follow these steps:

1. Click the object you want to anchor to one or more sides of the user interface window or autoresize.

2. Choose Tools ➤ Size Inspector, or press ⌘3. The Size window appears, displaying the Autoresizing box, as shown in Figure 14–13.

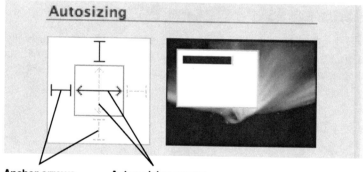

Anchor arrows   Autoresizing arrows

Figure 14–13. *The Autoresizing box lets you define how an object anchors or autoresizes.*

3. Click the vertical and/or horizontal autoresize arrow (inside the box) to define whether the object can expand in height or width if the user resizes the user interface window.

4. Click one or more anchor arrows (outside the box) to force the object to always stay within a fixed distance from the top, bottom, left, or right edges of the user interface window.

After you click the different anchor or autoresize arrows, the Example graphic to the right visually shows you how your choices will make your object behave if the user resizes the user interface window as long as you keep the mouse pointer over the Autosizing box.

Summary

To create a user interface, you have to use Interface Builder, which lets you visually drag and drop objects to create a user interface. A typical user interface consists of a single .xib file that contains pull-down menus and a window. However, you can add as many additional .xib files as necessary to create your program's user interface.

After you drag and drop objects on your user interface, you need to customize the appearance of each object by moving or resizing it. You can use the mouse to drag an object to the right position on the window or to resize its height or width. For more precision, you can choose View ➤ Utilities ➤ Size to open the Size window and type in a specific value for an object's width, height, or X and Y positions relative to the bottom-left corner of the user interface window.

To make sure your user interface remains consistent no matter how the user resizes the user interface window, you can anchor and autoresize each user interface object. Anchoring forces an object to maintain a fixed distance from one or more edges of a window. Autoresizing lets an object expand or shrink its height and/or width depending on how the user expands or shrinks the user interface window.

The basic idea behind designing a user interface is to drag and drop objects on a window, customize those user interface objects, and then connect them to your Objective-C code, which is what you'll learn to do in the next chapters in this part of the book.

Chapter 15

Choosing Commands with Buttons

The user interface lets you communicate with a program. In the old days, you had to type a command to make a program do something. If you didn't know the command to type or if you misspelled it, your command wouldn't work, and the program wouldn't respond to your actions.

Fortunately, today's programs use a graphical user interface (GUI) that displays options on the screen for the user to select using the mouse or keyboard. For most programs, the simplest way to offer options for the user to select involves using buttons.

A button typically appears on the screen as a rectangular object with a descriptive command displayed inside such as the word *Print* or *Cancel*. However, buttons can appear in different sizes, shapes, and colors, as shown in Figure 15–1, which you can display by choosing Tools ➤ Library.

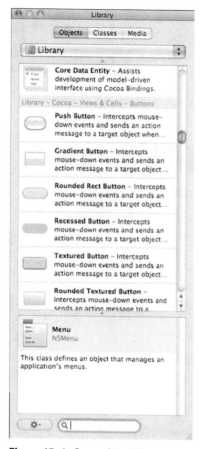

Figure 15–1. *Some of the different types of buttons you can create*

In this chapter, you'll learn how to create and customize different buttons and connect them to your Objective-C code to make them work.

Creating a Button

These are some of the more common types of buttons available for your user interface:

- Push Button
- Gradient Button
- Rounded Rect Button
- Rounded Textured Button
- Textured Button
- Recessed Button
- Disclosure Triangle

- Square Button
- Help Button
- Disclosure Button
- Round Button
- Bevel Button

All buttons work alike, but they just look different. The Push Button is the standard button appearance for Mac programs, but you can just as easily replace it with a Recessed Button or Square Button instead.

Some buttons, such as the Round Button, can't display as much text as the Push Button or Rounded Rect Button. Others types of buttons, such as the Help Button and Disclosure Button, don't display any text inside them at all, as shown in Figure 15–2.

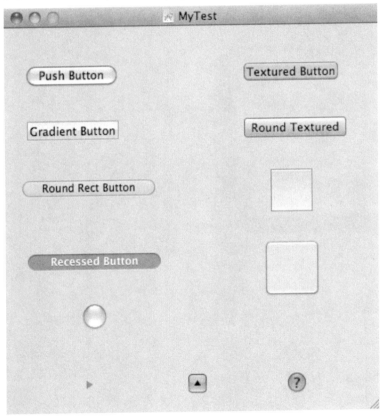

Figure 15–2. *The appearance of different types of buttons*

The basic idea behind all of these buttons is to provide the user with one-click access to a single command. Generally, use buttons when you need to give the user a limited number of options, such as two or three choices. If you display too many buttons on the screen at once, you may just wind up confusing the user and making your user interface look too cluttered.

There are two ways to create a button. First, you can scroll through the Object Library window (see Figure 15–1), find the type of button you want such as a Bevel Button or Round Button, and then drag and drop that button on your user interface.

Second, you can drag and drop any button on the user interface and then change it to another button style by following these steps:

1. Click a button on your user interface that you want to change.

2. Choose Tools ➤ Attributes Inspector to display the Attributes Inspector.

3. Click the Bezel pop-up menu, and choose the button type you want, as shown in Figure 15–3.

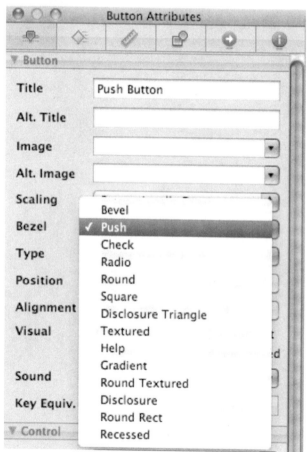

Figure 15–3. *Clicking the Bezel pop-up menu lets you change a button's appearance.*

Creating a Button Title

Nearly all types of buttons (with the exception of Disclosure Triangles, Disclosure Buttons, and Help Buttons) let you display a title inside the button. This title typically displays the name of the command that the button represents such as Save, OK, or Options.

There are two ways to create a title on a button. First, you can double-click the button directly and, when the button's title appears highlighted, type any text that you want to appear on the button.

A second way is to open the Attributes window, which not only lets you type text into the Title field to display text on a button but also lets you align text on a button as left-justified, centered, justified, or right-justified, as shown in Figure 15–4.

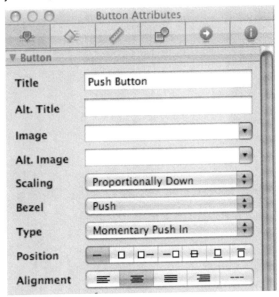

Figure 15–4. *The Attributes window lets you type and align text on a button.*

The Alternate field is used to define text that appears on a button that toggles between displaying the Title field text and the Alternate field text. Any text in the Alternate field appears only if the button's Type is set to Toggle.

The toggle feature can replace two separate buttons with a single button. For example, you might have one button that displays Go and a second button that displays Stop. Rather than clutter your user interface with two buttons, you could have one button that initially displays Go, and after the user clicks it, the button changes its text to display Stop. Of course, you'd have to write additional Objective-C code to make the button behave differently when displaying different text, but toggling lets you eliminate the need for two separate buttons.

To see how to display alternate text on a button, follow these steps:

1. Open the MyTest program you created in the previous chapter.

2. Double-click `MainMenu.xib` file inside the Resources folder to switch to Interface Builder.

3. Click the Window icon in Interface Builder window. Your user interface appears.

4. Click the button that appears on the user interface. (If a button does not appear, drag and drop a Push Button object on the window.)

5. Choose Tools ➤ Attributes Inspector. The Attributes Inspector appears.

6. Click the Type pop-up menu, and choose Toggle, as shown in Figure 15–5.

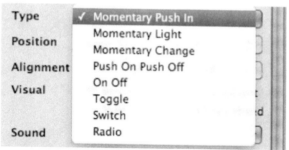

Figure 15–5. *The Object Attributes window lets you type and align text on a button.*

7. Click in the Title field, and replace the current text with new text such as **On**.

8. Click in the Alternate field, and type new text such as **Off**.

9. Choose File ➤ Save or press ⌘S to save your changes.

10. Switch to Xcode; click the Build and Run button, or choose Build ➤ Build and Run. A blank window appears on the screen with the button you placed on the window.

11. Click the On button on your user interface. Notice that it now toggles to display Off, as shown in Figure 15–6.

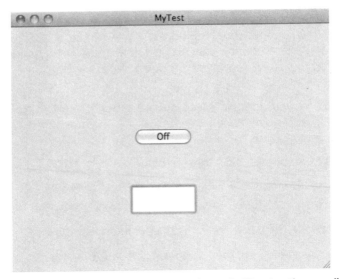

Figure 15–6. *A button that toggles can change its title when the user clicks it.*

12. Click the Off button. Notice that it now reads On.

13. Quit the program by choosing MyTest ➤ Quit.

Adding a Graphic Image

Besides displaying a title, most buttons can also display a graphic image that appears next to a button's title or replaces it altogether. To add a graphic image, you need to use the Image, Alternate, Position, and Scaling options in the Attributes Inspector, as shown in Figure 15–7.

Image	
Alt. Image	
Scaling	Proportionally Down
Bezel	Push
Type	Toggle
Position	☐ ☐— —☐ ☐ ☐ ☐

Figure 15–7. *The Image, Alt. Image, Position, and Scaling options for displaying graphic images on a button.*

The Image and Alternate pop-up menus let you choose from various icons commonly found in Mac programs. Any images defined by the Alt Image pop-up menu appear only if you have also set the button's Type option to Toggle.

Turning on this toggle feature would let a button display an initial image, and then after the user selects that button, a new image appears on that button. For example, a button might display a green traffic light, and then when the user clicks it, the image changes to a red traffic light, allowing the button to visually represent a toggled state, such as allowing or blocking something.

The Position options let you define how your graphic image should appear on the button next to any existing title. The Scaling pop-up menu lets you define how the graphic image should appear if the button gets resized.

To see how to add graphic images to a button, follow these steps:

1. Open the MyTest program you created in the previous section, and double-click MainMenu.xib file inside the Resources folder to switch to Interface Builder.

2. Click the Window icon in Interface Builder window. Your user interface appears.

3. Click the button on your user interface, and then choose Tools ➤ Attributes Inspector. The Attributes Inspector appears.

4. Make sure that Toggle appears in the Type option (see Figure 15–5).

5. Click the Image pop-up menu, and choose any option. Graphic images appear as class names such as NSUser or NSColorPanel, as shown in Figure 15–8.

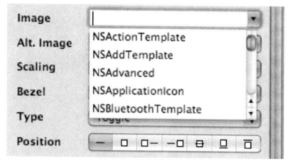

Figure 15–8. *The Image, Alt. Image, Position, and Scaling options for displaying graphic images on a button.*

6. Click the Alt. Image pop-up menu, and choose any option, preferably a different option than the one you chose in step 5.

7. Click an icon in the Position group (see Figure 15–8). The straight line represents your button's title, and the square represents your button's graphic image.

8. Choose File ➤ Save or press ⌘S to save your changes.

9. Switch to Xcode; click the Build and Run button, or choose Build ➤ Build and Run. A blank window appears on the screen with the button you placed on the window. Notice that the button now displays a graphic image.

10. Click the button. Notice that the button now displays a different graphic image, defined by the Alt. Image pop-up menu.

11. Quit the program by clicking the Stop button or choosing Product ➤ Stop from the Xcode pull-down menus.

> **NOTE:** To delete an option displayed in the Image or Alt. Image options, just highlight the currently displayed option and press the Delete or Backspace key.

Customizing the Visual Behavior of a Button

In most cases, you'll just need to create a button on a user interface, change its title, and be done. Occasionally, you may want to modify the appearance of a button to hide (or display) a border, as shown in Figure 15–9.

Figure 15–9. A border with a button and the identical button without a border

To hide (or display) a button's border, you just need to select (or clear) the Bordered check box in the button's Attributes Inspector, as shown in Figure 15–10. By default, the Bordered check box is selected to display a border around a button since the border helps identify the button's boundaries so the user knows where to click.

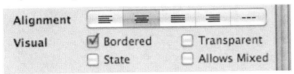

Figure 15–10. Clearing or selecting the Bordered or Transparent check box can hide (or display) the button border or the entire button.

One curious option is the ability to make a button transparent, which essentially makes it invisible. By making a button transparent or just removing its border, you could overlap a button on another object, such as placing a borderless or transparent button over different parts of a map. Now instead of seeing the button, users would see the map and be able to click an object that really has a button overlaid on top of that object.

Another way to customize the behavior and appearance of a button is to modify its Type, which defines how the button behaves when the user clicks it. Normally when the user clicks a button, that button appears highlighted momentarily until the user releases the mouse button. However, a button can also remain highlighted even after the user releases the mouse button or moves the mouse away from the button.

The default behavior is called Momentary Push In, which is where the button appears highlighted as long as the user holds the mouse button down while pointing at the button. To change a button's behavior, click in the Type pop-up menu, and choose a different option, as shown in Figure 15–11.

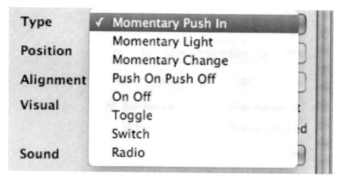

Figure 15–11. *The Type pop-up menu lets you change how a button appears when the user clicks it.*

Making Buttons Easier to Use

Buttons are one of the simplest user interface objects available since most users know that they can click a button to choose that particular command. However, you can make your buttons even easier to use by adding tooltips, sound, or keystrokes that allow users to choose a button by pressing the keyboard rather than using the mouse.

Creating Tooltips

Tooltips are short, descriptive text that appears if the user leaves the mouse pointer over a button for a few seconds. The tooltip text appears next to the button, displaying a short description of the button's purpose, as shown in Figure 15–12.

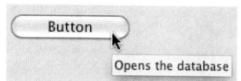

Figure 15–12. *A tooltip can describe the button's purpose before the user clicks it.*

To create a tooltip, click a button, and then choose Tools ➤ Identity Inspector to open the Identity Inspector. Then click in the Tooltip field, and type the text you want to appear as your tooltip, as shown in Figure 15–13.

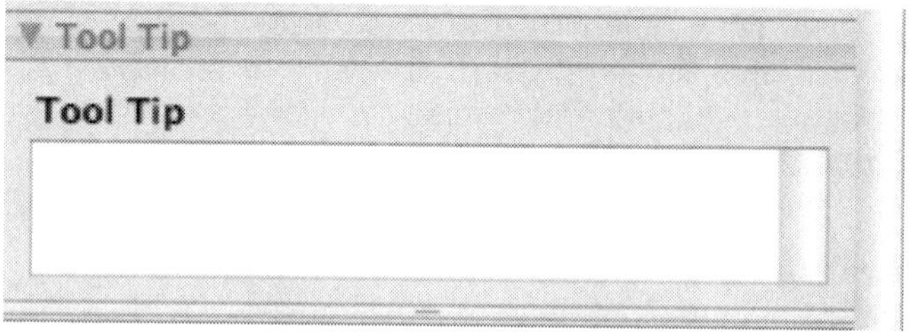

Figure 15–13. *The Tool Tip field appears in the Identity Inspector.*

Adding Sound

Normally when users click a button, the only feedback the user gets is the visual change in the button's appearance. To give the user audible feedback when the user has clicked a button, you can add simple sounds.

To add a sound to a button, click the button, choose Tools ➤ Attributes Inspector, and click in the Sound pop-up menu, as shown in Figure 15–14.

Figure 15–14. *The Sound pop-up menu lets you choose from a variety of sound effects.*

After you choose a sound, that sound will play every time the user clicks that button. To remove a sound, select the currently displayed sound effect in the Sound pop-up menu, and press the Backspace or Delete key.

Choosing a Button with a Keystroke Combination

Normally you can select a button only by clicking it with the mouse. In case you want to give users an alternative way of selecting a button, you can assign keystroke combinations to that button, such as ⌘F10.

To assign a keystroke combination to a button, click the button, and choose Tools ➤ Attributes Inspector. Click in the Key Equivalent field, and press a keystroke combination that you want to assign to your button, as shown in Figure 15–15.

Figure 15–15. *The Keystroke Equivalent field appears in the Object Attributes window.*

Keystroke combinations typically consist of a modifier key followed by another key such as a letter key or a function key such as F8. The four common types of modifier keys are as follows:

- ⌘ (Command)
- ⇧ (Shift)
- ⌥ (Option)
- ^ (Control)

Connecting a Button to an IBAction

When you create a button using Interface Builder, you can make that button look as pretty as you like, but whether you add graphics or change the size of the button, it won't do anything until you connect that button to a method written in Objective-C.

Methods that respond to user interface objects are called IBAction methods (Interface Builder Action). To connect a button to an Objective-C method, you must write the method in a class file (in both the header and implementation files) and then connect the button to that method.

> **NOTE:** You can identify methods that respond to the user interface because they include the word IBAction as their data type such as –(IBAction) methodName.

An IBAction method in the header (.h) file looks like this:

```
-(IBAction)methodName : (id) sender;
```

The method name is any descriptive name. The (id) sender portion of the method name identifies which user interface object is calling that IBAction method to run since it's possible to have two or more user interface objects connected to the same IBAction method.

To see how to create and connect an IBAction method to a button, follow these steps:

1. Open the MyTest program you created in the previous section. The MainMenu.xib user interface file should already have a button on the user interface window. If not, then add a button to the user interface window.

2. Click in the MyTestAppDelegate.h file stored in the Classes folder, and add the bold code as follows:

```
#import <Cocoa/Cocoa.h>

@interface MyTestAppDelegate : NSObject <NSApplicationDelegate> {
    NSWindow *window;
}

@property (retain) IBOutlet NSWindow *window;

-(IBAction)testMessage:(id)sender;

@end
```

3. Choose File ➤ Save or press ⌘S to save your changes.

4. Click in the MyTestAppDelegate.m file stored in the Classes folder, and add the bold code as follows:

```
#import "MyTestAppDelegate.h"

@implementation MyTestAppDelegate
```

```
@synthesize window;

- (void)applicationDidFinishLaunching:(NSNotification *)aNotification {
    // Insert code here to initialize your application
}

- (void)dealloc {

    [window release];
    [super dealloc];
}

-(IBAction)testMessage:(id)sender
{
    NSLog (@"The button works!");
}

@end
```

5. Choose File ➤ Save or press ⌘S to save your changes.

6. Double-click the `MainMenu.xib` file in the Resources folder to open Interface Builder.

7. Click the Window icon that appears in the Interface Builder window. The user interface's window appears, displaying the button you created earlier.

8. Choose one of the following three methods to connect your `IBAction` method to your button:

    ▪ Click the button, and choose Tools ➤ Connections Inspector to display the Connections Inspector, as shown in Figure 15–16.

    ▪ Right-click the button to display a heads-up window, as shown in Figure 15–17. Note that this heads-up window is identical to the Connections Inspector in Figure 15–16.

    ▪ Move the mouse over the button, hold down the Control key, and drag the mouse over the App Delegate icon to display a heads-up display.

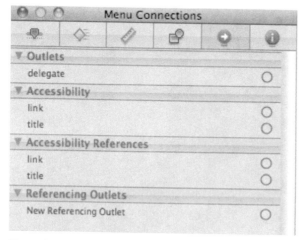

Figure 15–16. *The Connections Inspector*

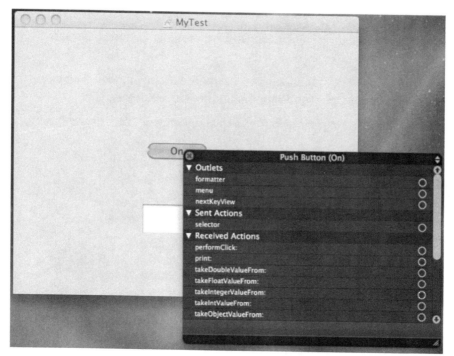

Figure 15–17. *The heads-up version of the Connections Inspector appears when you right-click a user interface object*

9. Move the mouse pointer over the circle that appears to the right of *selector*, which appears under the Sent Actions heading.

10. Drag the mouse from the selector circle over the icon that represents the Test App Delegate, as shown in Figure 15–18.

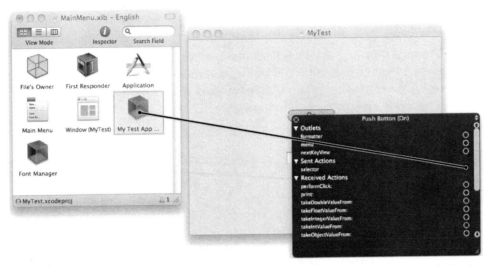

Figure 15–18. *Dragging the button's selector over the App Delegate icon lets you connect that button to an* `IBAction` *method.*

11. Release the mouse button while keeping the mouse pointing over the Test App Delegate icon. A pop-up menu of all available `IBAction` methods appears. In this case, the only `IBAction` method available is called `testMessage`.

12. Click `testMessage` inside this pop-up menu. You've now connected your button to an `IBAction` method.

13. Choose File ➤ Save or press ⌘S to save your changes.

14. Switch to Xcode; click the Build and Run button, or choose Build ➤ Build and Run. A blank window appears on the screen with the button you placed on the window.

15. Click the button on your user interface. You won't see anything since the button runs the `testMessage` `IBAction` method, which uses the `NSLog` command to print a message to the log window.

16. Quit the program by choosing MyTest ➤ Quit.

17. Choose Run ➤ Console, or press ⇧⌘R. You should see the printed statements created by the `NSLog` command:

```
2010-09-16 18:35:46.668 UITest[15098:a0f] The button works!
```

Alternate Dragging Option

In step 8, you dragged from the push button to the App Delegate icon that contains your `IBAction` method. You can also go in reverse and drag from the App Delegate icon (or any icon that represents a class file) and connect it to a button on the user interface. To use this method, follow these steps:

1. Within Interface Builder, right-click the icon that represents the class file that contains the IBAction method you want to connect to a user interface object. A heads-up window appears, listing all the available IBAction methods under the Received Actions category, as shown in Figure 15–19.

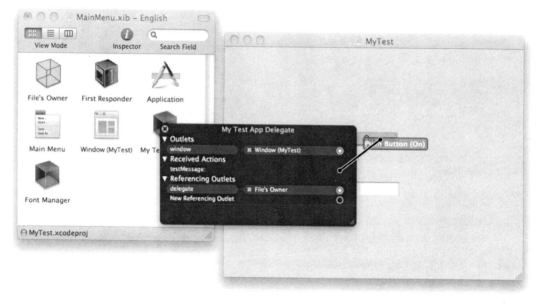

Figure 15–19. *Right-clicking a class file icon displays available* IBAction *methods.*

2. Move the mouse pointer over the circle that appears to the right of the IBAction method you want to use (which is testMessage in Figure 15–18), and drag the mouse over the button that you want to connect to your IBAction method.

3. Release the mouse button when the mouse pointer appears over the button that you want to connect to the IBAction method. Your button is now connected to your IBAction method.

Breaking a Link to an IBAction Method

A button can link to only one IBAction method at a time, although multiple buttons can link to the same IBAction method. If you want to link a button to a different IBAction method, you can connect it to a different IBAction method, which breaks the link to any previously connected IBAction method.

To break a link to an IBAction method, you have three options:

- Click the button, and choose Tools Connections Inspector. Then click the close icon that appears to the left of the currently connected user interface object, as shown in Figure 15–20.

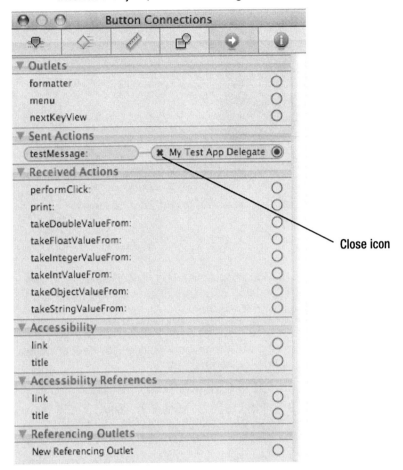

Close icon

Figure 15–20. *The close icon lets you break the connection between a button and an* IBAction *method.*

- Right-click the button to display a heads-up version of the Connections Inspector. Then click the close icon that appears to the left of the currently connected user interface object.

- Right-click the class file icon (such as App Delegate) that contains the IBAction method that you want to disconnect. This displays a heads-up window where you can click the close icon that appears to the left of the user interface object under the Received Actions category, as shown in Figure 15–21.

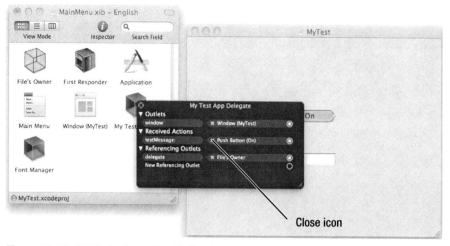

Figure 15–21. *Right-clicking a class file icon lets you break the connection to its* IBAction *methods.*

Summary

The most common type of button found in Mac programs is the Push Button, but there are a variety of other types of buttons that you can choose that look differently but act the same by displaying a command directly on the button.

Although buttons represent the simplest way to display commands on the user interface, there are many ways to customize a button beyond its size, position, and title text. You can also display graphic images on a button.

If you choose the Toggle option for a button's Type, you can make the button display different title text and graphic images each time the user clicks that button. To make buttons easier for users, you can also add tooltips to display brief, descriptive information about a button when the user moves the mouse pointer over that button.

To provide auditory feedback, you can add sounds that play every time the user clicks a button. In case you want to give users the option of selecting a button without using the mouse, you can assign keystroke combinations to choose a button without clicking it.

No matter how you customize the appearance of a button, you'll eventually need to connect it to a special method called an IBAction method. After you write an IBAction method in Objective-C and store it in a class file, you'll need to connect your IBAction method code to the actual button on your user interface. If you make a mistake or change your mind, you can always break a connection between a button and an IBAction method.

Buttons represent one of the more common ways for users to control a program. Use buttons sparingly because too many buttons on a user interface tends to clutter the screen and overwhelm the user with too many choices. Buttons may be simple, but there are so many choices that you can modify a button to make it unique to your particular Mac program.

Chapter 16

Making Choices with Radio Buttons and Check Boxes

Buttons let the user choose a single command. However, many times, you may need to present the user with several options. You could display multiple buttons, where each button represents a single option, but this could look cluttered and messy. A more compact solution is to use radio buttons and check boxes.

Both options let you display choices to the user and provide visual feedback so the user knows which options they have selected. Radio buttons and check boxes act as a way to input data into the computer and also offer a limited way to display information back to the user.

The main difference between the two is that when a program displays a group of radio buttons, the user can select only one radio button in that group at a time, whereas when a program displays check boxes, the user can select multiple check boxes, as shown in Figure 16–1.

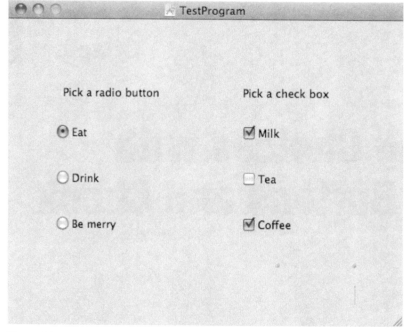

Figure 16–1. *The visual difference between radio buttons and check boxes*

Radio Buttons

Most car radios have buttons that let you assign a different station to each button. By pressing a button, you can quickly select your favorite radio station. Computer radio buttons work the same way, displaying multiple options but allowing the user to select only one option at a time. The moment the user chooses a different option, the previously selected option is no longer selected.

Creating and Adding Radio Buttons

Interface Builder treats radio buttons as cells in a table of rows and columns. To create a group of radio buttons, you just need to drag the Radio Group object from the Object Library and drop it on your user interface, as shown in Figure 16–2.

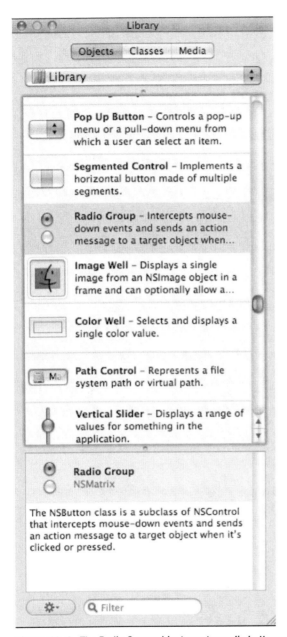

Figure 16–2. *The Radio Group object creates radio buttons on your user interface.*

By default, the Radio Group object creates a matrix of two radio buttons. To add more radio buttons, you can add additional rows or columns.

To add (or remove) additional radio buttons to (from) a radio group, follow these steps:

1. Click the Radio Group you want to modify. Handles appear around the edges of your Radio Group.

2. Choose Tools ➤ Attributes Inspector.

3. Click the up or down arrow next to the Rows text box or Columns text box, shown in Figure 16–3. Each time you click the up arrow, you add another row or column of radio buttons. Each time you click the down arrow, you remove a row or column of radio buttons.

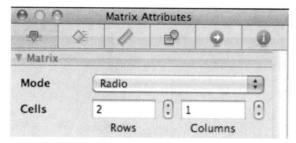

Figure 16–3. *The Attributes Inspector window lets you add rows or columns to a Radio Group.*

When you add new rows or columns to a Radio Group, you may wind up with an equal number of radio buttons in adjacent columns, such as three radio buttons in one column and three more radio buttons in an adjacent column.

If you need to display an odd number of radio buttons, such as three radio buttons in one column and two radio buttons in an adjacent column, you need to make one or more radio buttons transparent so they don't appear.

To make a radio button transparent so it doesn't appear on the user interface, follow these steps:

1. Double-click the radio button that you want to hide. Your selected radio button appears highlighted, as shown in Figure 16–4.

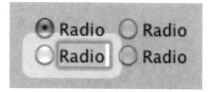

Figure 16–4. *Double-clicking a radio button selects that radio button.*

2. Choose Tools ➤ Attributes Inspector.

3. Select the Transparent check box, as shown in Figure 16–5.

Figure 16–5. *Selecting the Transparent check box makes a radio button disappear from view.*

4. Click a different radio button. The radio button you designated to be transparent should disappear. To make the radio button visible again, just repeat these steps except clear the Transparent check box in step 3.

Creating a Radio Button Title

Every radio button usually needs a title that represents an option for the user to choose. There are two ways to create a title on a radio button. First, you can double-click the radio button directly and, when the button's title appears highlighted, type any text that you want to appear on the radio button. A second way is to open the Attributes Inspector window, which lets you type text into the Title field to display text on a button.

Defining a Radio Button's State

A radio button can be in one of two states: On or Off. When On, the radio button appears selected. When Off, the radio button appears clear. Normally, only one radio button in a Radio Group can appear selected at a time.

To set a radio button's state, follow these steps:

1. Double-click the radio button that you want to modify.

2. Choose Tools ➤ Attributes Inspector.

3. Select (or clear) the State check box.

Determining Which Radio Button a User Selected

After you've created a Radio Group, you may need to identify which radio button the user selected. To get this information, you first need to realize that the entire Radio Group is based on a class called NSMatrix, and each radio button within that Radio Group is based on the NSButtonCell class. To determine which radio button the user clicked, you can use either of two properties of the NSButtonCell class: title or tag.

The title property identifies the actual text of the radio button that the user clicked. The tag property identifies an arbitrary numeric value assigned to each radio button. With either property, you must make sure that radio buttons have different title or tag values.

To see how to identify a radio button using the `title` property, follow these steps:

1. Open the MyTest program you created in the previous chapter.

2. Double-click the `MainMenu.xib` file stored in the Resources folder. Interface Builder appears, displaying your user interface window.

3. Choose Tools ➤ Library.

4. Drag and drop the Radio Group anywhere on your user interface window. Two radio buttons initially appear.

5. Double-click the top radio button. The radio button's title appears highlighted.

6. Type **Top** and press Return.

7. Double-click the bottom radio button. When the radio button's title appears highlighted, type **Bottom** and press Return. (You may need to drag the side handle of the Radio Group so the radio button titles don't appear cut off.) Your user interface should display two radio buttons, similar to Figure 16–6.

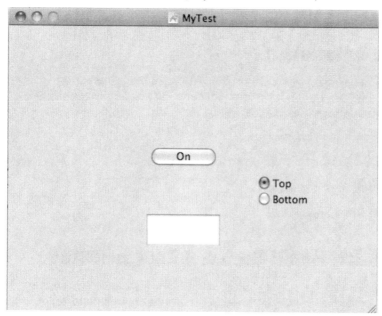

Figure 16–6. *The appearance of your user interface with two radio buttons added*

8. Choose File ➤ Save or press ⌘S to save your changes.

9. Switch to Xcode, click the `MyTestAppDelegate.h` file stored in the Classes folder, and modify the code as follows:

```
#import <Cocoa/Cocoa.h>

@interface MyTestAppDelegate : NSObject <NSApplicationDelegate> {
```

```
    NSWindow *window;
}

@property (retain) IBOutlet NSWindow *window;

-(IBAction)findSelectedButton:(id)sender;

@end
```

10. Choose File ➤ Save or press ⌘S to save your changes.

11. Click the MyTestAppDelegate.m file stored in the Classes folder and modify the code as follows:

```
#import "MyTestAppDelegate.h"

@implementation MyTestAppDelegate

@synthesize window;

- (void)applicationDidFinishLaunching:(NSNotification *)aNotification {
    // Insert code here to initialize your application
}

- (void)dealloc {

    [window release];
    [super dealloc];
}

-(IBAction)findSelectedButton:(id)sender {
    NSButtonCell *selCell = [sender selectedCell];
    //NSLog (@"Title cell is %@", [selCell title]);
    NSLog (@"Title cell is %@", selCell.title);
}

@end
```

In the findSelectedButton method, you have a choice of how you want to access the radio button's title property. You can use the square bracket method like this:

```
[selCell title];
```

Or you can use the dot notation method like this:

```
selCel.title
```

Both methods are equivalent, but the dot notation method is preferred because it's simpler to understand.

12. Choose File ➤ Save or press ⌘S to save your changes.

13. Double-click the MainMenu.xib file in the Resources folder. Interface Builder appears, displaying your user interface window with its two radio buttons.

14. Right-click the Radio Group. A heads-up window appears.

15. Move the mouse pointer over the circle that appears to the right of `selector`, under the Sent Actions category, and drag the mouse to the MyTest App Delegate icon, as shown in Figure 16–7.

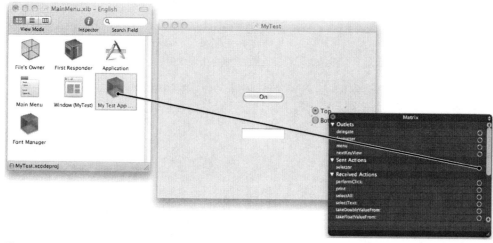

Figure 16–7. *Dragging the Radio Group's selector button connects it to your Objective-C method.*

16. Release the mouse button while the mouse pointer is over the My Test App Delegate icon. A pop-up window appears, listing all the `IBAction` methods available in that class file.

17. Choose the `findSelectedButton` method.

18. Choose File ➤ Save or press ⌘S to save your changes.

19. Switch to Xcode and click the Build and Run button or choose Build ➤ Build and Run. A blank window appears on the screen with the radio buttons you placed on the window.

20. Click the radio button named Bottom. Nothing will happen because the radio button is using the `NSLog` command to write to the log window.

21. Click the radio button named Top.

22. Quit your program by choosing MyTest ➤ Quit.

23. Choose Run ➤ Console or press ⇧⌘R. You should see the printed statements created by the `NSLog` command:

```
2010-09-18 12:15:39.772 UITest[22255:a0f] Title cell is Bottom
2010-09-18 12:15:40.927 UITest[22255:a0f] Title cell is Top
```

If you want to identify radio buttons using the `tag` property, you must first give each radio button a unique tag value by following these steps:

1. Double-click the radio button that you want to modify.

2. Choose Tools ➤ Attributes Inspector. The Attributes Inspector window appears.

3. Scroll down the Attributes Inspector window until you see the tag field under the Control category, as shown in Figure 16–8.

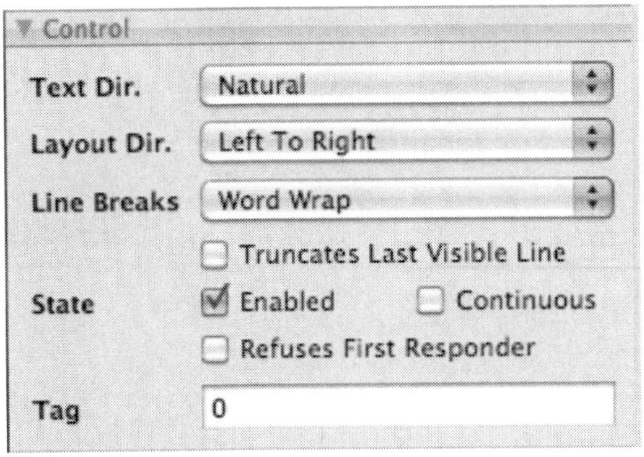

Control	
Text Dir.	Natural
Layout Dir.	Left To Right
Line Breaks	Word Wrap
	☐ Truncates Last Visible Line
State	☑ Enabled ☐ Continuous
	☐ Refuses First Responder
Tag	0

Figure 16–8. *The Tag field appears under the Control category in the Attributes Inspector window.*

4. Click in the tag field and type a number.

5. Repeat steps 1 to 4 for each radio button in the Radio Group. Be sure to give each radio button a unique tag value.

To use the `tag` property to identify which radio button the user clicked, you just have to look for the `tag` property:

```
-(IBAction)findSelectedButton:(id)sender {
    NSButtonCell *selCell = [sender selectedCell];
    NSLog(@"Tag value of the cell is %d", selCell.tag);
    // NSLog(@"Tag value of the cell is %d", [selCell tag]);
}
```

Just as with the `title` property, you can access the `tag` property using the square brackets method or the dot notation method.

Check Boxes

Radio buttons typically display multiple options but let the user choose only one option at a time. Check boxes also display multiple options, but the user can select zero or more options at the same time. When choices aren't mutually exclusive, use check boxes.

Creating Check Boxes

To create a check box, just drag a Check Box object from the Object Library and drop it on your user interface, as shown in Figure 16–9.

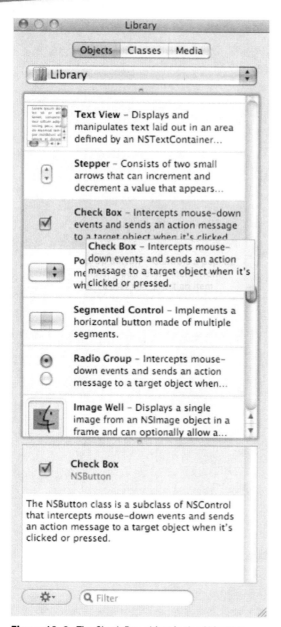

Figure 16–9. *The Check Box object in the Object Library*

Dragging and dropping a Check Box object creates only a single check box at a time. You'll need to drag and drop additional Check Box objects if you need more check boxes.

Defining a Check Box's Title and State

The title of a check box displays the option that the check box represents. The state defines whether the check box is selected or cleared.

There are two ways to create a title on a check box. First, you can double-click the check box directly and, when the check box's title appears highlighted, type any text that you want to appear.

Second, you can click a check box, choose Tools ➤ Attributes Inspector to open the Attributes Inspector window, and then click in the Title field and type the text you want to appear on the check box.

The Attributes Inspector window is also where you can define the check box's State property, using the check boxes that appear next to State under the Control category, as shown in Figure 16–10.

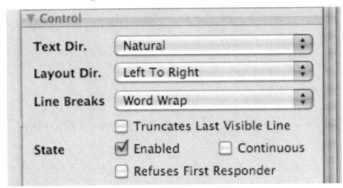

Figure 16–10. *The Enabled check box*

To determine the state property of a check box, you need to check if the state property is equal to NSOnState or NSOffState. To see how to identify a check box, follow these steps:

1. Open the MyTest program you modified in the previous section.

2. Double-click the MainMenu.xib file stored in the Resources folder. Interface Builder appears and displays your user interface window.

3. Choose Tools ➤ Library.

4. Drag and drop a Check Box object anywhere on your user interface window so that it looks similar to Figure 16–11.

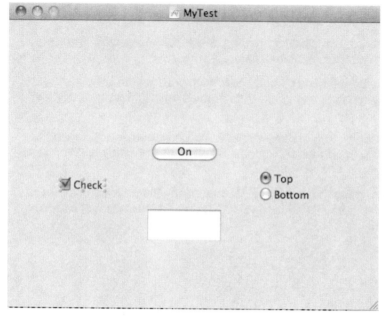

Figure 16–11. *Placing a check box on your user interface*

5. Click the MyTestAppDelegate.h file stored in the Classes folder and modify the code as follows:

```
#import <Cocoa/Cocoa.h>

@interface MyTestAppDelegate : NSObject <NSApplicationDelegate> {
    NSWindow *window;
}

@property (retain) IBOutlet NSWindow *window;

-(IBAction)checkBox:(id)sender;

@end
```

6. Choose File ➤ Save or press ⌘S to save your changes.

7. Click the MyTestAppDelegate.m file stored in the Classes folder and modify the code as follows:

```
#import "MyTestAppDelegate.h"

@implementation MyTestAppDelegate

@synthesize window;

- (void)applicationDidFinishLaunching:(NSNotification *)aNotification {
    // Insert code here to initialize your application
}
```

```
- (void)dealloc {

    [window release];
    [super dealloc];
}

-(IBAction)checkBox:(id)sender
{
    NSButton *check = sender;
    NSLog (@"Title = %@", check.title);
    switch ([check state])
    {
        case NSOnState:
            NSLog (@"Check box is On");
            break;
        case NSOffState:
            NSLog (@"Check box is Off");
            break;
    }
    NSLog (@"*****");
}

@end
```

8. Choose File ➤ Save or press ⌘S to save your changes.

9. Double-click the MainMenu.xib file in the Resources folder. Interface Builder appears, displaying your user interface window.

10. Right-click the check box. A heads-up window appears.

11. Move the mouse pointer over the circle that appears to the right of selector, under the Sent Actions category, and click and drag the mouse to the My Test App Delegate icon.

12. Release the mouse button while the mouse pointer is over the My Test App Delegate icon. A pop-up window appears, listing all the IBAction methods available in that class file.

13. Choose the checkBox method.

14. Choose File ➤ Save or press ⌘S to save your changes.

15. Switch to Xcode and click the Build and Run button or choose Build ➤ Build and Run. A blank window appears on the screen with the check box you placed on the window.

16. Click the check box two times to see each state of the check box.

17. Quit your program by choosing MyTest ➤ Quit.

18. Choose Run ➤ Console or press ⇧⌘R. You should see the printed statements created by the NSLog command:

```
2010-09-18 21:45:28.606 UITest[23899:a0f] Title = Check
2010-09-18 21:45:28.613 UITest[23899:a0f] Check box is Off
2010-09-18 21:45:28.614 UITest[23899:a0f] *****
2010-09-18 21:45:29.742 UITest[23899:a0f] Title = Check
2010-09-18 21:45:29.744 UITest[23899:a0f] Check box is On
2010-09-18 21:45:29.744 UITest[23899:a0f] *****
```

Summary

When you need to display multiple options to the user, use radio buttons or check boxes. Radio buttons let you display mutually exclusive choices, while check boxes let the user select zero or more options.

When you create a Radio Group, you're initially creating two radio buttons that work together, although you can add more radio buttons by adding rows or columns. In a Radio Group, only one radio button can be selected at any given time.

When you create a check box object, you create only a single check box at a time. You need to add additional check boxes manually.

To identify which radio button or check box the user clicked, you can use the Title property. To identify the state of a check box, you need to examine the State property to see if it equals NSOnState or NSOffState.

Radio buttons and check boxes are handy when you need to display a small number of options for the user to select. The more options you need to display, the more cluttered your user interface can look with multiple radio buttons or check boxes.

Chapter 17

Making Choices with Pop-Up Buttons

Radio buttons and check boxes let users select from multiple options. Unfortunately, each time you need to display another option, you also need to display another radio button or check box, which takes up space. The more radio buttons or check boxes displayed, the more cluttered and confusing your user interface will look.

To avoid this problem, you can also display options to the user through pop-up buttons. A pop-up button takes up a minimal amount of space, but when the user clicks it, a list of options appears that can be far more numerous than the limited number of choices you could display through multiple radio buttons or check boxes.

When you need to display a large number of options and need to conserve space on your user interface, use a pop-up button in place of multiple radio buttons or check boxes. The drawback is that all the available options won't be visible to the user at all times. The advantage is that hiding all the available options prevents your program from overwhelming the user with too many choices.

Pop-Up Button Basics

Like radio buttons, a pop-up button lets the user select only from a predefined list of options. Unlike radio buttons, a pop-up button always takes up a fixed amount of space no matter how many options you want to display to the user.

A pop-up button displays the currently selected option as a wide but short button. As soon as the user clicks the button, the pop-up menu expands to show a list of options, as shown in Figure 17–1. From this expanded list, the user can click one of the many available options.

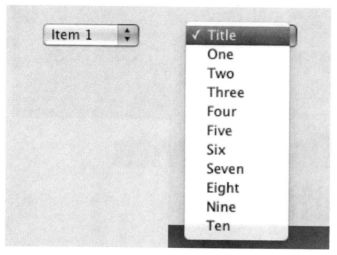

Figure 17–1. *A pop-up button takes up minimal amount of space, but can provide a list of choices when clicked.*

To create a pop-up button, just open the Library window in Interface Builder by choosing Tools ➤ Library. Then drag the Pop Up Button object from the Object Library (see Figure 17–2) to your user interface.

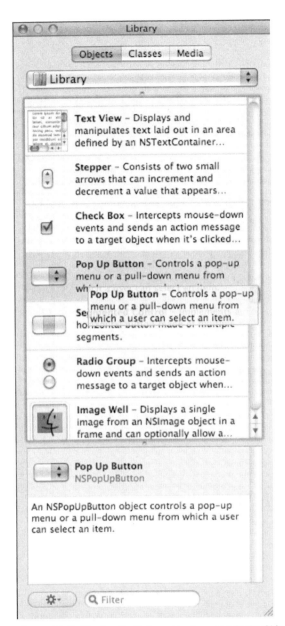

Figure 17–2. *The Pop Up Button object appears in the Object Library.*

After you've placed a Pop Up Button object on your user interface window, the next step is to fill its list with different choices. There are two ways to create and edit a pop-up button list:

- In Interface Builder
- Using Objective-C code

Using Interface Builder is simple since you just need to type or edit a list of options. However, once your program starts running, your pop-up button list remains fixed. Using Objective-C code to create a pop-up button list is much harder, but it gives you the flexibility of changing the list as your program runs.

You can use either method separately or both in combination. For example, you might create your initial pop-up button list in Interface Builder, and then modify it using Objective-C code as your program runs. Let's see how to do so now.

Creating a Pop-Up Button List in Interface Builder

By default, every pop-up button comes with three items, labeled Item 1, Item 2, and Item 3. To create your own list of choices, you have to rename these existing default choices and add or delete additional items, depending on how many choices you want to offer. To create a pop-up button and edit its existing three items, follow these steps:

1. Open the MyTest program that you modified in Chapter 16.

2. Double-click on the MainMenu.xib file in the Resources folder to open Interface Builder. Your user interface appears.

3. Choose Tools ➤ Library to make the Object Library window appear.

4. Drag a Pop Up Button object from the Object Library and drop it on your user interface window.

5. Double-click the pop-up button. A list of three items appears, as shown in Figure 17–3.

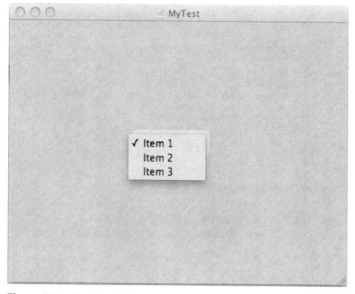

Figure 17–3. *Double-clicking a pop-up button displays its menu contents.*

6. Double-click each item in the menu (such as Item 1) and type a new word or phrase. Repeat for each item that you want to change.

Adding (and Deleting) Items on a Pop-Up Button List

By default, a pop-up button lists only three menu items. Chances are good you'll need more (or less) than exactly three menu items, so you can add or delete menu items at any time. To add new items to a pop-up button's list, make sure that the pop-up button appears on your user interface in Interface Builder and then follow these steps:

1. Open the MyTest program that you modified in the previous section (If it isn't already open).

2. Double-click the `MainMenu.xib` file located in the Resources folder. Interface Builder appears and displays your user interface.

3. Double-click the pop-up button you want to modify. A list of currently stored menu items appears, as shown in Figure 17–3.

4. (Optional) Click the menu item that you want to delete and press Delete or Backspace. Your selected menu item disappears.

5. Choose Tools ➤ Library to make the Library window appear.

6. Scroll down the Library window until you see the Menu Item object, as shown in Figure 17–4.

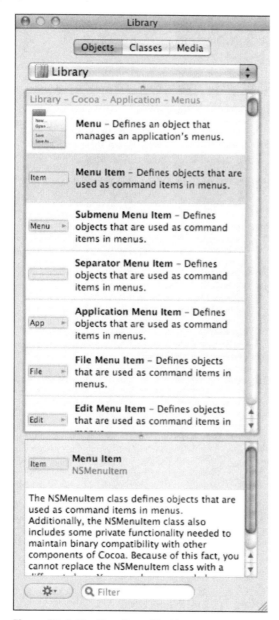

Figure 17–4. *The Menu Item object lets you add new items to a pop-up button's menu.*

7. Drag the Menu Item object over the pop-up button's menu until you see a white plus sign inside a green circle, as shown in Figure 17–5.

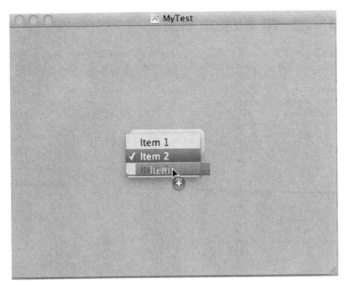

Figure 17–5. *A plus sign appears when you've placed a menu item inside a pop-up button's menu.*

8. Release the mouse button. Your newly added menu item appears in the pop-up button's menu. Repeat this step for each additional menu item you want to add.

9. (Optional) Drag a Separator Menu Item object or Submenu Menu Item object to your pop-up button's menu. The Separator Menu Item object displays a line to group related menu items together. The Submenu Menu Item object lets you create an additional submenu that you can fill with additional menu items. Both are shown in action in Figure 17–6.

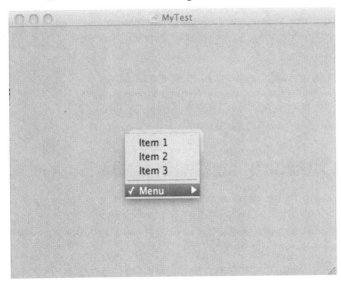

Figure 17–6. *A separator and submenu can further enhance the appearance of your menus.*

Renaming an Item in a Pop-Up Button List

After adding or deleting items in a pop-up button's list, you need to rename the items so they don't display a generic title like Item 2 or Item 3. There are two ways to rename an item, as shown in Figure 17–7:

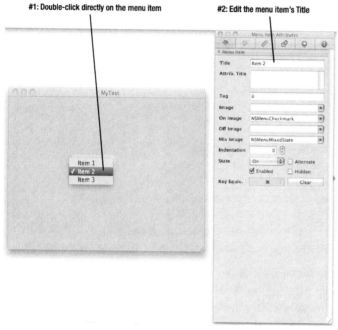

Figure 17–7. *The two ways to rename an item displayed in a pop-up button's list*

- Double-click the pop-up button directly on your user interface to display its list of choices. Then double-click the item that you want to rename and type new text.

- Double-click the pop-up button directly on your user interface to display its list of choices. Then click the item in the list that you want to rename. Choose Tools ➤ Attributes Inspector to open the Object Attributes window, and type new text in the Title field.

Modifying a Pop-Up Button's List with Code

Another way to modify a pop-up button's list of choices is to create an array and then load that array of data into the pop-up button's list. This option requires writing Objective-C code and connecting your code to the pop-up button on your user interface.

To connect your Objective-C code to a user interface object, you must create something called an IBOutlet. Basically, any variable declared as an IBOutlet can display data to a user interface object, such as a pop-up button.

Next, you need to create an array and fill it with data. Then you need to store this array of data in your IBOutlet variable that's connected to your pop-up button, which will display your data on the screen.

To see how to create an array and connect this data to a pop-up menu button, follow these steps:

1. Open the MyTest program from earlier in the chapter.

2. Click the MyTestAppDelegate.h file located in the Classes folder and type the following bold text in the existing Objective-C code:

```
#import <Cocoa/Cocoa.h>

@interface MyTestAppDelegate : NSObject <NSApplicationDelegate> {
    NSWindow *window;

    NSPopUpButton *myPopUp;
    }

@property (retain) IBOutlet NSWindow *window;
@property (retain) IBOutlet NSPopUpButton *myPopUp;

@end
```

The myPopUp pointer name is arbitrary, but this will represent your pop-up button.

3. Choose File ➤ Save or press ⌘S to save your changes.

4. Click the MyTestAppDelegate.m file and type the following bold text in the existing Objective-C code:

```
#import "UITestAppDelegate.h"

@implementation MyTestAppDelegate

@synthesize window;
@synthesize myPopUp;

- (void)applicationDidFinishLaunching:(NSNotification *)aNotification {
    // Insert code here to initialize your application
    NSString *object1 = @"Electric trains";
    NSString *object2 = @"Bicycles";
    NSString *object3 = @"Video games";
    NSString *object4 = @"Skateboards";
    NSMutableArray *myArray;
    myArray= [NSMutableArray arrayWithObjects: object1, object2, object3, object4, nil];
    [myPopUp removeAllItems];
    [myPopUp addItemsWithTitles: myArray];
}

- (void)dealloc {
    [myPopup release];
    [window release];
    [super dealloc];
}
```

@end

This applicationDidFinishLaunching method creates four string objects, declares an NSMutableArray, stuffs the four string objects into this array, uses the removeAllItems method to get rid of the three default items normally stored in the pop-up button, and finally adds the array item to the pop-up button using the addItemsWithTitles method and the array itself.

5. Choose File ➤ Save or press ⌘S to save your changes.

6. Double-click the MainMenu.xib file located in the Resources folder. Interface Builder appears and displays your user interface window.

7. Right-click the My Test App Delegate icon. A heads-up window appears.

8. Move the mouse pointer over the circle that appears to the right of myPopUp, which appears under the Outlets category. Click and drag the mouse pointer over the pop-up button on your user interface and release the mouse button to connect the user interface object to the myPopUp pointer, as shown in Figure 17–8.

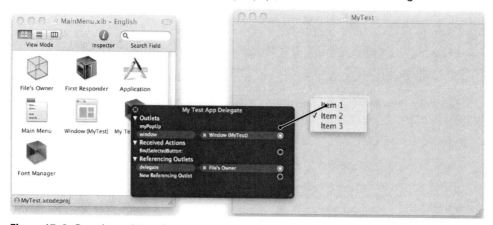

Figure 17–8. *Dragging and dropping connects the* myPopUp IBOutlet *to your actual pop-up button object on the user interface.*

As an alternative to step 8, you can right-click the pop-up button on the user interface to display a heads-up window. Then click and drag the circle to the right of New Referencing Outlet under the Referencing Outlets category and drop it over the class file icon that contains the IBOutlet you want to use, as shown in Figure 17–9.

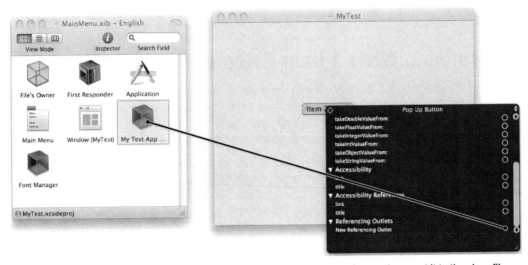

Figure 17–9. *You can right-click the Pop Up Button object on the user interface and connect it to the class file that contains the* IBOutlet *that represents the pop-up button.*

9. Choose File ➤ Save or press ⌘S to save your changes.

10. Switch back to Xcode and click the Build and Run button or choose Build ➤ Build and Run. As long as you didn't mistype anything, you should see a window pop up with your pop-up button on it.

11. Click the pop-up button and you'll see the contents of your array displayed in the pop-up button's list, as shown in Figure 17–10.

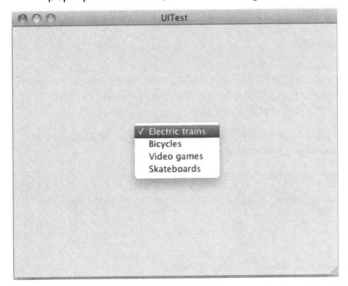

Figure 17–10. *The array contents appear in the pop-up button's list of choices.*

12. Quit your program by choosing MyTest ➤ Quit.

Determining What a User Selected

If you define your pop-up button's list of choices through Interface Builder, you can identify each choice by the title or tag property. If you create your pop-up button's list of choices with an array using Objective-C code, you can identify what the user selected through the text of that item or the index position of the selected item.

The Title property identifies the actual text of the option that the user clicked. The Tag property identifies an arbitrary numeric value assigned to each option through the Object Attributes window. With either property, you must make sure that all your pop-up button's options have different Title or Tag values.

The problem with identifying menu items through the Title value is that you must identify the text exactly. If the menu item is "Open File" and your Objective-C code searches for "open file" instead, the code won't work since the text isn't exactly the same. For that reason, you may prefer to identify a selected menu item by using its index position.

The first (top) menu item is considered at index position 0, the second at index position 1, and so on. By searching for index position, you don't have to worry about the actual text displayed by each menu item.

To retrieve the index position of an item in a menu, you need to retrieve the value of the index item, stored in the indexOfSelectedItem property. After you retrieve this index value, you need to store it in a variable such as:

```
-(IBAction)findSelectedButton:(id)sender;
{
    NSInteger index = [sender indexOfSelectedItem];
    NSLog(@"Selected item index is %i", index);
}
```

If the preceding method were connected to a pop-up button, the sender would retrieve the item that the user selected in the pop-up button, and the indexOfSelectedItem property would retrieve that selected item's index position.

To see how to identify a selected item chosen from a pop-up button by its displayed text (Title property) or its index position, follow these steps:

1. Open the MyTest program you modified in the previous section.

2. Click the MyTestAppDelegate.h file located in the Classes folder and modify its code as follows:

```
#import <Cocoa/Cocoa.h>

@interface MyTestAppDelegate : NSObject <NSApplicationDelegate> {
    NSWindow *window;

    NSPopUpButton *myPopUp;
}
```

```
@property (retain) IBOutlet NSWindow *window;
@property (retain) IBOutlet NSPopUpButton *myPopUp;

-(IBAction)findSelectedButton:(id)sender;

@end
```

3. Choose File ➤ Save or press ⌘S to save your changes.

4. Click the MyTestAppDelegate.m file located in the Classes folder and modify the code as follows:

```
#import "MyTestAppDelegate.h"

@implementation MyTestAppDelegate

@synthesize window;
@synthesize myPopUp;

- (void)applicationDidFinishLaunching:(NSNotification *)aNotification {
    // Insert code here to initialize your application
    NSString *object1 = @"Electric trains";
    NSString *object2 = @"Bicycles";
    NSString *object3 = @"Video games";
    NSString *object4 = @"Skateboards";
    NSMutableArray *myArray;
    myArray= [NSMutableArray arrayWithObjects: object1, object2, object3, object4, nil];

    [myPopUp removeAllItems];
    [myPopUp addItemsWithTitles: myArray];
}

- (void)dealloc {
    [myPopUp release];
    [window release];
    [super dealloc];
}

-(IBAction)findSelectedButton:(id)sender {
    NSPopUpButtonCell *selCell = [sender selectedCell];
    //NSLog(@"Selected cell is %d", [selCell tag]);
    NSLog (@"Selected cell is %d", selCell.tag);
    //NSLog (@"Title cell is %@", [selCell title]);
    NSLog (@"Title cell is %@", selCell.title);

    NSInteger index = [sender indexOfSelectedItem];
    NSLog(@"Selected item index is %i", index);
}

@end
```

In the findSelectedButton method, you have a choice of how you want to access the Title property; you can use square brackets like this,

```
[selCell title];
```

or you can use the dot notation method like this:

`selCel.title`

Both methods are equivalent and you can choose whichever method you prefer, although the dot notation method is now considered the preferred method to use.

5. Choose File ➤ Save or press ⌘S to save your changes.

6. Double-click the `MainMenu.xib` file located in the Resources folder. Interface Builder appears and displays your user interface window.

7. Right-click the pop-up button on the user interface. A heads-up window appears.

8. Move the mouse pointer over the circle that appears to the right of `selector`, under the Sent Actions category, and click and drag the mouse to the Test App Delegate icon.

9. Release the mouse button while the mouse pointer is over the Test App Delegate icon. A pop-up window appears, listing all the `IBAction` methods available in that class file.

10. Choose the `findSelectedButton` method.

11. Choose File ➤ Save or press ⌘S to save your changes.

12. Switch to Xcode and click the Build and Run button or choose Build ➤ Build and Run. A blank window appears on the screen with the radio buttons you placed on the window.

13. Click the pop-up button. A list of options appears.

14. Click an option such as `Bicycles`.

15. Click the pop-up button again and click a different option such as `Skateboards`.

16. Quit your program by choosing MyTest ➤ Quit.

17. Choose Run ➤ Console or press ⇧⌘R. You should see the printed statements created by the `NSLog` command:

```
2010-12-06 09:36:11.435 NewTest[15438:a0f] Selected cell is 0
2010-12-06 09:36:11.439 NewTest[15438:a0f] Title cell is Bicycles
2010-12-06 09:36:11.443 NewTest[15438:a0f] Selected item index is 1
2010-12-06 09:36:14.222 NewTest[15438:a0f] Selected cell is 0
2010-12-06 09:36:14.222 NewTest[15438:a0f] Title cell is Skateboards
2010-12-06 09:36:14.223 NewTest[15438:a0f] Selected item index is 3
```

Notice that the Tag property of both items is 0 because you didn't define this value. If you created your pop-up button's list of options through Interface Builder, you could set this Tag property of each item through the Object Attributes window.

Summary

Think of pop-up buttons as an alternative to radio buttons. Whenever your number of options starts to get too numerous to display as multiple radio buttons, switch to a pop-up button that can take up a minimal amount of space and still display a huge list of options for the user to select. The only drawback is that, whereas radio buttons make the options clearly visible at all times, a pop-up button requires that the user click it to see the list of choices.

The simplest and most straightforward way to create a list of options to display on a pop-up button is to expand the icon view that appears between the left and middle pane of the Xcode window. Then you can add, delete, or rename items that you want to appear as choices in your pop-up button list.

If you just want to rename the list of items in the pop-up button, you can either double-click the pop-up button directly to view and edit its list of choices, or you can double-click the pop-up button directly, click each item in the list, and open its Object Attributes window to edit the Title text and add a distinct value to each item's Tag property.

If you need to change the list of items displayed in a pop-up button, you can create its list of choices using Objective-C code. First, you need to create an IBOutlet variable to connect with your pop-up menu. Then, you need to connect your pop-up button on the user interface to the IBOutlet variable. Finally, you need to create an array of your pop-up button options, and then store this array in the IBOutlet variable that represents your pop-up button. Linking this IBOutlet variable to your pop-up button on the user interface allows the array data to appear as the pop-up button's list of choices.

Whenever you need to display a large number of choices in a small amount of space, use a pop-up button. By filling a pop-up button's list using an array and Objective-C code, you can even change the pop-up button's list of choices while your program runs.

Chapter 18

Inputting and Outputting Data with Labels, Text Fields, and Combo Boxes

Radio buttons, check boxes, and pop-up buttons let the user choose from a fixed list of choices. However, many times a program may need to request data that won't fit easily into a limited number of choices, such as asking for the user's name.

To accept data, a program needs to let the user type in data. To display data, a program can use a text field or a label. A label basically can display only text, but a text field can display text or allow the user to type in text. With a text field, users can type in any type of data such as text or numbers.

For even greater flexibility, you can use a combo box, which lets the user type in data or select from a list of choices, just like a pop-up button. By using a text field, label, or combo box, your user interface can display information and accept data to use.

Using Labels

A label serves two purposes. First, it can display static information to the user, such as listing short instructions explaining the purpose of other user interface objects. For example, if your program displays a text field, the user may have no idea what type of information your program expects to receive in that text field. However, if you put a label next to that text field and display the word "Name" in that label, it becomes clear what type of information the user needs to type into that text field.

Labels can also be used to display information to the user, such as a warning. For example, if the user types in an incorrect password, a label can display a message telling the user what happened. When you need to display static or changing information, you can use a label.

Adding a Label to Your User Interface

A label is useful for displaying text on the user interface, such as instructions to the user or brief descriptions of what other controls might do, such as a label that identifies a slider for adjusting the volume. To create a label, follow these steps:

1. Double-click the .xib user interface file that contains the window to which you want to add a label. Interface Builder appears.

2. Choose Tools ➤ Library to display the Library window.

3. Scroll through the Object Library and look for the Label object, as shown in Figure 18–1.

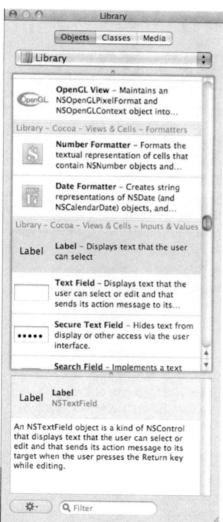

Figure 18–1. *The Label object in the Object Library*

4. Drag the Label object from the Object Library and drop it on your user interface.

Editing Text on a Label

When you first place a label on the user interface, it displays the generic text *Label*, which probably isn't what you want. To display custom text in a label, you have three options:

- Double-click the label and type or edit text

- Click the label, choose Tools ➤ Attributes Inspector, and edit the label's title property

- Assign a string to the label's stringValue property using Objective-C code:

```
labelStatic.stringValue = @"Type a name:";
```

The first two options let you modify a Label's text at design time when you're creating your program, but the text remains static once your program runs. The last option that uses Objective-C code to change a label's text lets you change the label's text while your program is running, which lets you create dynamic text that can change based on the user's actions.

To see how to use a label to display static text and dynamic text, follow these steps:

1. Open the MyTest program that you modified in Chapter 17.

2. Double-click the MainMenu.xib file stored in the Resources folder. Interface Builder appears and displays your user interface window.

3. Click any items currently displayed on the user interface and press Delete to remove them.

4. Add two Label objects, one Text Field object, and one Push Button object so that your user interface looks like Figure 18–2.

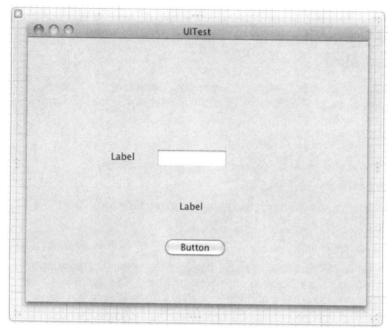

Figure 18–2. *The design of a simple user interface with two labels, a push button, and a text field*

5. Resize both labels so they are at least 125 in width. To resize a label, click on it so handles appear and drag a handle to the left or right.

6. Choose File ➤ Save or press ⌘S to save your changes.

7. Click the MyTestAppDelegate.h file and modify the code as follows:

```
#import <Cocoa/Cocoa.h>

@interface MyTestAppDelegate : NSObject <NSApplicationDelegate> {
    NSWindow *window;
    NSTextField *labelStatic;
    NSTextField *labelDynamic;
    NSTextField *textInput;
}

@property (retain) IBOutlet NSWindow *window;
@property (retain) IBOutlet NSTextField *labelStatic;
@property (retain) IBOutlet NSTextField *labelDynamic;
@property (retain) IBOutlet NSTextField *textInput;

-(IBAction)displayMessage:(id)sender;

@end
```

8. Choose File ➤ Save or press ⌘S to save your changes.

9. Click the MyTestAppDelegate.m file and modify the code as follows:

```
#import "MyTestAppDelegate.h"

@implementation MyTestAppDelegate

@synthesize window;
@synthesize labelStatic;
@synthesize labelDynamic;
@synthesize textInput;

- (void)applicationDidFinishLaunching:(NSNotification *)aNotification {
    // Insert code here to initialize your application
    labelStatic.stringValue = @"Type a name:";
}

- (void)dealloc {

    [window release];
    [super dealloc];
}

-(IBAction)displayMessage:(id)sender
{
    NSMutableString *greeting;
    greeting = [NSMutableString stringWithString: @"Hello, "];
    [greeting appendString: textInput.stringValue];
    labelDynamic.stringValue = greeting;
}

@end
```

10. Choose File ➤ Save or press ⌘S to save your changes.

11. Double-click the MainMenu.xib file stored in the Resources folder. Interface Builder appears and displays your user interface window.

12. Right-click the My Test App Delegate icon. A heads-up window appears.

13. Move the mouse pointer over the circle that appears to the right of labelDynamic, which appears under the Outlets heading. Click and drag the mouse pointer over the label on your user interface and release the mouse button to connect the label to the labelDynamic property, as shown in Figure 18–3.

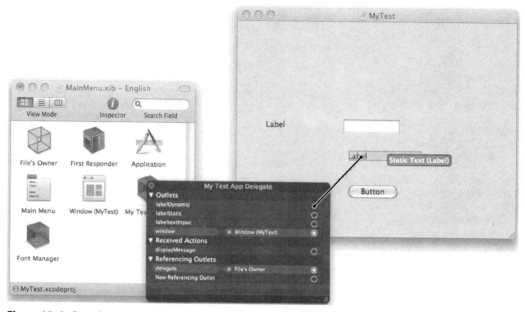

Figure 18–3. *Dragging and dropping connects the* `labelDynamic` `IBOutlet` *to your label on the user interface.*

NOTE: As an alternative to step 13, you can right-click the label on the user interface to display a heads-up window. Then click and drag the circle to the right of New Referencing Outlet under the Referencing Outlets category and drop it over the class file icon that contains the `IBOutlet` you want to use.

14. Move the mouse pointer over the circle that appears to the right of `labelStatic`, which appears under the Outlets heading. Click and drag the mouse pointer over the label on your user interface and release the mouse button to connect the label to the `labelStatic` property, as shown in Figure 18–4.

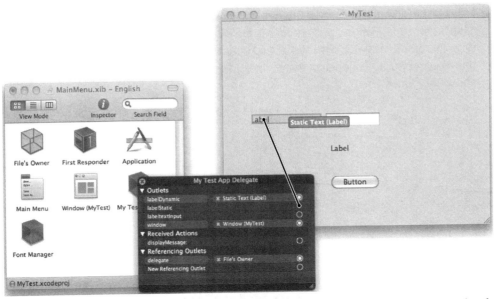

Figure 18–4. *Dragging and dropping connects the* `labelStatic IBOutlet` *to your label on the user interface.*

15. Move the mouse pointer over the circle that appears to the right of `labelTextInput`, which appears under the Outlets heading. Click and drag the mouse pointer over the text field on your user interface and release the mouse button to connect the text field to the `LabeltextInput` property, as shown in Figure 18–5.

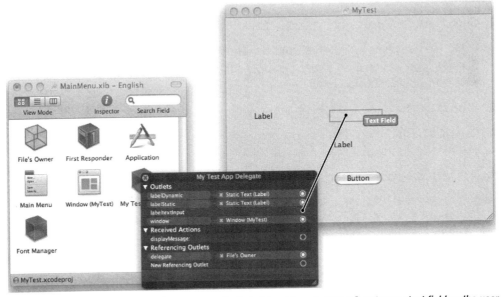

Figure 18–5. *Dragging and dropping connects the* `LabeltextInput IBOutlet` *to your text field on the user interface.*

16. Move the mouse pointer over the circle that appears to the right of `displayMessage`, which appears under the Received Actions heading. Click and drag the mouse pointer over the push button on your user interface and release the mouse button to connect the push button to the `displayMessage` method, as shown in Figure 18–6.

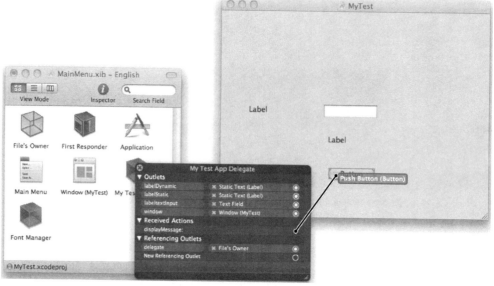

Figure 18–6. *Dragging and dropping connects the* `displayMessage` *method to your push button on the user interface.*

17. Choose File ➤ Save or press ⌘S to save your changes.

18. Switch to Xcode and click the Build and Run button or choose Build ➤ Build and Run. As long as you didn't mistype anything, you should see a window pop up with your pop-up button on it.

19. Click in the text field and type a name, such as **Joe** or **Mary**.

20. Click the push button. The label underneath displays the message with the name you typed into the text field, such as "Hello, Joe."

21. Quit your program by choosing MyTest ➤ Quit.

Although the program you just created is fairly simple, it demonstrates how to change a label's text using by using Objective-C code and the label's `stringValue` property. To change a label's text with Objective-C code, you also need to connect your label objects to variables.

Changing a label's text using Objective-C code isn't as straightforward as changing a label's text when you're designing your user interface, but using Objective-C lets you create dynamic text that changes based on the user's actions.

Using Text Fields

A text field can display text or let the user type in new text. As a result, a text field can get data from the user and display information for the user to see and edit, which isn't possible with a label. If you just need to display information, use a label. If you need to accept data and allow editing, use a text field.

Adding a Text Field to Your User Interface

To create a text field on your user interface, follow these steps:

1. Double-click the .xib user interface file that contains the window to which you want to add a text field. Interface Builder appears.

2. Choose Tools ➤ Library to display the Object Library.

3. Scroll through the Object Library and look for the Text Field object, as shown in Figure 18–7.

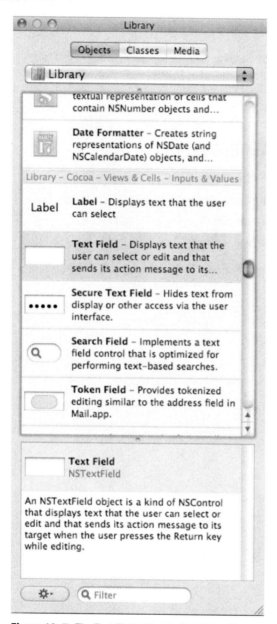

Figure 18–7. *The Text Field object in the Object Library*

4.   Drag the Text Field object from the Object Library and drop it on your user interface.

Editing Text in a Text Field

When you first place a text field on the user interface, it will be empty. To display custom text in a text field, you have three options:

- Double-click the text field and type or edit text

- Click the text field, choose Tools ➤ Attributes Inspector, and edit the text field's title property

- Assign a string to the text field's stringValue property using Objective-C code

When creating a text field on a user interface, you can customize two types of text in the text field. First, you can type text into the Title field, which displays text that the user can then edit or delete. Second, you can define something called *placeholder text* in the Placeholder field, as shown in Figure 18–8.

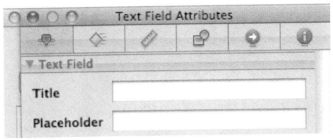

Figure 18–8. *The Placeholder field in the Object Attributes window*

Any text that you type in the Placeholder field appears inside your text field faintly dimmed when the text field is empty. The purpose of such placeholder text is to provide a brief description or instruction to help a user understand what to type inside a particular text field.

For example, if you wanted a user to type a name into a text field, you could type **First Name** in the Placeholder field. This text will appear dimmed in the text field, as shown in Figure 18–9, but as soon as the user clicks in that text field, the placeholder text completely vanishes.

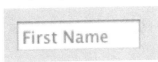

Figure 18–9. *Placeholder text appears dimmed inside a text field.*

Retrieving Data from a Text Field

Part of the usefulness of a text field is that it allows someone to type something into the text field that your program can then retrieve. To enable your program to retrieve the data a user types into a text field, you need to declare an NSTextField variable, which is what holds the data displayed or typed into a text field. Declaring an NSTextField variable in the header (.h) file might look like this:

```
@interface UITestAppDelegate : NSObject <NSApplicationDelegate> {
    NSWindow *window;
    NSTextField *textInput;
}

@property (retain) IBOutlet NSWindow *window;
@property (retain) IBOutlet NSTextField *textInput;
```

After creating a variable to represent the NSTextField, you need to use the @synthesize command in the implementation (.m) file:

```
@synthesize textInput;
```

Finally, you need to connect the textInput variable to your actual text field on your user interface window. Now when the user types something in the text field, that data will get stored in the textInput variable, which you can retrieve through the stringValue property:

```
textInput.stringValue
```

Using Combo Boxes

With a text field, users have the option of typing in new data. However, what if you want to give users the option of either typing in data or selecting from a list of choices? You could use a text field along with a bunch of radio buttons or a single pop-up button. As a simpler solution, you can use a combo box, which combines the features of a text field and a pop-up button in a single object.

Adding a Combo Box to Your User Interface

To create a combo box on your user interface, follow these steps:

1. Double-click the .xib user interface file that contains the window to which you want to add a combo box. Interface Builder appears.

2. Choose Tools ➤ Library to display the Object Library.

3. Scroll through the Object Library and look for the Combo Box object, as shown in Figure 18–10.

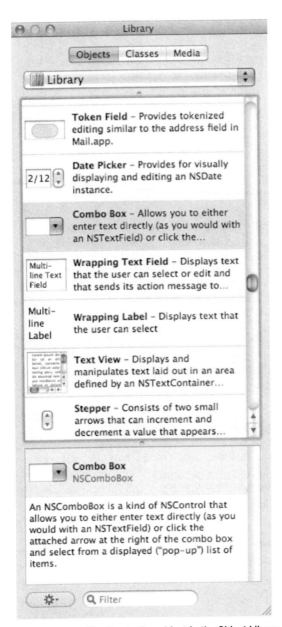

Figure 18–10. *The Combo Box object in the Object Library*

4. Drag the Combo Box object from the Object Library and drop it on your user interface.

Now that the combo box is in place, you can create a list for it.

Creating a List for a Combo Box

A combo box, like a pop-up button, can store multiple choices that the user can view and select. To fill a combo box with choices, you just need to use the `addItemsWithObjectValues` method:

```
NSString *object1 = @"Electric trains";
NSString *object2 = @"Bicycles";
NSString *object3 = @"Video games";
NSString *object4 = @"Skateboards";
NSMutableArray *myArray;
myArray= [NSMutableArray arrayWithObjects: object1, object2, object3, object4, nil];

[myCombo addItemsWithObjectValues: myArray];
```

The first four lines simply define four different string objects. The fifth line declares `myArray` as an `NSMutableArray`. Then the next line stuffs the four string objects into `myArray`.

The last line assumes that you have created a `myCombo` variable to represent the `NSComboBox`. This last line uses the `addItemsWithObjectValues` method to store the `myArray` list in the `myCombo` variable.

> **NOTE:** After storing data into a variable, the final step to make this data appear in a combo box is to connect the `myCombo` variable to the actual combo box on your user interface.

Retrieving a Value from a Combo Box

Whether the user types in data or selects from a combo box's list of choices, you can retrieve that data through the combo box's `stringValue` property. A combo box is an object created from the `NSComboBox` class. However, the portion of the combo box that holds the data typed in or selected is the `NSComboBoxCell` class, which is derived from the `NSTextField` class.

To retrieve data from a combo box, you must first declare an `IBOutlet` variable as an `NSComboBox` in a header (.h) file:

```
@interface MyTestAppDelegate : NSObject <NSApplicationDelegate> {
    NSWindow *window;
    NSComboBox *myCombo;
}

@property (retain) IBOutlet NSComboBox *myCombo;
@end
```

Next, in the implementation (.m) file, you need to use the `@synthesize` command:

```
@synthesize myCombo;
```

Finally, you need to connect the variable (myCombo) to your actual combo box on the user interface. Now whatever value appears in the combo box will get stored in the myCombo stringValue property.

To see how to fill a combo box with data and retrieve the user's selection (or typed in data), follow these steps:

1. Open the MyTest program that you modified in the previous section.

2. Double-click the MainMenu.xib file stored in the Resources folder. Interface Builder appears and displays your user interface window.

3. Click any items currently displayed on the user interface and press Delete to remove them.

4. Drag and drop one Combo Box object on your user interface window.

5. Click the MyTestAppDelegate.h file stored in the Classes folder and modify the code as follows:

```
#import <Cocoa/Cocoa.h>

@interface MyTestAppDelegate : NSObject <NSApplicationDelegate> {
    NSWindow *window;
    NSComboBox *myCombo;
}

@property (retain) IBOutlet NSWindow *window;
@property (retain) IBOutlet NSComboBox *myCombo;

-(IBAction)displayMessage:(id)sender;

@end
```

6. Choose File ➤ Save or press ⌘S to save your changes.

7. Click the MyTestAppDelegate.m file stored in the Classes folder and modify the code as follows:

```
#import "MyTestAppDelegate.h"

@implementation MyTestAppDelegate

@synthesize window;
@synthesize myCombo;

- (void)applicationDidFinishLaunching:(NSNotification *)aNotification {
    // Insert code here to initialize your application

    NSString *object1 = @"Electric trains";
    NSString *object2 = @"Bicycles";
    NSString *object3 = @"Video games";
    NSString *object4 = @"Skateboards";
    NSMutableArray *myArray;
    myArray= [NSMutableArray arrayWithObjects: object1, object2, object3, object4, nil];
```

```
        [myCombo addItemsWithObjectValues: myArray];

}

- (void)dealloc {
    [myCombo release];
    [window release];
    [super dealloc];
}

-(IBAction)displayMessage:(id)sender
{
    NSLog (@"Selected item = %@", myCombo.stringValue);
}

@end
```

8. Choose File ➤ Save or press ⌘S to save your changes.

9. Double-click the MainMenu.xib file stored in the Resources folder. Interface
    Builder appears and displays your user interface window.

10. Right-click the My Test App Delegate icon. A heads-up window appears.

11. Click the circle that appears to the right of myCombo under the Outlets heading and
    drag and drop it over the combo box on the user interface, as shown in Figure
    18–11.

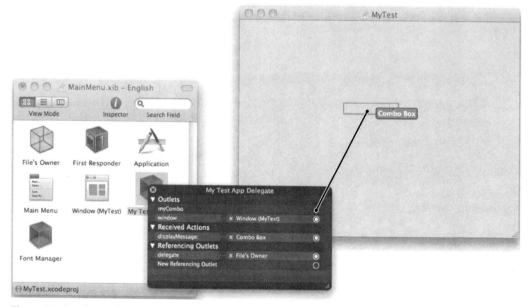

Figure 18–11. *Connecting the* myCombo *IBOutlet variable to the combo box on the user interface*

12. Connect `displayMessage` (under Received Actions) to the combo box on the user interface.

13. Choose File ➤ Save or press ⌘S to save your changes.

14. Switch to Xcode and click the Build and Run button or choose Build ➤ Build and Run. As long as you didn't mistype anything, you should see a blank window pop up.

15. Click the combo box and select an option such as `Electric trains`.

16. Click the combo box a second time and type some text, such as **Teddy bear**, and press Return.

17. Quit your program by choosing MyTest ➤ Quit.

18. Choose Run ➤ Console or press ⇧⌘R. You should see the printed statements created by the `NSLog` command:

```
2010-09-22 14:22:44.802 UITest[4027:a0f] Selected item = Electric trains
2010-09-22 14:22:53.758 UITest[4027:a0f] Selected item = Teddy bear
```

This program shows how to retrieve data from a combo box whether the user selects a choice from the combo box's menu or types in new data. By giving users the ability to select a choice from a pull-down menu or type something else instead, a combo box combines the flexibility of a text field with a pop-up button's list of fixed choices in a menu.

Wrapping Labels and Text Fields

Text fields and labels typically display a single line of text. If you want to display multiple lines, you need to use a Wrapping Label object or Wrapping Text Field object, either of which lets you resize its height to handle multiple lines of text. The Wrapping Label and Wrapping Text Field objects appear next to each other in the Object Library, as shown in Figure 18–12.

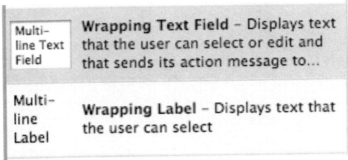

Figure 18–12. *The Wrapping Label and Wrapping Text Field objects in the Object Library*

To display text on either a wrapping label or wrapping text field, you can double-click that object directly in Interface Builder and then type whatever text you want to appear in the wrapping label or wrapping text field.

If you want to change the text in a wrapping label or wrapping text field through Objective-C code, you need to define an NSTextField property variable in a header (.h) file:

```
#import <Cocoa/Cocoa.h>

@interface MyTestAppDelegate : NSObject <NSApplicationDelegate> {
    NSWindow *window;
    NSTextField *bigText;
    NSTextField *labelText;
}

@property (retain) IBOutlet NSWindow *window;
@property (retain) IBOutlet NSTextField *bigText;
@property (retain) IBOutlet NSTextField *labelText;

@end
```

Then add the @synthesize command in the implementation (.m) file like this:

```
@synthesize bigText;
@synthesize labelText;
```

After you connect these NSTextField properties to a wrapping label and wrapping text field on your user interface, you'll be able to put text into either object using its stringValue property:

```
labelText.stringValue = @"This text can appear inside a Wrapping Label";
bigText.stringValue = @"This text can appear in a Wrapping Text Field";
```

You can just as easily retrieve the text stored in a wrapping label or a wrapping text field by using the stringValue property again:

```
NSLog (@"Wrapping Label text = %@", labelText.stringValue);
NSLog (@"Wrapping Text Field contents = %@", bigText.stringValue);
```

Summary

Labels are handy for displaying text to identify parts of your user interface or just to provide instructions or information for the user to read. Text fields are designed to allow the user to type in text so that your program can retrieve and manipulate that data.

If you need to display multiple lines of text, you can use a Wrapping Label object or a Wrapping Text Field object. With both labels and text fields, you can double-click the object directly on your user interface and type text that you want to appear on that label or text field; you can modify the Title property of each item via the Attributes Inspector; or you can assign a string to the label's stringValue property using Objective-C code.

Double-clicking and typing directly on the label or text field may be the simplest method, but using the Object Attributes window for a text field lets you define placeholder text, which appears dimmed to display a brief description of what type of information the user needs to type into that text field.

A combo box combines the features of a text field with a pop-up button, allowing users to either select from a list of choices or type in their own option. With the combo box, labels, and text fields, you must always connect your IBOutlet variables to the actual user interface item.

Labels, text fields, and combo boxes provide different ways to display information to the user and (for text fields and combo boxes) accept data from the user.

Chapter **19**

Inputting Data with Sliders, Date Pickers, and Steppers

When you need to let the user choose from a limited list of options, radio buttons, check boxes, and pop-up buttons will work just fine. When you need to let the user type in data, a text field or combo box will be a better choice. However, if you want the user to select a numeric value, a predefined list of options may be too limited and clumsy, and forcing the user to type in a number might not work if you want to restrict the number to a specific range. In this case, you may want to use a horizontal, vertical, or circular *slider*.

A slider lets you define a minimum and maximum value so the user can choose any number in between by moving the slider up and down or left and right. Sliders also let you define increments, such as allowing the user to select only even numbers or only numbers in increments of 0.5.

Another way to let the user input numeric values is to use a *stepper*, which looks like a tiny up and down arrow. Like a slider, a stepper lets you define a minimum and maximum value along with an increment value, so you could make the stepper count by ones, threes, fives, or any number you want.

Sliders and steppers can help users input a numeric value, but sometimes you may need the user to input a date. You could let the user type that information into a text field, but then you'll have the problem of enforcing a specific format, such as August 10, 2012 or 8/10/12. If the user misspells a month or uses dashes instead of slashes (8-10-12), your program might get confused if it doesn't expect anyone to type in a data using dashes.

To avoid this problem, you can use an object called a *date picker*. Instead of forcing users to type a date, a date picker displays a calendar so users can pick a date without typing. A date picker makes choosing dates convenient for the user while also simplifying receiving dates for your program.

The main purpose of all these controls is to prevent the user from giving your program invalid information, such as typing "Twelve" instead of using the number 12. By preventing the user from entering invalid data, your user interface can protect your program from crashing due to unexpected data, which increases the reliability of your program.

Using Sliders

The main purpose of a slider is to let the user drag it to select a value. The following are the three types of sliders, as shown in Figure 19–1:

Horizontal

Vertical

Circular

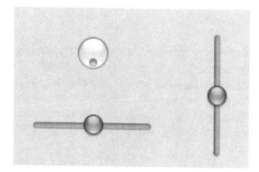

Figure 19–1. *The three types of sliders*

To create a slider, follow these steps:

1. Open a .xib user interface file in Interface Builder.

2. Choose Tools ➤ Library to open the Library window.

3. Drag the Horizontal Slider object, Vertical Slider object, or Circular Slider object from the Object Library (as shown in Figure 19–2) and drop it on your user interface window.

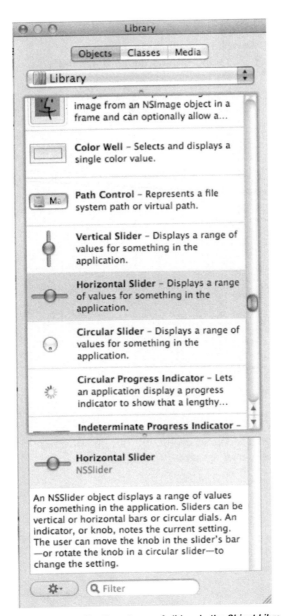

Figure 19–2. *The three types of sliders in the Object Library*

Defining Values

For every slider, you can define a Minimum, Maximum, and Current value. The Minimum value represents the lowest value the slider (left on a horizontal slider or bottom on a vertical slider) can return. The Maximum value represents the highest value the slider (right on a horizontal slider or top on a vertical slider) can return.

The Current value defines the value displayed on the slider. By modifying this value, you can set the slider's position. You can set all three values in the slider's Attributes Inspector window, shown in Figure 19–3, which you can open by clicking a slider and then choosing Tools ➤ Attributes Inspector.

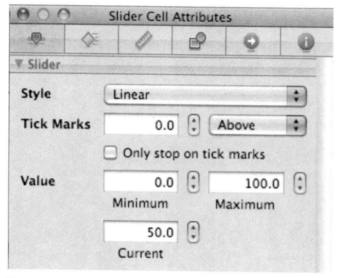

Figure 19–3. *The Minimum, Maximum, and Current values of a slider*

Displaying Tick Marks

Tick marks can appear above or below a horizontal slider, on the left or right side of a vertical slider, or around the edges of a circular slider, as shown in Figure 19–4.

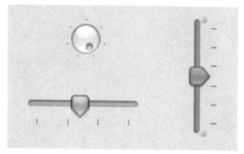

Figure 19–4. *Tick marks around, below, and to the right of three sliders*

When displaying tick marks, you can choose in which position (above/below, left/right, around) you want the tick marks to appear for a slider, the number of tick marks to display, and whether you want to restrain the slider to move only in increments defined by the tick marks. To define the appearance of tick marks, you need to modify the following in the slider's Attributes Inspector window (see Figure 19–3):

The position of the tick marks

Number of tick marks to display (this value must be 1 or greater to display tick marks)

Whether the slider can move only in increments defined by the tick marks

Retrieving and Displaying a Slider's Value

When the user manipulates a slider, the slider constantly changes its current value. However, you won't be able to see this change in value unless you display that value in another object such as a label.

To use a label to display a slider's current value, you need to follow these steps:

1. Double-click on the MainMenu.xib file in the Resources file to open Interface Builder.

2. Choose Tools ➤ Library to open the Library window.

3. Drag one Label object and one Slider object from the Object Library and drop them on the user interface window.

4. Right-click the Label object to display a heads-up window.

5. Click the circle that appears to the right of `takeIntegerValueFrom` under the Received Actions category and drag and drop it on the slider object, as shown in Figure 19–5. (If you wanted the label to display decimal numbers, you would drag the `takeFloatValueFrom` circle to the slider instead.)

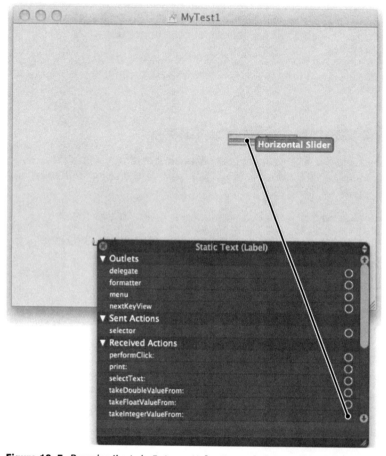

Figure 19–5. *Dragging the* `takeIntegerValueFrom` *circle to a slider links that slider's value to the label.*

6. Choose File ➤ Save or press ! S to save your changes.

7. Switch to Xcode and click the Build and Run button or choose Build ➤ Build and Run.

8. Drag the slider. Notice that the current value of the slider now appears inside your label.

9. Quit your program.such as pressing ! Q.

> **NOTE:** A circular slider works identically to how a horizontal or vertical slider works, except that the user must spin the slider around to change its value.

Using a Date Picker

A date picker lets the user enter a date and time by clicking a choice instead of typing the whole date or time in. There are three ways to display a date picker, as shown in Figure 19–6:

Textual: Displays a text field that automatically formats dates and times

Textual with Stepper: Displays dates and times that allow you to increase/decrease the month, day, and year using the stepper (up/down arrows)

Graphical: Displays a monthly calendar and a clock

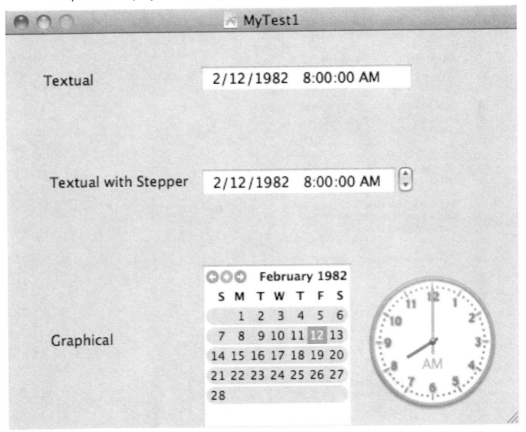

Figure 19–6. *The three different appearances for a date picker.*

To create a date picker, follow these steps:

1. Open a `.xib` user interface file in Interface Builder.

2. Choose Tools ➤ Library to open the Library window.

3. Drag the Date Picker object from the Object Library (as shown in Figure 19–7) and drop it on your user interface window.

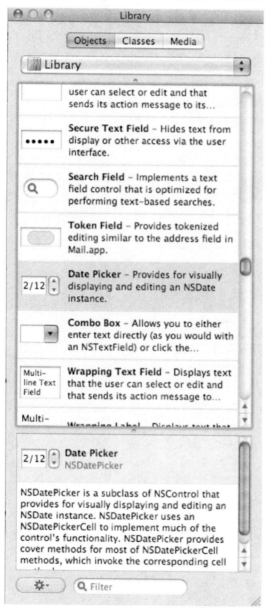

Figure 19–7. *The Date Picker object in the Object Library*

After you create a date picker, you can modify one or more of the following by clicking the Date Picker object and opening its Attributes Inspector window (by choosing Tools ➤ Attributes Inspector), as shown in Figure 19–8:

Style: Defines how to display the date picker (Textual, Textual with Stepper, or Graphical)

Selects: Defines whether the user can select only a single date or a range of dates

Elements: Defines whether to include the month, day, and year along with hours, minutes, and seconds

Date: Determines the currently displayed date

Minimum Date: Defines the earliest valid date

Maximum Date: Defines the latest possible valid date

Display: Defines whether a background color and/or border appears around the calendar

Text: Defines the color of text displayed on the date picker

Background: Defines the background color of the date picker

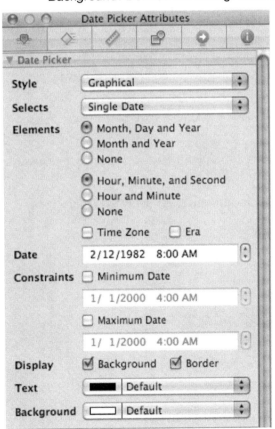

Figure 19–8. *The properties you can modify for a date picker*

Retrieving a Date from a Date Picker

To retrieve a date from a date picker, you need to declare an NSDatePicker variable in a header (.h) file:

`NSDatePicker *myDate;`

`@property (retain) IBOutlet NSDatePicker *myDate;`

Then, use the @synthesize command in the implementation (.m) file:

`@synthesize myDate;`

You need to connect this myDate variable to the actual date picker on your user interface. Now if you want to retrieve the value from the date picker, you just need to use the dateValue property:

`myDate.dateValue`

To see how to use a date picker, follow these steps:

1. Open the MyTest program that you modified in the previous chapter.

2. Double-click the MainMenu.xib file stored in the Resources folder. Interface Builder appears and displays your user interface window.

3. Click any items currently displayed on the user interface and press Delete to remove them.

4. Drag and drop one Push Button object and one Date Picker object on your user interface window.

5. Click the Date Picker object and choose Tools ➤ Attributes Inspector to display the Attributes Inspector window.

6. Click the Style pop-up button and choose Graphical, as shown in Figure 19–9.

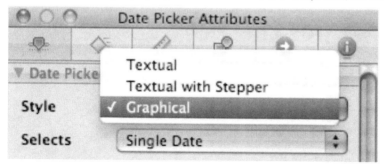

Figure 19–9. *The Graphical option in the Attributes Inspector window*

7. Click the Selects pop-up button and choose Single Date.

8. Under the Elements category, select the Month, Day, and Year radio button and the Hour, Minute, and Second radio button.

9. Click the MyTestAppDelegate.h file stored in the Classes folder and modify the code as follows:

```
#import <Cocoa/Cocoa.h>

@interface MyTestAppDelegate : NSObject <NSApplicationDelegate> {
    NSWindow *window;

    NSDatePicker *myDate;
}

@property (retain) IBOutlet NSWindow *window;
@property (retain) IBOutlet NSDatePicker *myDate;

-(IBAction) displayDate:(id)sender;

@end
```

10. Choose File ➤ Save or press ! S to save your changes.

11. Click the MyTestAppDelegate.m file stored in the Classes folder and modify the code as follows:

```
#import "MyTestAppDelegate.h"

@implementation MyTestAppDelegate

@synthesize window;
@synthesize myDate;

- (void)applicationDidFinishLaunching:(NSNotification *)aNotification {
    // Insert code here to initialize your application
}
- (void)dealloc {
    [myDate release];
    [window release];
    [super dealloc];
}

-(IBAction) displayDate:(id)sender
{
    NSLog (@"Date = %@", myDate.dateValue);
}

@end
```

12. Choose File ➤ Save or press ! S to save your changes.

13. Double-click the MainMenu.xib file stored in the Resources folder. Interface Builder appears and displays your user interface window.

14. Right-click the My Test App Delegate icon in the MainMenu.xib window. A heads-up window appears.

15. Click the circle that appears to the right of myDate under the Outlets heading and drag and drop it over the date picker on the user interface.

16. Click the circle that appears to the right of displayDate (under Received Actions) and drag and drop it over the push button on the user interface.

17. Choose File ➤ Save or press ! S to save your changes.

18. Switch to Xcode and click the Build and Run button or choose Build ➤ Build and Run. As long as you didn't mistype anything, you should see a blank window pop up.

19. Click a date displayed by the date picker.

20. Click a time displayed by the date picker.

21. Click the push button.

22. Quit your program.

23. Choose Run ➤ Console or press " ! R. You should see the printed statements created by the NSLog command:

```
2010-09-24 16:32:36.299 UITest[13123:a0f] Date = 2011-02-01 08:00:00 -0800
```

Using Steppers

A stepper lets the user increment a value by a fixed amount, such as 1. A stepper lets the user select from a range of valid values but takes up less space than a slider.

To create a stepper, follow these steps:

1. Open a .xib user interface file in Interface Builder.

2. Choose Tools ➤ Library to open the Library window.

3. Drag the Stepper object from the Object Library (as shown in Figure 19–10) and drop it on your user interface window.

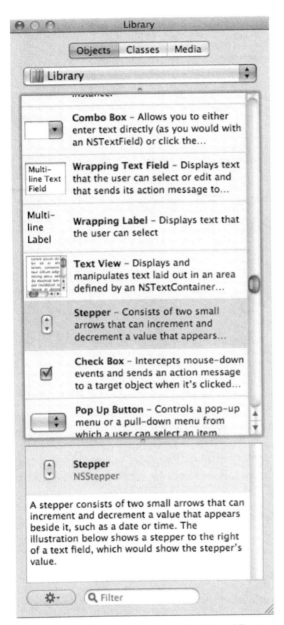

Figure 19–10. *The Stepper object in the Object Library*

After you create a stepper, you can modify one or more of the following, as shown in Figure 19–11:

> *Value Wraps*: Defines whether the stepper stops when its minimum or maximum value is reached (unchecked) or "wraps around" and allows the stepper to jump from the minimum value to the maximum value and vice versa (checked)

Auto Repeats: Defines whether the user can hold down the stepper's up or down arrow to keep incrementing (checked) or must click the stepper up/down arrow each time to increment/decrement the value (unchecked)

Minimum: Defines the minimum value

Maximum: Defines the maximum value

Increment: Defines the increment by which the stepper increases/decreases its value each time the user clicks the up/down arrow

Current: Determines the current value stored in the stepper

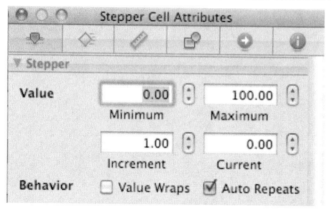

Figure 19–11. *Defining the behavior of a stepper in the Attributes Inspector window*

One problem with the stepper is that as you click to change its value, you can't see your changes. To display your changes, you can link a `Label` object to the Stepper object so that the value always appears in the `Label`.

In case you need to retrieve the value from the stepper, you can use the `doubleValue` property:

```
myStepper.doubleValue
```

To see how to use a stepper, follow these steps:

4. Open the MyTest program that you modified in the previous section.

5. Double-click the `MainMenu.xib` file stored in the Resources folder. Interface Builder appears and displays your user interface window.

6. Click any items currently displayed on the user interface and press Delete to remove them.

7. Drag one Push Button object, one Label object, and one Stepper object and drop them on your user interface window.

8. Click the Stepper object and choose Tools ➤ Attributes Inspector to display the Attributes Inspector window.

9. Click to select the Value Wraps check box. (If the Auto Repeats check box is clear, click to select it.)

10. Click in the Maximum text field, type **5**, and press Return.

11. Click the `MyTestAppDelegate.h` file stored in the Classes folder and modify the code as follows:

```
#import <Cocoa/Cocoa.h>

@interface MyTestAppDelegate : NSObject <NSApplicationDelegate> {
    NSWindow *window;

    NSStepper *myValue;
 }

@property (retain) IBOutlet NSWindow *window;
@property (retain) IBOutlet NSStepper *myValue;

-(IBAction) displayValue:(id)sender;

@end
```

12. Choose File ➤ Save or press ! S to save your changes.

13. Click the `MyTestAppDelegate.m` file stored in the Classes folder and modify the code as follows:

```
#import "MyTestAppDelegate.h"

@implementation MyTestAppDelegate

@synthesize window;
@synthesize myValue;

- (void)applicationDidFinishLaunching:(NSNotification *)aNotification {
    // Insert code here to initialize your application
}

- (void)dealloc {
    [myValue release];
    [window release];
    [super dealloc];
}

-(IBAction) displayValue:(id)sender
{
    NSLog (@" Value = %f", myValue.doubleValue);
}

@end
```

14. Choose File ➤ Save or press ! S to save your changes.

15. Double-click the `MainMenu.xib` file stored in the Resources folder. Interface Builder appears and displays your user interface window.

16. Right-click the My Test App Delegate icon in the MainMenu.xib window. A heads-up window appears.

17. Click the circle that appears to the right of `myValue` under the Outlets heading and drag and drop it over the stepper on the user interface.

18. Click the circle that appears to the right of `displayValue` (under Received Actions) and drag and drop it over the push button on the user interface.

19. Right-click the label on your user interface window. A heads-up window appears.

20. Click the circle that appears to the right of `takeDoubleValueFrom` and drag and drop it over the stepper on the user interface. This links the label to the value of the stepper.

21. Choose File ➤ Save or press ⌘ S to save your changes.

22. Switch to Xcode and click the Build and Run button or choose Build ➤ Build and Run. As long as you didn't mistype anything, you should see a blank window pop up.

23. Click the up or down arrow on the stepper. Notice that the value appears in the label.

24. Click the push button.

25. Quit your program.

26. Choose Run ➤ Console or press " ⌘ R. You should see the printed statements created by the `NSLog` command:

```
2010-09-24 18:50:59.519 UITest[13551:a0f]  Value = 4.000000
```

Summary

Sliders and steppers let the user select a numeric value that falls within a fixed range. To display the value of a slider or stepper, you may need to link a label to the slider or stepper so that the value always appears on the label, making it visible to the user.

The date picker lets the user select a date by either typing in an actual numeric value or clicking a displayed date. Sliders, steppers, and date pickers are just a few of the ways to provide a limited number of valid choices that the user can select.

Chapter 20

Using Built-In Dialog Boxes

Apple provides plenty of prewritten and tested code you can reuse from the Cocoa framework. Besides letting you create a program faster, prewritten code also ensures that your program looks and behaves like a typical Mac program. One of the common elements of every Mac program are dialog boxes, which are windows that pop up and allow the user to print, open, or save a file. Rather than force you to create these common user interface elements yourself, Apple provides you with built-in dialog boxes that you can plug into your own program.

One common built-in dialog box is an alert panel that pops up on the screen to alert the user to something, such as confirming that the computer is about to delete a file if the user confirms this delete action. Another common type of dialog box display is an Open or Save dialog box that lets the user select a folder and a file. By using these common user interface items in your programs, you can create programs that look and behave just like Apple's own programs such as iPhoto and iTunes.

Using Alert Dialog Boxes

An alert dialog is used whenever your program needs to bring something to the user's attention. To use an alert dialog box, you need to create and customize it, display it on the screen, and then retrieve any choices that the user made, such as clicking an OK or Cancel button.

The first step in creating an alert dialog box is to define a pointer to the NSAlert class and then initialize that pointer like this:

```
NSAlert *alert = [[NSAlert alloc] init];
```

After creating an alert dialog box, the next step is to define the type of dialog box to display, as shown in Figure 20–1. The following are the three types of alert dialog boxes:

- NSWarningAlertStyle: Displays the default style used to warn the user about an impending event

- NSInformationalAlertStyle: Creates a dialog box to warn the user of an event; looks identical to the NSWarningAlertStyle

- NSCriticalAlertStyle: Displays a caution icon, used to caution the user about an event that could have consequences

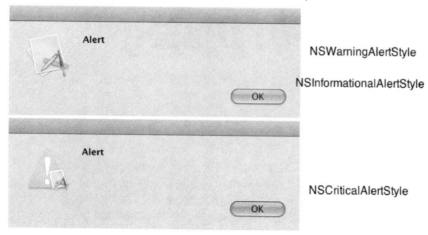

Figure 20–1. *The appearance of the different dialog box styles*

To define the type of dialog box style, just use alertStyle and specify the style you want to use like this:

```
NSAlert *alert = [[NSAlert alloc] init];
alert.alertStyle = NSWarningAlertStyle;
```

NOTE: The icon displayed in a dialog box is the icon assigned to your program. If you do not assign an icon to your program, the icon will be the default application icon (see Figure 20–1).

To make the alert dialog box actually appear (and release its memory usage when it's done), you need to add two additional lines of code:

```
NSAlert *alert = [[NSAlert alloc] init];
alert.alertStyle = NSWarningAlertStyle;
[alert runModal];
[alert release];
```

The [alert runModal] line makes your dialog box actually appear on the screen. While these four lines create and display a dialog box, you'll probably want to customize the dialog box with text and buttons, which the following sections explain.

Displaying Text on a Dialog Box

By default, a dialog box simply displays the word "Alert." To customize a dialog box, you can define message text and informative text. Message text appears in bold to catch the user's eye, while informative text appears underneath and provides additional explanation about the dialog box's message, as shown in Figure 20–2.

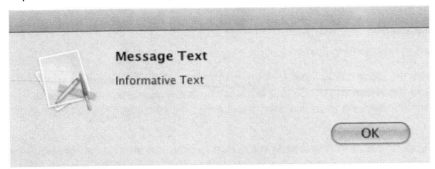

Figure 20–2. *The appearance of message and informative text on a dialog box*

After you've created a dialog box, you can use `messageText` and `informativeText` to define the text to display on your dialog box:

```
alert.messageText = @"Message Text";
alert.informativeText = @"Informative Text";
```

Displaying a Suppression Check Box

If you've ever used a new browser for the first time, you may have seen a dialog box pop up asking if you want to make the browser your default browser. This dialog box lets you click Yes or No, but it also includes a check box called a *suppression check box*, which you can check to make sure the dialog box doesn't keep popping up again and again, as shown in Figure 20–3.

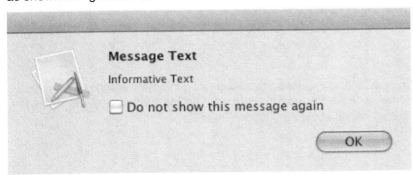

Figure 20–3. *The suppression check box displays "Do not show this message again."*

To create a suppression check box, use `suppressionButton` and set it to YES:

```
alert.showsSuppressionButton: = YES;
```

Displaying Buttons on a Dialog Box

By default, a dialog box appears with only an OK button (see Figure 20–2). If you just need to alert the user about something noncritical, the user can acknowledge getting that message and remove the dialog box by clicking the OK button.

However, many times you may want to display more than one button and display custom text on each button. To do both, you need to use the addButtonWithTitle method and define the text that you want to appear on the button:

```
[alert addButtonWithTitle:@"OK"];
```

The first button you add to a dialog box appears on the far right. Each additional button you add appears to the left of the preceding button. Generally you don't want to use more than three or four buttons because then the dialog box starts to get cluttered and more confusing.

When the user clicks any button displayed on the dialog box, the dialog box immediately disappears. If you have two or more buttons displayed on the dialog box, you may want to know which button the user chose.

To determine the button that the user clicked, you can use a switch statement along with the NSAlertFirstButtonReturn, NSAlertSecondButtonReturn, and NSAlertThirdButtonReturn constants:

```
switch ([alert runModal])
    {
        case NSAlertFirstButtonReturn:
            NSLog (@"First button clicked");
            break;

        case NSAlertSecondButtonReturn:
            NSLog (@"Second clicked");
            break;

        case NSAlertThirdButtonReturn:
            NSLog (@"Third clicked");
            break;

        default:
            break;
    }
```

The [alert runModal] command displays the dialog box. The first button on the dialog box is the button on the far right, the second button is the button that appears to the left of the first button, and so on, as shown in Figure 20–4.

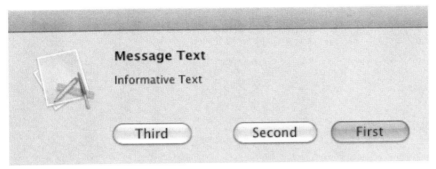

Figure 20-4. *Identifying the first, second, and third buttons on a dialog box*

If you have more than three buttons on a dialog box, you can identify each additional button by checking for NSAlertThirdButton + x, where x is a number that represents an additional button beyond the third one.

To see how to create and display a dialog box, follow these steps:

1. Open the MyTest program that you modified in the previous chapter.

2. Double-click the MainMenu.xib file stored in the Resources folder. Interface Builder appears and displays your user interface window.

3. Click any items currently displayed on the user interface and press Delete to remove them.

4. Drag and drop one Push Button object on your user interface window.

5. Click the MyTestAppDelegate.h file stored in the Classes folder and modify the code as follows:

```
#import <Cocoa/Cocoa.h>

@interface MyTestAppDelegate : NSObject <NSApplicationDelegate> {
    NSWindow *window;
}
@property (retain) IBOutlet NSWindow *window;

-(IBAction) displayDialog:(id)sender;

@end
```

6. Choose File ➤ Save or press ⌘S to save your changes.

7. Click the MyTestAppDelegate.m file stored in the Classes folder and modify the code as follows:

```
#import "MyTestAppDelegate.h"

@implementation MyTestAppDelegate

@synthesize window;
```

```objc
- (void)applicationDidFinishLaunching:(NSNotification *)aNotification {
    // Insert code here to initialize your application
}

- (void)dealloc {

    [window release];
    [super dealloc];
}

-(IBAction) displayDialog:(id)sender
{
    NSAlert *alert = [[NSAlert alloc] init];
    alert.salertStyle = NSWarningAlertStyle;

    [alert addButtonWithTitle:@"OK"];
    [alert addButtonWithTitle:@"Cancel"];

    alert.messageText = @"Message Text";
    alert.informativeText = @"Informative Text";

    switch ([alert runModal])
    {
        case NSAlertFirstButtonReturn:
            NSLog (@"OK clicked");
            break;

        case NSAlertSecondButtonReturn:
            NSLog (@"Cancel clicked");
            break;

        default:
            break;
    }

    [alert release];
}

@end
```

NOTE: After you create an alert dialog box, you need to use the `release` method (such as `[alert release];`) to remove the object from memory. If you fail to do this, each time the user opens the dialog box, it will gobble up memory and eventually could cause your program to crash when there's no more memory available.

8. Choose File ➤ Save or press ⌘S to save your changes.

9. Double-click the `MainMenu.xib` file stored in the Resources folder. Interface Builder appears and displays your user interface window.

10. Right-click the My Test App Delegate icon in MainMenu.xib window. A heads-up window appears.

11. Click the circle that appear to the right of `displayDialog` under the Received Actions heading and drag the mouse to the push button on the user interface.

12. Choose File ➤ Save or press ⌘S to save your changes.

13. Switch to Xcode and click the Build and Run button or choose Build ➤ Build and Run. As long as you didn't mistype anything, you should see a blank window pop up.

14. Click the push button. Your dialog box appears.

15. Click the OK button. The dialog box disappears.

16. Repeat steps 14 and 15 except click the Cancel button.

17. Quit your program.

18. Choose Run ➤ Console or press ⇧⌘R. You should see the printed statements created by the `NSLog` command:

```
2010-09-25 22:44:52.232 UITest[19293:a0f] OK clicked
2010-09-25 22:44:54.426 UITest[19293:a0f] Cancel clicked
```

Creating an Open Panel

Many Mac programs need to let the user choose a file stored on a computer. To present this option in a consistent way, almost every Mac program uses a special window called an *Open panel*, as shown in Figure 20–5.

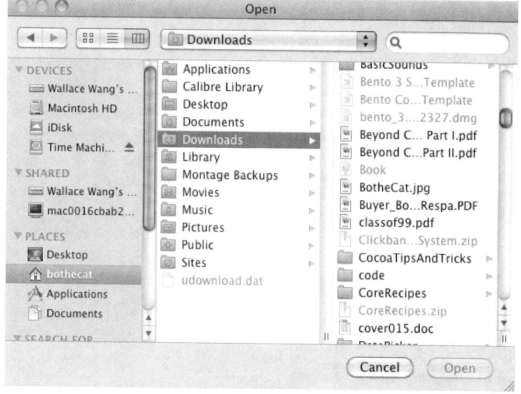

Figure 20–5. *An Open panel lets you select files on a computer.*

To create an Open panel, you need to use the NSOpenPanel class like this:

```
NSOpenPanel *myPanel = [NSOpenPanel openPanel];
```

This creates an Open panel, but you still need to display it and determine which button the user clicked (NSOKButton or NSCancelButton) and which file the user selected.

To display an Open panel, you need to use the runModal method, which looks like this:

```
[myPanel runModal];
```

This line of code returns an integer value that identifies which button the user clicked to make the Open panel disappear. To identify which button the user clicked (Open or Cancel), you need to check if the value of [myPanel runModal] is equal to the constant value NSOKButton (which represents the Open button):

```
if ([myPanel runModal] == NSOKButton)
    {
        // If the user selected a file, retrieve that file name
    }
```

If the user clicked the Cancel button, then there's no need to do anything else. However, if the user clicked the Open button (identified by the NSOKButton constant), then the user must have also selected a file from the Open panel.

To retrieve this file name (plus its directory path), you must use the URLs property, which contains an array of all the files that the user selected. (Most users will select only a single file, but it's possible to allow the user to select multiple files.) To use the URLs property, you must declare an NSArray like this:

```
NSArray *filenamesArray = myPanel.URLs;
```

Once the list of selected file names gets stored in an array, the second step is to retrieve each file name from this array. If the Open panel allowed the user to select only a single file, then you need to retrieve only the first item in the array, located at index position 0:

```
NSString *filename = [filenamesArray objectAtIndex:0];
```

The string stored in the filename string now identifies the file name (and directory path) of the file that the user chose.

To see how to create and display an Open panel, follow these steps:

1. Open the MyTest program that you modified in the previous section.

2. Double-click the MainMenu.xib file stored in the Resources folder. Interface Builder appears and displays your user interface window.

3. Click any items currently displayed on the user interface and press Delete to remove them.

4. Drag and drop one Push Button object on your user interface window.

5. Click the MyTestAppDelegate.h file stored in the Classes folder and modify the code as follows:

```
#import <Cocoa/Cocoa.h>

@interface MyTestAppDelegate : NSObject <NSApplicationDelegate> {
    NSWindow *window;
}
@property (retain) IBOutlet NSWindow *window;

-(IBAction) displayPanel:(id)sender;

@end
```

6. Choose File ➤ Save or press ⌘S to save your changes.

7. Click the MyTestAppDelegate.m file stored in the Classes folder and modify the code as follows:

```
#import "MyTestAppDelegate.h"

@implementation MyTestAppDelegate

@synthesize window;

- (void)applicationDidFinishLaunching:(NSNotification *)aNotification {
    // Insert code here to initialize your application
```

```
}

- (void)dealloc {

    [window release];
    [super dealloc];
}

-(IBAction) displayPanel:(id)sender
{
    NSOpenPanel *myPanel = [NSOpenPanel openPanel];

    if ([myPanel runModal] == NSOKButton)
    {
        NSArray *files = myPanel.URLs;
        NSURL *filename = [files objectAtIndex:0];
        NSLog (@"File = %@", filename);
    }
}

@end
```

8. Choose File ➤ Save or press ⌘S to save your changes.

9. Double-click the `MainMenu.xib` file stored in the Resources folder to open Interface Builder.

10. Click the Window (My Test) icon in the MainMenu.xib window. Your user interface window appears.

11. Right-click the My Test App Delegate icon. A heads-up window appears.

12. Click the circle that appears to the right of `displayPanel` under the Received Actions category and drag it to the push button on the user interface.

13. Choose File ➤ Save or press ⌘S to save your changes.

14. Switch to Xcode and click the Build and Run button or choose Build ➤ Build and Run. As long as you didn't mistype anything, you should see a blank window pop up.

15. Click the push button. The Open panel appears.

16. Click a file (open up different folders if you wish), and click the Open button.

17. Quit your program.

18. Choose Run ➤ Console or press ⇧⌘R. You should see the printed statements created by the `NSLog` command:

```
2010-09-26 20:48:21.314 UITest[21836:a0f] File = /Users/JohnDoe/Documents/About
Stacks.pdf
```

Limiting File Types

The Open panel normally displays every file type on your computer. However, you can limit the Open panel to make available only certain types of files, such as PDF or Microsoft Word (.doc and .docx) files.

To define the types of files to allow the user to select, you must first create an array that lists all the file extensions that define all the files you want to allow the user to select, such as in this example:

```
NSArray *fileTypes = [NSArray arrayWithObjects:@"doc",  @"pdf", nil];
```

This code would force the Open panel to display only .doc or .pdf files. Any file with a different file extension, such as .tif or .jpg, would appear dimmed so the user can't select it. By limiting the types of files the user can select, you can ensure that the user won't select an inappropriate file that won't work in your program.

After you've defined a list of acceptable file extensions, the next step is to tell the Open panel which files are acceptable by using the allowedFilesTypes property like this:

```
NSArray *fileTypes = [NSArray arrayWithObjects:@"doc", @"jpg", @"pdf", nil];
myPanel.allowedFileTypes = fileTypes;
```

Allowing Multiple File Selections

In most cases, you may want the user to select only a single file from the Open panel. However, you can let the user select multiple files, by holding down the ⌘ key while clicking each file to select. To allow the user to select multiple files, you need to turn on this multiple selection option by using the setAllowsMultipleSelection method like this:

```
[myPanel setAllowsMultipleSelection:YES];
```

When you allow the user to select multiple files, you have no idea how many files the user might have selected. To retrieve each file name, you must use a loop that keeps retrieving each selected file name until it finds them all:

```
if ([myPanel runModal] == NSOKButton)
    {
        NSArray *filenamesArray = myPanel.URLs;
        for (NSURL *element in filenamesArray) {
            NSLog(@"File = %@", element);
        }
    }
```

The for loop keeps repeating until it retrieves all the file names from filenamesArray, which holds the list of the multiple files the user selected.

To see how to limit the file types the user can select and allow the user to select multiple files, follow these steps:

1. Open the MyTest program that you modified in the previous section.

2. Double-click the MainMenu.xib file stored in the Resources folder. Interface Builder appears and displays your user interface window. One push button should appear on the user interface. If not, delete anything currently displayed and then drag and drop one Push Button object on the user interface window.

3. Click the MyTestAppDelegate.m file stored in the Classes folder and modify the code as follows:

```
#import "MyTestAppDelegate.h"

@implementation MyTestAppDelegate

@synthesize window;

- (void)applicationDidFinishLaunching:(NSNotification *)aNotification {
    // Insert code here to initialize your application
}

- (void)dealloc {

    [window release];
    [super dealloc];
}

-(IBAction) displayPanel:(id)sender
{

    NSOpenPanel *myPanel = [NSOpenPanel openPanel];

    NSArray *fileTypes = [NSArray arrayWithObjects:@"doc", @"jpg", @"pdf", nil];
    myPanel.allowedFileTypes = fileTypes;

    myPanel.allowsMultipleSelection = YES;

    if ([myPanel runModal] == NSOKButton)
    {
        NSArray *filenamesArray = myPanel.URLs;
        for (NSURL *element in filenamesArray) {
            NSLog(@"File = %@", element);
        }
    }
}

@end
```

4. Choose File ➤ Save or press ⌘S to save your changes.

5. Double-click the MainMenu.xib file stored in the Resources folder. Interface Builder appears and displays your user interface window.

6. Right-click the My Test App Delegate icon in the MainMenu.xib window. A heads-up window appears. Make sure the `displayPanel` method is connected to the push button on your user interface. If not, click the circle that appears to the right of `displayPanel` under the Received Actions category and drag it to the push button on the user interface.

7. Choose File ➤ Save or press ⌘S to save your changes.

8. Switch to Xcode and click the Build and Run button or choose Build ➤ Build and Run. As long as you didn't mistype anything, you should see a blank window pop up.

9. Click the push button. The Open panel appears.

10. Hold down the ⌘ key and click two or more files. Then click the Open button.

11. Quit your program.

12. Choose Run ➤ Console or press ⇧⌘R. You should see the printed statements created by the NSLog command:

```
2010-09-27 21:26:24.726 UITest[984:a0f] File =
/Users/bothecat/Documents/ComputorEdge/Fig-3.jpg
2010-09-27 21:26:24.726 UITest[984:a0f] File =
/Users/bothecat/Documents/ComputorEdge/Fig-5.jpg
```

In this example, the user clicked two files, named Fig-3.jpg and Fig-5.jpg. Depending on which files you selected, you'll see those file names displayed instead.

Creating a Save Panel

A Save panel is similar to an Open panel except that the Save panel lets you create a file by typing a new file name and selecting a folder in which to store that new file. (The Save panel won't actually create the file, though; you'll need to write Objective-C code that does this for you.)

To create a Save panel, you must create a pointer to the NSSavePanel class:

```
NSSavePanel *myPanel = [NSSavePanel savePanel];
```

Then to display the Save panel, you need to use the runModal method and check if the user clicked the Save button (represented by the NSOKButton constant). Then you need to retrieve the name of the file that the user typed, which gets stored in the URL or URL.lastPathComponent property. The URL property stores the entire path and file name, such as /Documents/filename, while the URL.lastPathComponent property just stores the file name. Depending on whether you want to retrieve the entire path or just the file name, you can use the URL or URL.lastPathComponent property like this:

```
if ([myPanel runModal] == NSOKButton)
    {
// URL returns the entire path and file name
        NSLog (@"Path chosen = %@", myPanel.URL);
```

```
//URL.lastPathComponent returns just the file name
      NSLog (@"File typed = %@", myPanel.URL);
   }
```

To see how to create and use a Save panel, follow these steps:

1. Open the MyTest program that you modified in the previous section.

2. Double-click the MainMenu.xib file stored in the Resources folder. Interface Builder appears and displays your user interface window. One push button should appear on the user interface. If not, delete anything currently displayed and drag and drop one Push Button object on the user interface window.

3. Click the MyTestAppDelegate.m file stored in the Classes folder and modify the code as follows:

```
#import "MyTestAppDelegate.h"

@implementation MyTestAppDelegate

@synthesize window;

- (void)applicationDidFinishLaunching:(NSNotification *)aNotification {
    // Insert code here to initialize your application

}

- (void)dealloc {

    [window release];
    [super dealloc];
}

-(IBAction) displayPanel:(id)sender
{
    NSSavePanel *myPanel = [NSSavePanel savePanel];

    if ([myPanel runModal] == NSOKButton)
    {
        NSLog (@"Path chosen = %@", myPanel.URL);
        NSLog (@"File typed = %@", myPanel.URL.lastPathComponent);
    }
}

@end
```

4. Choose File ➤ Save or press ⌘S to save your changes.

5. Switch to Xcode and click the Build and Run button or choose Build ➤ Build and Run. As long as you didn't mistype anything, you should see a blank window pop up.

6. Click the push button. The Save panel appears.

7. Click in the Save As text field and type a filename such as **My Files**.

8. Quit your program.

9. Choose Run ➤ Console or press ⇧⌘R. You should see the printed statement created by the NSLog command:

```
2010-09-28 13:57:15.920 MyTest[2250:a0f] Path chosen =
file://localhost/Users/JohnDoe/Documents/My%20Files
2010-09-28 13:57:15.920 MyTest[2250:a0f] File typed = My Files
```

Limiting File Types

The Save panel and the Open panel look and work similarly because the Save panel inherits features from the Open panel. As a result, the Save panel can also use the allowedFileTypes property to automatically add a specific extension to every file the user types in the Save panel.

To define a file extension, such as .xyz, you could use the following:

```
NSArray *fileTypes = [NSArray arrayWithObjects:@"xyz", nil];
```

If the user typed the file name "MyFiles" into the Save panel, the preceding code would tell your program to add the .xyz file extension so that the complete file name would be MyFiles.xyz. After you've defined a file extension, the next step is to tell the Save panel to use the allowedFilesTypes property:

```
NSArray *fileTypes = [NSArray arrayWithObjects:@"xyz", nil];
myPanel.allowedFileTypes = fileTypes;
```

Summary

Dialog boxes let you display short messages, temporarily interrupting the user. You can customize the text inside an alert dialog box to display different types of messages. Generally a dialog box can simply display information, but it can also retrieve the choice that the user picked so your program can respond accordingly.

If your program needs to open or save a file, you can use the built-in Open and Save panels. Both of these panels provide the standard Mac Open and Save panel that lets users switch between drives and folders to search for a file. To make these Open and Save panels actually work, you'll need to write Objective-C code to retrieve or save a file.

By using the built-in dialog boxes and Open and Save panels, you can create a program that looks and behaves like every Mac program. Users will be familiar with the way these dialog boxes and Open/Save panels work, so you can focus your time just writing the code needed to make your program do something useful.

Chapter 21

Creating Pull-Down Menus

The simplest user interface might consist of a window with a few buttons or check boxes on the screen. However, there's a limit to the number of options you can cram inside a window. Eventually, you may want to organize commands in categories and display those categories of commands in pull-down menus at the top of the screen.

Pull-down menus enable you to store and organize multiple commands, yet keep them tucked out of sight until the user actually needs them. In addition to menus, you can create submenus. You can also assign shortcut keystrokes to specific menu commands. By designing a pull-down menu for your program, you can simplify your user interface and provide a consistent Mac look and feel for your program without any additional programming whatsoever.

When you create a new program, Interface Builder automatically creates a standard pull-down menu for you. To make this pull-down menu work, you need to customize these menus and commands. In this chapter, you'll learn the steps involved in editing pull-down menus, linking menu commands and assigning keystrokes to them, and defining text inside dialog boxes.

Editing Pull-Down Menus

Every time you create a new project based on the Cocoa Application template, Xcode automatically creates a basic pull-down menu that contains common menus (File, Edit, View, etc.) along with common menu items (Cut, Copy, Paste, etc.), as shown in Figure 21–1.

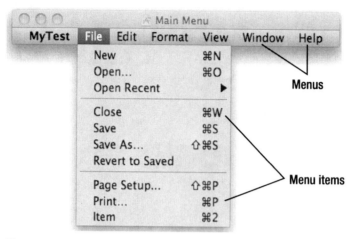

Figure 21-1. *Menus and menu items make up the pull-down menus.*

The following are the six pull-down menus that typically appear:

> *File*: Commands for manipulating files used by the program, such as opening, creating, printing, and saving

> *Edit*: Commands for editing data, such as Cut, Copy, and Paste

> *Format*: Commands for changing the appearance of data

> *View*: Commands for changing the appearance of data displayed in a window on the screen

> *Window*: Commands for manipulating multiple windows that display data

> *Help*: Commands for getting help using the program

Editing a Menu or Menu Item

Since Xcode creates generic pull-down menus for your Cocoa application automatically, you'll need to customize these menus and menu items. To edit a pull-down menu, follow these steps:

1. Double-click the `MainMenu.xib` file that contains the pull-down menu you want to edit. Interface Builder appears.

2. Double-click the Main Menu icon inside the MainMenu.xib window to display the pull-down menu bar.

3. Double-click the menu object that you want to edit. For example, if you want to change the name of the Format menu, you would double-click Format. Your chosen menu appears highlighted.

4. Type new text or use the arrow keys to edit the existing menu title.

To edit a menu item that appears in a pull-down menu, follow these steps:

5. Double-click the MainMenu.xib file that contains the pull-down menu you want to edit.

6. Double-click the Main Menu icon inside the MainMenu.xib window to display the pull-down menu bar.

7. Click the menu that contains the menu item you want to edit. A pull-down menu appears.

8. Double-click the menu item that you want to edit. Your chosen item appears highlighted, as shown in Figure 21–2.

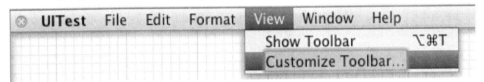

Figure 21–2. *Double-clicking highlights a menu or menu item.*

9. Type new text or use the arrow keys to edit the existing menu item title.

You can also edit a menu or menu item by clicking it and then choosing Tools ➤ Attributes Inspector. You then can edit the menu or menu item in the Attributes Inspector window, as shown in Figure 21–3.

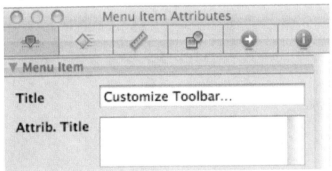

Figure 21–3. *The Attributes Inspector window lets you edit a menu or menu item in the Title field.*

Moving a Menu or Menu Item

Sometimes a pull-down menu or menu item may not appear in the order you want, in which case you can move it to another position. To move a menu, follow these steps:

1. Double-click the MainMenu.xib file that contains the pull-down menu you want to move.

2. Double-click the Main Menu icon inside the MainMenu.xib window to display the pull-down menu bar.

3. Click on the menu that you want to move (such as Edit or View) and drag the mouse left or right. As you move the mouse, a vertical line indicates where the menu will appear when you release the mouse button.

4. Release the mouse button when you're happy with the new position of the menu.

To move a menu item, follow these steps:

5. Double-click the `MainMenu.xib` file that contains the pull-down menu in which the menu item you want to move appears.

6. Double-click the Main Menu icon inside the MainMenu.xib window to display the pull-down menu bar.

7. Click the menu (such as File or Edit) that contains the menu item you want to move. The pull-down menu appears.

8. Click the menu item that you want to move and drag the mouse up or down. As you move the mouse, a horizontal line indicates where the menu item will appear when you release the mouse button, as shown in Figure 21–4.

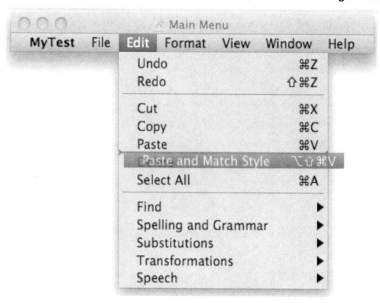

Figure 21–4. *Dragging a menu item to change its position*

9. Release the mouse button when you're happy with the new position of the menu item.

Deleting Menus and Menu Items

Chances are good that the default pull-down menu that Xcode creates will contain menus and menu items that your program won't need. To delete a pull-down menu (and all menu items stored in that pull-down menu), follow these steps:

1. Double-click the `MainMenu.xib` file that contains the pull-down menu you want to delete.

2. Double-click the Main Menu icon inside the MainMenu.xib window to display the pull-down menu bar.

3. Click the menu that you want to delete. The menu's pull-down menu appears.

4. Click the menu again. The menu's pull-down menu now disappears.

5. Press Delete or Backspace to delete your selected menu.

To delete a menu item, follow these steps:

1. Double-click the MainMenu.xib file that contains the pull-down menu in which the menu item you want to delete appears.

2. Double-click the Main Menu icon inside the MainMenu.xib window to display the pull-down menu bar.

3. Click the menu that contains the menu item you want to delete. Its pull-down menu appears.

4. Click the menu item you want to delete.

5. Press Delete or Backspace to delete your selected menu item.

NOTE: If you delete a menu or menu item by mistake, you can undo the deletion and retrieve it by pressing ⌘Z.

Creating New Menus and Menu Items

After deleting, editing, and rearranging menus and menu items, you may eventually need to add your own menus and menu items to the pull-down menus. To add a new menu, follow these steps:

1. Double-click the `MainMenu.xib` file stored in the Resources folder. Interface Builder appears.

2. Double-click the Main Menu icon inside the MainMenu.xib window to display the pull-down menu bar.

3. Choose Tools ➤ Library to open the Library window.

4. Scroll through the Object Library until you find a Menu Item object such as File Menu Item or Text Menu Item, as shown in Figure 21–5.

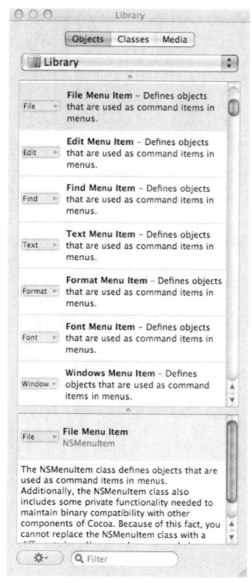

Figure 21–5. *The Menu Item objects appear in the Object Library.*

5. Drag the Menu Item object over your pull-down menu bar. A vertical line indicates where your newly added menu will appear when you release the mouse button.

6. Release the mouse button to drop the menu in place.

7. Double-click the menu to highlight it.

8. Type or edit the menu title.

9. Choose File ➤ Save or press ⌘S to save your changes.

To add a new menu item to an existing pull-down menu, follow these steps:

1. Double-click the `MainMenu.xib` file stored in the Resources folder. Interface Builder appears.

2. Double-click the Main Menu icon inside the MainMenu.xib window to display the pull-down menu bar.

3. Click the menu to which you want to add a new item. So, for example, if you want to add a new menu item to the File menu, you would click the File menu to display its menu.

4. Choose Tools ➤ Library to open the Library window.

5. Scroll through the Object Library until you find the Menu Item object, as shown in Figure 21–6.

Figure 21–6. *The Menu Item object in the Library window.*

6. Drag the Menu Item object over the pull-down menu. A horizontal line indicates where your menu item will appear when you release the mouse button.

7. Release the mouse button to drop the menu item in place.

8. Double-click your newly added menu item.

9. Type or edit the menu item.

10. Choose File ➤ Save or press ⌘S to save your changes.

Linking Menu Commands

After creating a new menu item, you need to connect it to a method to make it actually work. Just as you can connect a push button or any user interface object to a method, you can connect a menu item to a method in the same fashion.

To see how to connect a menu item to a method, follow these steps:

1. Open the MyTest program that you modified in the previous chapter.

2. Click the MyTestAppDelegate.h file stored in the Classes folder and modify the code as follows:

```
#import <Cocoa/Cocoa.h>

@interface MyTestAppDelegate : NSObject <NSApplicationDelegate> {
    NSWindow *window;

}

@property (retain) IBOutlet NSWindow *window;

-(IBAction) displayDialog:(id)sender;

@end
```

3. Choose File ➤ Save or press ⌘S to save your changes.

4. Click the MyTestAppDelegate.m file stored in the Classes folder and modify the code as follows:

```
#import "MyTestAppDelegate.h"

@implementation MyTestAppDelegate

@synthesize window;

- (void)applicationDidFinishLaunching:(NSNotification *)aNotification {
    // Insert code here to initialize your application

}

- (void)dealloc {

    [window release];
    [super dealloc];
}

-(IBAction) displayDialog:(id)sender
{
    NSAlert *alert = [[NSAlert alloc] init];
    alert.alertStyle = NSWarningAlertStyle;

    alert.messageText = @"It worked!";
    alert.informativeText = @"The displayDialog method ran.";
```

```
    [alert runModal];
    [alert release];
}

@end
```

5. Choose File ➤ Save or press ⌘S to save your changes.

6. Double-click the `MainMenu.xib` file stored in the Resources folder to open your user interface.

7. Double-click the Main Menu icon inside the `MainMenu.xib` window to display the pull-down menu bar.

8. Click the File menu to display its pull-down menu.

9. Choose Tools ➤ Library to open the Library window.

10. Scroll through the Object Library until you see the Menu Item object.

11. Drag the Menu Item object and drop it near the bottom of the File menu.

12. Right-click the menu item you just added. A heads-up window appears, as shown in Figure 21–7.

Figure 21–7. *The Connections window lets you link a menu item to a method.*

NOTE: You can also choose Tools ➤ Connections Inspector to view the Connections Inspector window.

13. Move the mouse pointer over the circle that appears to the right of `selector` under the Sent Actions heading.

14. Click and drag the mouse pointer over the My Test App Delegate icon. A menu of methods appears.

15. Choose `displayDialog`.

16. Choose File ➤ Save or press ⌘S to save your changes.

17. Switch to Xcode and click the Build and Run button or choose Build ➤ Build and Run. As long as you didn't mistype anything, you should see a blank window pop up.

18. Choose File ➤ Item. An alert dialog box pops up to let you know that the `displayDialog` method ran.

19. Click the OK button to make the alert dialog box go away.

20. Quit your program.

Assigning Keystrokes to a Menu Item

To make choosing a particular menu command easy, many programs assign shortcut keystrokes. Instead of clicking a menu title to display a pull-down menu, and then clicking a command, the user can just press the assigned keystroke combination and your program chooses the command without requiring the user to fumble with the pull-down menus at all.

To assign a keystroke combination to a menu command, follow these steps:

1. Double-click the `MainMenu.xib` file that contains the pull-down menu in which the menu command appears.

2. Double-click the Main Menu icon inside the `MainMenu.xib` window to display the pull-down menu bar.

3. Click the menu to display the pull-down menu of menu items.

4. Click a menu item to which you want to assign a keystroke.

5. Choose Tools ➤ Attributes Inspector to display the Attributes Inspector window.

6. Click in the Key Equiv. field.

7. Press the keystroke combination you want to assign to the currently selected command. Make sure you choose a keystroke combination that isn't used by another command. Your chosen keystroke combination appears on the pull-down menu, as shown in Figure 21–8. Now when your program runs, users can choose the command by pressing its keystroke combination.

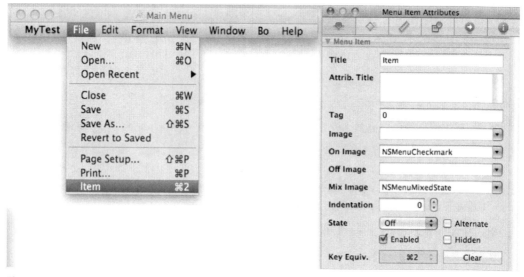

Figure 21–8. *Pressing keys in the Keystroke Equiv. field displays those keystrokes on the pull-down menu.*

Summary

When you need to provide the user with multiple commands, you probably won't want to clutter your user interface with multiple push buttons or check boxes. Instead, you can store related commands in their own menu that users can pull down when they want to choose a particular command.

To make choosing a menu command even easier, you can assign a unique keystroke combination to that command. Then a user can just press that keystroke combination to choose the command without displaying the pull-down menu at all.

To edit, rearrange, or delete menu titles and menu commands, you can click the pull-down menu directly. If you want to add new menus or menu items, just drag a menu or menu item from the Library window and drop it directly on the pull-down menu bar or on a menu.

In general, use the standard commands in every menu whenever possible, such as the Cut, Copy, and Paste commands under the Edit menu or the Save, Print, and Open commands under the File menu. Users expect to find common commands under certain menu titles, so delete, edit, or move them only when absolutely necessary to ensure that your program looks and behaves like a typical Mac application.

Chapter **22**

Designing Your Own Programs

Every program starts off with a problem. Typically the best problems for computers to solve involve something that humans find tedious, tiresome, or error-prone to do themselves. For example, people used to calculate formulas by hand. If they made one mistake, any formulas relying on the flawed data would calculate incorrect answers. To make calculating multiple formulas faster and more accurate, programmers invented the spreadsheet.

The invention of the spreadsheet provided a general-purpose tool that a wide variety of people could use, from business executives calculating financial results to engineers calculating scientific results. However, programs can also solve more specific types of problems.

A lottery-number prediction program might store all previously drawn numbers and calculate which numbers appear most often. Based on this information, the program could show only those numbers with the highest chance of getting picked, theoretically giving you a greater chance of winning the lottery.

Whether you want to create a general-purpose tool like a spreadsheet or a more specialized tool like a lottery number predictor, the goal of any program is always the same. Identify a problem, define how to solve this problem, and then write step-by-step instructions to create a program.

When creating a program, the most important work isn't the actual writing of commands in a specific programming language like Objective-C. Instead, the most important work involves identifying the problem to solve, identifying the best way to solve this problem in a way that's easiest for the user, and identifying how to turn this design into an actual working program.

> **NOTE:** One major reason why programs fail is because the programmers never identified a clear problem to solve. If a program can't solve a problem, then there's no use for that program.

Identifying the Right Problem

The best person to identify the problem you need to solve is the person who will be using your program. If you identify a problem and rush out to write a program to solve that problem, you may later find out that you've solved a problem that isn't that important after all.

For example, suppose you wrote a program that stored data on a racehorse. Based on this horse's past six races and the racing history of all the other horses in the same race, your program might calculate which horse seems mostly likely to win.

However, what the user might really want is a program that uses the current odds to determine the type of bet with the highest probability of winning and returning the highest payoff possible. Betting on the winning horse might be pointless if the payoff is low. However, betting on a horse to come in second or third might pay far more if that horse had high odds.

Therefore, the real problem isn't picking the winning horse but in choosing the horse most likely to return the highest payoff, which may not always be the winning horse. The real goal is to make the most money with the highest probability of success. If you fail to identify the real problem your users want solved, you'll fail to meet the needs of your customers.

The key to identifying the real problem your program should solve is to simply ask the potential users of your program what they really need.

If you fail to ask the users what they need, chances are good that you'll create a program that solves the wrong problem. As a result, users won't find your program useful, nobody will want it, and you'll have wasted your time creating it.

Since users may not be clear on exactly what they want, always ask what's the most painful problem that annoys people the most and causes the most frustration and agony. Once you can identify this single, most pressing problem, the next step is deciding whether this problem can be solved with a program and, if so, how to solve this problem in a way that provides the most relief to the user.

What Programs Do Well

Every problem is also an opportunity, but not every problem can be solved with a computer program. If you own a bar and your problem is that underage people keep trying to sneak into your building, a computer program probably won't be as helpful as hiring extra doormen and bouncers to guard all the doors and check the IDs of everyone who wants to get in.

Any problem that involves a physical presence (like a security guard) is probably best left for real people. However, any problem that requires mental activities that need speed and accuracy are perfect problems for a computer program to solve.

For example, how do you calculate the best time to buy a particular stock during the hectic commotion of the stock market? For a human, trying to capture rapidly changing data and make sense of it means taking too long with a high risk of inaccuracy. For a computer, making sense of rapidly changing data and calculating a result is simple and easy.

The two keys of most programs are speed and accuracy. A program designed to navigate an airplane must be accurate and fast. Even the most accurate airplane computer is worthless if it can't calculate an alternate path around a mountain in time.

Computers excel at speed and accuracy, which makes them perfect for any tedious jobs that humans would rather not do. Before spreadsheets, people had to use adding machines to calculate long lists of figures. Before word processors, people had to use typewriters and physical blocks of letters to create text and print newspapers. Before databases, people had to use filing cabinets stuffed with drawers full of files that were nearly impossible to search quickly and accurately.

Once you've identified a mental problem solvable by a computer, the next step is to determine how to solve it as a computer program.

Designing the Program Structure

In the past, once programmers identified a problem, they would rush off and start writing a program to solve that problem, often without the feedback of the people who would use that program. The end result would be a lot of wasted effort creating a program that didn't quite do what anyone wanted.

To avoid this trap, it's best to design your program on paper because it's easier and less time-consuming to scribble something on a sheet of paper than it is to write a program on your computer, only to throw away all your work afterward because you did it wrong.

There is no one best way to design a program, but there are general principles for designing a program. One common way to design a program involves breaking it into three parts called *model-view-controller*.

- The model portion does all the calculations that make your program create some useful result.

- The view portion displays your user interface that accepts input from the user and displays information back to the user.

- The controller portion acts as the bridge between the view and the model. The controller takes data from the user interface (the view) and sends it to the model to calculate a new result. The model returns its calculation to the controller, which passes the data back to the user interface (the view).

By dividing a program into a model, view, and controller, you can focus on different parts of your program at a time.

The Model

The model portion of your program typically includes one or more Objective-C class files that do all the necessary calculations so your program can solve a specific problem. The purpose of the model is to isolate the calculation portion of your program so it operates completely independently of the user interface. This gives you the flexibility to change the user interface without worrying about making any changes to the model portion of your program.

The Controller

The controller portion of your program consists of one or more Objective-C class files, which act as a middleman in between your model and your view portion of your program. The idea is to isolate your model portion of your program from the view portion of your program (the user interface). Whenever the model needs to interact with the user interface, it sends data or requests information through the controller.

The only way the model ever communicates with the view is through a controller. This lets you replace or modify the view at any time without worrying about its effect on the model. Likewise, this also lets you modify the model at any time without worrying about its effects on the view. Any time you make a change to either the model or the view, you just have to worry about making the appropriate changes to the controller.

Essentially, the controller keeps the model and the view separate so they act more like building blocks that can be easily swapped in and out of your program.

The View

The view portion of your program typically includes one or more .xib files that contain your user interface. In many cases, you can create a mock-up of your program's user interface and show this mock-up to potential users to get their feedback, as shown in Figure 22–1.

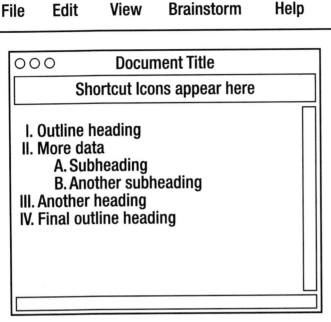

Figure 22–1. *Designing a mock-up of a user interface can be as simple as drawing it on a piece of paper or on the computer.*

A mock-up of your program's user interface lets you create a rough draft of your program without expending any effort writing an actual program. Instead, you just draw pictures, show users what the program could look like, and get their feedback on what's missing, what should be rearranged, and what should be eliminated altogether.

After potential users have examined your user interface and determined what and how it should work, you can take the next step and create that actual user interface as a .xib file using Interface Builder, as shown in Figure 22–2.

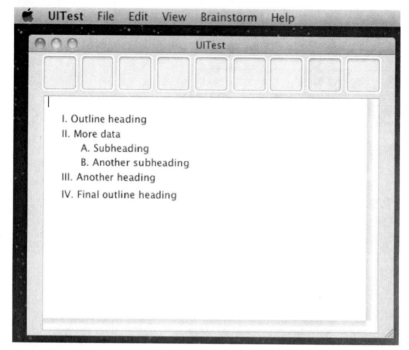

Figure 22–2. *Turning a rough draft of a user interface into an actual* `.xib` *file*

Although your program at this point will show only what your program might look like, it won't actually do anything. With a mock-up of your program, you can focus on the main features of your program and how they should work.

Remember, designing your user interface can be one of the hardest parts to creating your program because if your program works perfectly but nobody likes or can understand your program's user interface, nobody will want to use your program. Since there is no scientific measurement for what makes a good user interface, consider the following tips for creating your program's user interface.

Be Conventional

When designing a program, follow the basic conventions that users expect from a Mac program. That includes pull-down menus with familiar menu titles in the expected order (such as the File menu first followed by Edit, View, Window, and Help) along with windows and user interface elements that behave identically to other Mac programs.

Using the elements of a typical Mac user interface offers two huge benefits. First, users can immediately become familiar with the basic ways of controlling your program. As a result, they'll be more receptive to using it and will know how to find and choose commands to control your program.

Second, creating your user interface out of common Mac user interface elements also makes your job, as a programmer, much easier since Apple has already written the code needed to create common user interface elements such as windows and pull-down menus. All you have to do is connect these existing user interface elements to your program, and you can create a working program with little or no additional coding whatsoever.

Be Imitative

Look at some of your own favorite programs and ask yourself what makes them so useful. Chances are good that for each program you like, there are probably a handful of rival programs offering the same, or maybe even more, features, so what is it about the program you use that makes it stand out?

You might like the way the program looks on the screen because the information and commands you need are thoughtfully laid out. Maybe you like the way the program guides you from one task to another, making the transition effortlessly while showing you relationships between diverse information that you may never have spotted on your own. Perhaps you like the way a program provides power features for advanced users yet remains accessible to novices.

Whatever you find useful in other programs, see whether you can adapt those designs in your own program. By doing so, you can take the best features from multiple programs and use them to create a great program that other users will rave about.

Besides looking at other programs to imitate, look at physical, real-world objects that represent tools that users might already be familiar using. For example, the Stickies program on the Mac mimics those familiar sticky notes that people use to jot down notes and stick them on desks, monitors, and chairs to remind them of something. If you're creating a program that lets users jot down ideas and notes, modeling your program after physical sticky notes can make your program easier for users to understand and use, as shown in Figure 22–3.

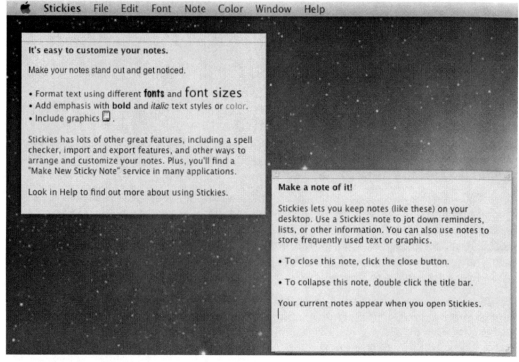

Figure 22–3. *The Stickies program mimics sticky notes that people use in an office.*

By studying existing programs and real-world tools that your program may be mimicking, you may be able to discover the optimum appearance for displaying information and allowing input for your program.

Be Unusual

Closely adhering to conventional user interface designs like pull-down menus and resizable windows can make your program more comfortable and easier to use. However, take a moment to think how your program might need to behave in unconventional ways that actually might make your program easier and more intuitive to use.

For example, suppose your program displayed a 3D image of a piece of equipment such as a tractor or a missile. You could display pull-down menu commands that would let you rotate that image, you might display a horizontal and vertical slider that would let you rotate that image by dragging the mouse, or you could throw all conventional user interface ideas away and design your own user interface that lets the user directly manipulate the item by dragging the mouse or by tracking finger gestures on a trackpad.

By offering a specialized way of interacting with the 3D image, your program might not look and work like anything the user might have ever used before, but it could make your program more intuitive and simpler to use.

As a general rule, use standard user interface elements whenever possible, but don't be afraid to create custom interface elements. Creating such custom user interface elements will take time to design, write, and test, but the end result can be a user interface uniquely customized for your users and program.

Thinking in Objects

With object-oriented programming languages like Objective-C, you need to think of how to divide your program into objects. Ideally, each object should represent a distinct part of your program.

For example, if you were creating a program to create and manipulate outlines, each outline heading might be an object. If you were creating a video game, each displayed item, such as a character or an obstacle, could also be an object.

Don't worry about designing your program into objects perfectly at this point. Just identify the most likely parts of your program that can be represented by objects and then decide what type of properties and methods those objects might need.

An object representing an outline heading might need properties that define the text to display and its position in that outline on the screen. Such an outline heading object might also need a method for moving the heading and a second method for changing the formatting of the text.

An object representing a video game monster might need a property that represents its health and a method for moving and attacking another item on the screen.

The goal isn't to define every method and property for each object in your program, but to slowly flesh out the design of your program so you know how the different parts of your program might interact with each other.

There is no one best way to divide a program into objects. However, you should always strive to write as little code as possible to make your program easier to write. The easier a program is to write, the easier it will be to fix and modify, improving its reliability.

To achieve this goal, find the commonalities of the different parts of your program. For example, the common parts of a video game might be an object that represents a monster and an object that represents the player. Both the player and the monster need to move and fight, so it's natural to create a single class that contains a health property and a move method, as shown in Figure 22–4.

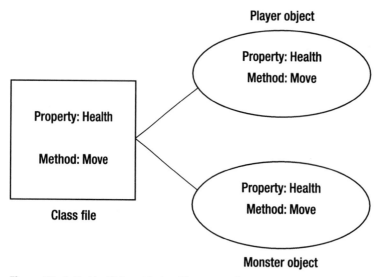

Figure 22–4. *By identifying objects with common features, you can design a single class to represent those objects.*

Searching for common features among objects means you can write less duplicate code. After you've identified the main types of objects in your program, you can go to the next step of actually writing Objective-C code to create your class files.

Picking a Data Structure

With a rough design of your program and a clear idea what problem your program needs to solve, another step to completing your program is deciding how your program will work. First you must consider what type of data your program will accept and manipulate to create a useful result for the user.

The type of data your program needs to store and the way it manipulates that data can determine the type of data structure you use. Choose the right data structure, and your program can be easy to write. Choose the wrong data structure, and you could wind up writing a lot of extra (and unnecessary) code to make your program work.

For example, suppose you created a simple database program for storing names. One option might be to store each name as a separate variable. Unfortunately, you may not know how many possible names someone might want to store, so you would have to create a large number of variables to store a fixed number of possible names, or you could choose a more flexible data structure such as an array, which can grow as the user adds more data.

By choosing the right data structure, you can greatly simplify the way your program works by writing less code and creating a more reliable program in the process.

Creating an Algorithm

Besides choosing the best data structure for your program, you must also know how to solve a particular problem step-by-step. (If you don't know how to do this, then you need to find someone who does because if no one knows how to solve a particular problem, the computer will never know how to do it either.)

The step-by-step instructions you need to solve a problem are called an *algorithm*. Since there might be a million different ways to solve the same problem, your goal is to find an algorithm that starts with the data a user might input into your program and then manipulates that data to achieve a specific result.

First, identify the end result. Next, identify the data that your program will start with. Now your goal is to find all the missing steps in between.

The type of algorithm you create depends on the type of data structures your program uses, so part of your algorithm will need to know how to accept data from the user, how to store data in a data structure, and how to send a new calculated result back to the user again.

One way to create an algorithm is to pick typical data that your program might accept, determine the result your program would calculate from this initial data, and then write out the steps you would need to solve that problem using a pencil and paper.

For example, suppose you wanted to implement a simple encryption algorithm known as the Caesar Cipher. The basic idea behind this cipher is to shift one letter a fixed number of places. So if you shifted all letters to the right by three places, the letter *D* would actually represent the letter *A*, the letter *E* would represent the letter *B*, and so on. Shifting all letters three places to the right would create a coded message "EDG" that would represent the actual message "BAD."

To implement such a simple letter substitution algorithm, we could start by assigning each letter a number. The number 0 would represent the letter *A*, the number 1 would represent the letter *B*, and so on. This could easily be implemented by creating an array, storing each letter in that array, and using the array index to represent each letter where the letter *A* would appear in the first array element, which has an index of 0, the letter *B* would appear in the second array element, which has an index of 1, and so on, as shown in Figure 22–5.

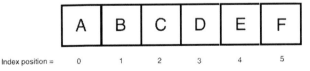

Figure 22–5. *The index position of an array can represent each stored letter.*

To encrypt a message, you need to define how many letters to shift to the right, which can be any value ranging from 1 to 25. (Shifting 0 places or 26 places essentially means that each letter represents itself, which would obviously not hide the actual message.)

To encrypt a message, the program needs two pieces of data:

- How many places to shift a letter to the right
- Which letter to shift

To encrypt a letter, you can use this simple encryption formula:

$$\text{Encryption}_n (x) = (x + n) \bmod 26$$

With this formula, the variable x represents the letter to shift (where 0 represents the letter A, 1 represents the letter B, and so on), and n represents the number of places to shift.

Defining an Algorithm

When you know what problem you want to solve and how you can solve it, you should write out those steps to look for any flaws in your logic. Essentially the steps to solve the problem of encrypting a text string might look like this:

1. Count the number of characters in a string, and store this string length in a variable.

2. Identify how many places to shift to the right, and store this numeric value in the n variable.

3. Strip away the first letter of the string, and save the remaining text in separate variables.

4. Associate the stripped character with its associated number representation, such as 0 for the letter A, 1 for the letter B, and so on. Store this numeric value into a variable.

5. Use the encryption formula to determine which letter to replace the current letter. So if the computer is encrypting the letter C, it would first store the value of 2 (representing the letter C). Next, it would store the number of places to shift in the n variable. If the value of n were equal to 4, the encryption formula would look like this:

$$\text{Encryption}_4 (2) = (2 + 4) \bmod 26$$

$$= 6$$

So, the encryption formula would replace the letter C with the letter represented by the number 6. Take this number and replace it with the letter associated with that number, such as replacing the number 6 with the letter G.

6. Repeat steps 3–5 using the string length as a counting variable.

7. Print out the final result:

Encoded text = GEX

Once you've created an algorithm, go through the steps manually to verify that they work. You may know how to solve a problem, but you may not have clearly stated all of the steps needed to solve that particular problem. By forcing yourself to follow the exact steps a computer would follow, you can see if you're missing a step or if a particular step isn't working right.

Ideally, have someone else go through the steps because that person won't have all the assumptions and knowledge about the algorithm beforehand, so they'll be more likely to follow your instructions literally, which is exactly how the computer will do it too.

Writing Pseudocode

When you're satisfied that your instructions are both accurate and complete, the next step is to translate your algorithm into a simplified programming language called *pseudocode*. The purpose of pseudocode is to write instructions like a programming language but without worrying about proper syntax or commands.

Examining the previous algorithm, you could break this down into pseudocode like this:

```
inputText = String to encrypt.
n = number of characters to shift
lengthString = length (inputText)
for I = 1 to lengthString)
        strippedText = first letter of inputText
        remainderText = remaining characters of inputText
        letterValue = numeric equivalent (strippedText)
        encryptedText = (letterValue + n) mod 26
        cipherText = letter equivalent (encryptedText)
        encodedText = encodedText + cipherText
Print encodedText.
```

The goal of translating your algorithm from a wordy description into shorter, more computer-like pseudocode is to gradually translate your algorithm from English to actual Objective-C code.

Writing Actual Code

When you've defined the steps to solving a problem using pseudocode, you can convert your defined steps and turn them into actual commands in any programming language. For Mac programming using Xcode, you'll be using Objective-C code. If you create a new Mac OS X Cocoa application, you can edit the AppDelegate.m file's applicationDidFinishLaunching method with the following Objective-C code:

```
- (void)applicationDidFinishLaunching:(NSNotification *)aNotification {
    // Insert code here to initialize your application
    NSString *object1 = @"A";
    NSString *object2 = @"B";
    NSString *object3 = @"C";
    NSString *object4 = @"D";
    NSString *object5 = @"E";
    NSString *object6 = @"F";
    NSString *object7 = @"G";
```

```
            NSString *object8 = @"H";
            NSString *object9 = @"I";
            NSString *object10 = @"J";
            NSString *object11 = @"K";
            NSString *object12 = @"L";
            NSString *object13 = @"M";
            NSString *object14 = @"N";
            NSString *object15 = @"O";
            NSString *object16 = @"P";
            NSString *object17 = @"Q";
            NSString *object18 = @"R";
            NSString *object19 = @"S";
            NSString *object20 = @"T";
            NSString *object21 = @"U";
            NSString *object22 = @"V";
            NSString *object23 = @"W";
            NSString *object24 = @"X";
            NSString *object25 = @"Y";
            NSString *object26 = @"Z";

        NSArray *letterArray;
        letterArray = [NSArray arrayWithObjects: object1, object2, object3, object4,
    object5, object6, object7, object8, object9, object10, object11, object12, object13,
    object14, object15, object16, object17, object18, object19, object20, object21,
    object22, object23, object24, object25, object26, nil];

        NSString *inputText;
        inputText = @"CAT";
        int lengthString = [inputText length];

        NSMutableString *plainText; // = [[NSMutableString alloc] init];
        plainText = [NSMutableString stringWithString: inputText];

        NSMutableString *encodedText; // = [[NSMutableString alloc] init];
        encodedText = [NSMutableString stringWithString: @""];

        NSString *remainderText;
        NSString *strippedText;
        NSInteger letterValue;
        NSInteger encryptedText;
        NSString *cipherText;
        NSInteger n; //Shift
        n = 4;

        //Loop -- Strip away first character and leave remaining characters behind
        int i;
        for (i = 1; i <= lengthString; i++)
        {
            remainderText = [plainText substringFromIndex:1];
            strippedText = [plainText substringToIndex:1];

            NSLog (@"Stripped character = %@", strippedText);
            plainText = [NSMutableString stringWithString: remainderText];
            NSLog (@"Plaintext left = %@", plainText);

            letterValue = [letterArray indexOfObject: strippedText];
```

```
    encryptedText = (letterValue + n) % 26;

    cipherText = [letterArray objectAtIndex: encryptedText];
    [encodedText appendString: cipherText];
    NSLog (@"Encoded text = %@", encodedText);
    NSLog (@"**********");
    }
    // End loop
}
```

This Objective-C code stores the letters of the alphabet into an array where the index position of each character represents its numeric value, so the letter *A* is located at index position 0, the letter *B* is located at index position 1, and so on.

This code also uses a fixed value for the input text (CAT) and the number of places to shift the characters (4). Ideally, you'll want to allow the user to input different values for the text and the number of places to shift. If you ran this code, the NSLog commands would print the following to show you how the program strips away each character of the input text and creates a new coded version of that text, converting the string CAT to GEX:

```
2010-12-12 16:08:33.418 Cipher[27523:a0f] Stripped character = C
2010-12-12 16:08:33.420 Cipher[27523:a0f] Plaintext left = AT
2010-12-12 16:08:33.421 Cipher[27523:a0f] Encoded text = G
2010-12-12 16:08:33.421 Cipher[27523:a0f] **********
2010-12-12 16:08:33.422 Cipher[27523:a0f] Stripped character = A
2010-12-12 16:08:33.423 Cipher[27523:a0f] Plaintext left = T
2010-12-12 16:08:33.424 Cipher[27523:a0f] Encoded text = GE
2010-12-12 16:08:33.424 Cipher[27523:a0f] **********
2010-12-12 16:08:33.425 Cipher[27523:a0f] Stripped character = T
2010-12-12 16:08:33.425 Cipher[27523:a0f] Plaintext left =
2010-12-12 16:08:33.426 Cipher[27523:a0f] Encoded text = GEX
2010-12-12 16:08:33.426 Cipher[27523:a0f] **********
```

Prototyping Your Program

For small projects, you can start creating a simple version of your program right away. However, for a large project, you may want to take one additional step and create a prototype of your program.

Just as architects often build miniature skyscrapers out of cardboard or plastic to help them visualize the final appearance of a project, so do computer programmers create a prototype of their program using a variety of tools. When you create a prototype of a program, your prototype simply shows what the program will look like and how it will behave, but your prototype isn't an actual program.

For example, you might create a rough design of your program using a presentation program like PowerPoint or Keynote where each slide represents a different part of your user interface. Clicking various commands or buttons displays a different slide, depending on how your program works.

Prototyping lets potential users see and use your program so they can provide feedback on the user interface, what features the program needs, and what features may need to be changed or eliminated altogether.

Other prototyping tools might include simple drawing and paint programs or web page–designing programs that let you create a series of web pages that represent different appearances of your working program. You could even create a prototype of your program by simply drawing pictures on different sheets of paper.

The goal of a prototype is to create the appearance and behavior of your program without forcing you to spend a lot of time creating that prototype so it doesn't matter how you create your prototype. This lets you freely modify and change the prototype until it behaves and looks exactly the way you want. After you've finalized the design of your program by creating a prototype, then you'll be ready to create your actual program.

Writing and Testing Your Program

You're not going to write your entire program in one try. Instead, you'll gradually create a program and add more features one by one until you finally create the program you initially envisioned. Think of creating a program like shaping a clay sculpture. You would never take a chunk of clay, throw it on a table, and expect it to be perfect right away. Instead, you'd take that lump of clay and gradually shape it into the form you want. You might add a little extra clay here, remove a chunk of clay there, and move clay to one spot and slap it on a different spot.

In the same way that you'd create a work of art by starting with a lump of clay and gradually shaping it into your final design, so will you gradually create your program a little bit at a time. Testing your program doesn't mean waiting until the whole thing is complete. Instead, testing means you create a little bit of your program, test to make sure that the little bit you added works as expected, and then add another little bit to your program and test how that newly added portion of your program works.

Each time you add a new portion to your program, you'll need to test that new portion to make sure it works correctly and then test how that new portion interacts with the rest of your program.

When writing your program, divide your program into specialized parts and reusable parts. A specialized part of your program might perform unique calculations, such as a stock market prediction program that uses an algorithm to analyze stock price data and calculate which stocks will likely rise in the near future.

A reusable part of your program might be the part of your program that retrieves data from the Internet, such as stock market data. Retrieving data from the Internet might be handy to use in another program, such as one that needs to retrieve updated weather reports from the Internet. By clearly dividing your program into specialized and reusable, general portions, you can gradually create a library of your general-purpose code so you can plug each bit into future programs, allowing you to create new programs quickly, easily, and reliably.

By building your program slowly and testing each newly added feature along the way, you can catch problems as they occur and fix them before you rush ahead and create the entire program and wind up spending all your time tracking down and fixing bugs in your software.

The first goal of your program is to get it to work. Once you've gotten one part of your program to work, you can see what needs to be fixed or modified. Maybe your program doesn't look the way you wanted, so you might need to change the user interface. Maybe the program runs too slowly. Then you might need to use a different data structure or create a better algorithm.

The more testing you can do, the better, so you can spot problems with your program before releasing it to your customers and users. (Fixing a bug-ridden program after you've sold or distributed it to people is rarely the quickest way to make others happy or look favorably at your programming abilities.)

When you've created a workable program with the majority of its features available, you might start testing your program with other people so they can give you feedback on what they like, what they didn't like, and what changes you should make. At this point, you can choose to make those changes (or ignore them if you have a good reason for doing so), and then after you modify your program, you can repeat the whole testing cycle all over again.

Repeat several times, and you'll gradually create a working program that you can give away or sell to others. The whole process of designing, creating, and testing a program can be frustrating, fun, tiresome, and challenging all at the same time.

The more programs you create, the more confident you'll get and the more experience you'll have to avoid problems and take shortcuts to simplify your program. Like any skill, designing, writing, and testing a program may seem hard and confusing at first, but after enough practice, you'll soon find that it's not as difficult as you might have initially thought.

Summary

The most important task of writing a program is identifying the most important problem to solve. Once you've identified an important problem, you need to determine if it's even possible for a computer program to solve it. If so, then you'll be ready to start designing your program.

Designing your program is more than just designing a pretty user interface. The design of your program includes its structure, the data structures you use, the way you divide it into multiple objects, and the algorithm you use to solve a particular problem. None of these structural designs of your program may be readily seen by the user, but if they're missing or faulty, the user will know it through a slow, unresponsive, flawed program that doesn't work correctly.

Writing your program should be the last task you tackle. Before you write even one line of code, it's best to plan ahead how your program will work, how it will solve a particular problem, and, more importantly, what problem your program will solve in the first place.

Your program's user interface is all that people will see of your program, so it's important to design one that's easy to understand and use. Most of the time, designing a user interface involves using common interface elements such as dialog boxes, buttons, pull-down menus, and windows. However, you may want to customize your program's user interface to mimic a feature found in another program or to mimic a physical object that your program mimics such as sticky notes or a notepad.

Once you know the type of data your program needs to accept and manipulate, you can choose the best data structure to hold that data. By choosing the correct data structure, you can simplify the way your program works.

Besides choosing the right data structure, you also need to define the algorithm that your program will use to solve a problem, step-by-step. There is no one perfect algorithm for any program, so you just need to worry about creating a simple algorithm that works.

After you've decided on the rough design of your program, you may need to create a simple prototype to give potential users a chance to see what your program can do and how it might look and behave. A prototype can be as simple as drawings on a piece of paper or as sophisticated as a simplified version of your program running on a computer.

Prototyping helps users determine whether your program might be useful and what changes (if any) you might need to make before actually writing your program. After examining your prototype and making any final changes to your design or user interface, you can start writing the actual code to make your program work.

When creating a program, do it a little at a time, and test each new feature as you go along. In general, the more you plan ahead, the less time you'll need to rewrite your code or redesign your user interface. Instead, you'll be able to go from a working prototype to a working program relatively quickly, and the final result will be a working program that you can sell or give away to others.

Chapter 23

Working with Xcode

The most time-consuming part of creating your program will be writing the Objective-C code that makes your program do something. Since you'll be spending much of your time writing, testing, and rewriting code, you'll be using Xcode as your primary tool for hours at a time. Whereas much of this book showed you one way of using Xcode, this chapter will show you several tips and shortcuts for using Xcode that weren't covered previously.

By learning some of Xcode's hidden features, you can save time and work more efficiently. The less time you waste wrestling with Xcode, the more time you'll have to design, write, test, and market your finished program.

Creating New Folders

A single Xcode project typically consists of several files. To help organize those files, Xcode automatically creates several folders such as Classes and Resources. As your program grows in size and complexity, chances are good that even these default folders will get too cluttered. To solve that problem, you may need to create additional folders.

You can create as many folders as you need and name them anything you want. To create a new folder, follow these steps:

1. Right-click the folder in which you want to store your newly created folder. A pop-up menu appears, as shown in Figure 23–1. (If you wanted to create a new folder inside the Classes folder, right-click the Classes folder. If you right-click your project name, you'll be able to create a new folder at the same hierarchical level as the Classes and Resources folders.)

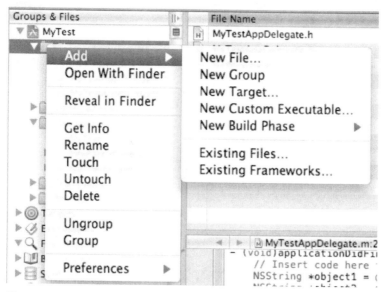

Figure 23–1. *Creating a new folder by right-clicking*

2. Choose Add ➤ New Group. Xcode displays your newly created folder called New Group.

3. Double-click the New Group name. Xcode highlights New Group.

4. Type a new name for your folder. At this point, you can drag and drop files from other folders and store them in your newly created folder.

NOTE: You can delete a folder at any time by right-clicking that folder to display a pop-up menu and then choosing Delete. Make sure you really want to delete a folder, because you'll also delete any files stored in that folder.

Fast Navigation Shortcuts

One of the biggest problems with creating a project is that your data winds up scattered all over the place. To navigate from one part of your program to another, you might have to switch to a different folder, then switch to a different file, then scroll through that file to find the method you want to edit.

To make navigating through your program faster and easier, Xcode offers pop-up buttons and icons that let you switch to a different part of your program quickly, as shown in Figure 23–2.

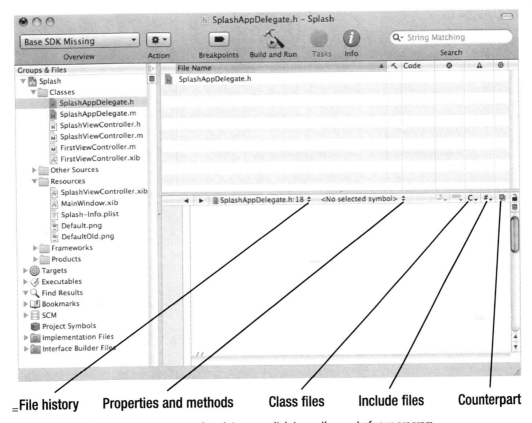

_File history   Properties and methods   Class files   Include files   Counterpart

Figure 23–2. *Clicking a pop-up button or icon lets you switch to another part of your program.*

Using the File History Pop-Up Button

The File History pop-up button stores a list of all the files you've opened. The idea is that if you opened a file once, you'll probably want to open and view that file again. Clicking the File History pop-up button displays a list of your recently opened files along with options to clear the entire history list or define how many files to store, as shown in Figure 23–3.

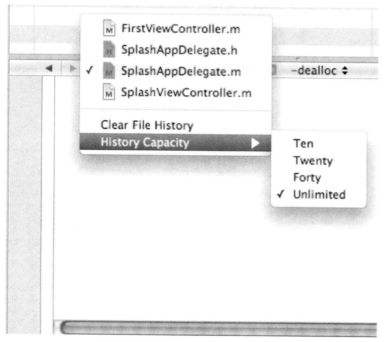

Figure 23–3. *The File History list lets you jump to a previously opened file.*

The File History button displays the currently displayed file plus the line number that the cursor is on, as shown in Figure 23–4.

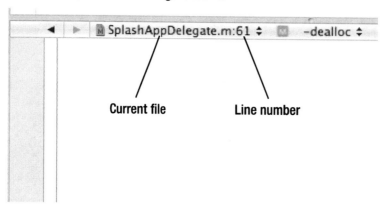

Figure 23–4. *The current file name and line number of the cursor's location appear on the File History pop-up button.*

Using the Properties and Methods Pop-Up Button

When you're viewing a file, you may want to jump to a particular variable (property) or method. Rather than scroll endlessly through the file, you can just click the Properties and Methods pop-up button and view a list of different items, as shown in Figure 23–5.

Figure 23–5. *You can jump to a specific property or method in a file.*

Just click a property or method name and Xcode displays your chosen method or property.

Using the Classes Menu

If you want to see the class that your currently displayed file is based on, click the Classes menu, as shown in Figure 23–6.

Figure 23–6. *The Classes menu displays the superclass of a file.*

Clicking the superclass file displays the Objective-C code for that superclass. In most cases, you probably won't modify this Objective-C code (although you could). Instead, you can study this code to better understand how it works.

Using the Include Menu

Most Objective-C files are interdependent on other files, so if you want to see which files depend on the currently displayed file, click the Include menu, as shown in Figure 23–7.

Figure 23–7. *The Include menu shows your interdependent files.*

Switching Between the .h File and .m File

Every time you create a class, you're actually creating two files: the header (.h) file and the implementation (.m) file. Almost every time you change one file, you'll need to change the other file. To make switching between the header file and implementation file easier, you can use the Counterparts icon by following these steps:

1. Open either the .h or .m file of a class.

2. Click the Counterparts icon. If you opened the .h file, the Counterparts icon displays the accompanying .m file. If you opened the .m file, the Counterparts icon displays the accompanying .h file.

Making Code Easier to Read

The more Objective-C code you write, the harder it can be to read, let alone understand. The problem is that more code means more instructions, which means more possible ways your program can do something wrong.

Ideally, you want to divide large chunks of code into multiple files and then store as little code as possible in each file to make it easier to read. Since this isn't always possible, Xcode offers *code folding*.

Code folding temporarily collapses code, such as a block of code inside a loop, switch statement, or a method, as shown in Figure 23–8.

```
- (void)reallyEmptyTrash:(id)sender {
#pragma unused (sender)
    NSLog(@"Yada.");
}

- (void)radioAction:(id)sender {
    currentRadioSetting = [sender tag];
}

- (void)switch1Action:(id)sender {
#pragma unused (sender)
    currentSwitch1Setting = (currentSwitch1Setting ? NO : YES);
}

- (void)switch2Action:(id)sender {
#pragma unused (sender)
    currentSwitch2Setting = (currentSwitch2Setting ? NO : YES);
}
```

```
- (void)reallyEmptyTrash:(id)sender {...}

- (void)radioAction:(id)sender {...}

- (void)switch1Action:(id)sender {...}

- (void)switch2Action:(id)sender {...}
```

Before code folding   After code folding

Figure 23–8. *Code folding temporarily hides a bracketed block of code.*

To fold code, you have three choices:

- Fold (unfold) all methods and functions

- Fold (unfold) a selected block of code, but leave all other blocks of code unchanged

- Fold (unfold) comments defined by the /* and */ symbols

Folding (or Unfolding) All Methods and Functions

To fold (or unfold) all methods and functions in a file, follow these steps:

1. Click a file that contains Objective-C code.

2. Choose View ➤ Code Folding ➤ Fold (Unfold) Methods & Functions. All methods and functions in the currently displayed file get folded (or unfolded).

Folding (or Unfolding) a Single Block of Code

Xcode can fold any bracketed chunk of code inside a method, loop, if statement, or switch statement. To fold a single block of code in a file, follow these steps:

1. Click a file that contains Objective-C code.

2. Move the cursor anywhere inside the block of code (defined by { } brackets) that you want to fold.

3. Choose View ➤ Code Folding ➤ Fold. Xcode displays an ellipse symbol in between curly brackets to identify folded code, as shown in Figure 23–9.

Figure 23–9. *An ellipse helps identify folded code.*

NOTE: A quick way to fold a block of code is to move the mouse pointer to the left of the method or function name until a gray arrow appears. Then click that gray arrow to fold your code.

To unfold a block of code, you have two options:

- Click the gray arrow that appears to the left of the folded code
- Click the ellipse symbol of the folded code

Folding (or Unfolding) a Block of Comments

If you used the /* and */ symbols to define multiple lines of comments, you can selectively fold (unfold) your comment block by following these steps:

1. Click a file that contains Objective-C code.

2. Move the cursor anywhere inside a comment defined by the /* and */ symbols.

3. Choose View ➤ Code Folding ➤ Fold (Unfold) Comment Blocks.

> **NOTE:** After you have folded a comment block, you can also unfold that comment block by clicking its ellipse symbol or the gray arrow that appears to the left of the folded comment block.

Unfolding Everything

If you want to unfold every method/function and comment block in a file, follow these steps:

4. Click a file that contains Objective-C code.

5. Choose View ➤ Code Folding ➤ Unfold All.

Splitting the Xcode Window

Usually the Xcode window displays either your Objective-C code or your user interface, but not both at the same time. However, you can split the Xcode window in half so you can see both your user interface and the editor split horizontally to show two different files containing Objective-C code, as shown in Figure 23–10.

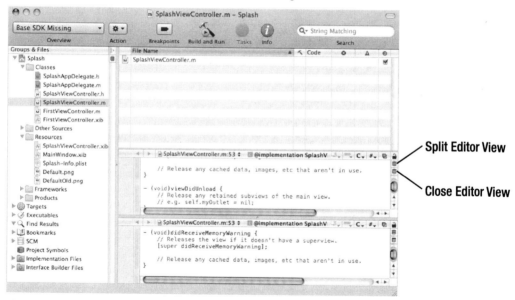

Figure 23–10. *The split view of the Xcode window*

To split the Xcode window, follow these steps:

1. Click the .h or .m file that you want to view.

2. Click the Split Editor View icon (or click the Close Editor View icon).

Summary

Xcode provides plenty of features to make programming easier, but you have to find out what those features are and learn how to use them. Initially as you're learning to program the Mac, just focus on learning the basic features of Xcode so you understand how to write Objective-C code, how to design a user interface, how to connect your user interface to your Objective-C code, and how to use the built-in classes provided for you by Apple's Cocoa framework.

Once you get familiar with these basic steps to Mac programming, then you'll be more comfortable exploring Xcode's other features. By using folders, you can organize your projects exactly the way you want. Then you can use the various pop-up buttons and icons to navigate your way around folders, files, and methods so you can quickly find what you need.

Ideally, you don't want a single file to get too crowded with code or else it will be harder to read, understand, and modify later. Since you can't always avoid this problem, you can do the next best thing and temporarily hide or fold code so only the method or function names appear but the actual code that makes those methods or functions work remains hidden. By selectively folding code, you can hide code that you don't need to examine and just focus on the code that you need to look at right now.

If you have a large monitor, you can even split the Xcode window to show two files. This lets you study two separate files full of Objective-C code.

Of course, you can selectively choose which Xcode features you want to use and ignore the rest. The more you get comfortable using Xcode, the more you'll find how Xcode can make programming even easier and faster than ever before, just as long as you take time to learn the basics of Mac programming first.

Chapter 24

Debugging Your Program

Programs rarely work right the first time. In most cases, you'll need to fix problems as they occur until your program finally works. However, just because a program seems to work doesn't mean that it will work, so that involves more testing and fixing, known as *debugging*.

After you've debugged your program so that it finally does what it's supposed to do without crashing, freezing, or wrecking other files on a computer, you may be ready to ship it. That's the point where you have an actual working program that you can sell and distribute to others.

The main goal of writing any program is to get it to work. Once you get your program to work, you can stop right there and celebrate. Once you release your program to the public, your users are sure to find problems or request additional features, so you'll constantly need to keep updating and fixing your program over time.

Debugging a Program

Trying to write a program correctly the first time is nearly impossible, especially when you're creating anything beyond a trivial program that displays "Hello, world!" on the screen. The bigger your program, the more potential for errors and the more possible problems you'll need to consider.

Debugging any program can be challenging because you may know that your program isn't working right, but you may have no idea *why* it's not working right or even where to look for the problem. In general, there are three types of common bugs or errors to look for:

- Syntax errors
- Logic errors
- Run-time errors

Syntax Errors

A syntax error occurs whenever you misspell a command or put a punctuation mark or symbol in the wrong place. In many cases, Xcode can immediately identify the problem, as shown in Figure 24–1.

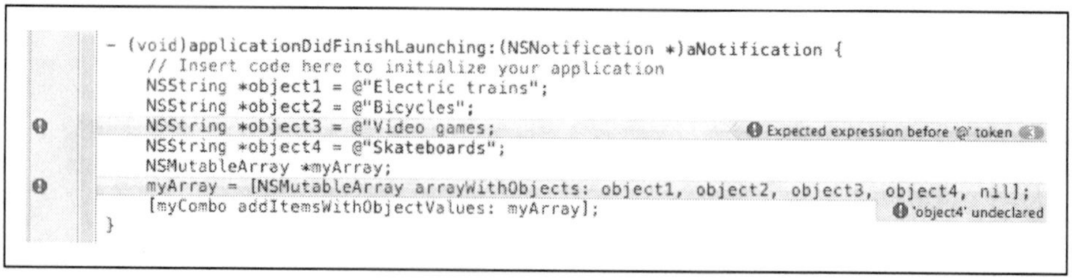

```
- (void)applicationDidFinishLaunching:(NSNotification *)aNotification {
    // Insert code here to initialize your application
    NSString *object1 = @"Electric trains";
    NSString *object2 = @"Bicycles";
    NSString *object3 = @"Video games;                    🔴 Expected expression before '@' token ◀
    NSString *object4 = @"Skateboards";
    NSMutableArray *myArray;
    myArray = [NSMutableArray arrayWithObjects: object1, object2, object3, object4, nil];
    [myCombo addItemsWithObjectValues: myArray];              🔴 'object4' undeclared
}
```

Figure 24–1. *Xcode can alert you to misspellings or unused variables.*

When Xcode highlights a potential problem, it displays a brief message bubble (located to the far right in Figure 24–1) that explains what the problem might be. In most cases, this message bubble may seem confusing because whatever error you created may have affected other parts of your code in an unintended way.

For example, if you forget to type a semicolon at the end of a line, Xcode will treat this line of code as part of the next line of code. Depending on what commands you've typed on each line, the problem can be fixed just by typing a semicolon in the right place, but Xcode's message bubble won't tell you that.

Some more common types of syntax errors that can affect how your program works include the following:

  ▪ Using = instead of == to compare two values

  ▪ Omitting a break statement in a switch statement

  ▪ Omitting the @ character when using strings of the NSString class

  ▪ Omitting the * symbol when using pointers

  ▪ Not creating a matching pair of property variables in the header (.h) file and defining a synthesized variable in the implementation (.m) file

Using One = Instead of == to Compare Values

The single equal sign (=) assigns a value, while the double equal signs (==) compares two values. In other programming languages, it's acceptable to use the single equal sign to assign values and compare values, but in Objective-C, this will prevent your program from working. For example, if you wrote the following:

```
if (myValue = 45)
{
   // Code goes here
}
```

the single equal sign simply assigns the value of 45 to the variable myValue. As a result, it never compares if 45 is equal to the value stored in the myValue variable, so the code inside the if statement always runs, which probably isn't what you want. Because your code works (but not in the intended way), this type of error can be difficult to identify.

One way to ensure that you don't accidentally use a single equal sign instead of a double equal sign is to place an actual value first followed by the variable:

```
if (45 == myValue)
{
    // Code goes here
}
```

Now if you mistakenly use a single equal sign, such as (45 = myValue), Xcode will flag this as an error.

Omitting break Statements in a switch Statement

Omitting the break statement in a switch statement means your code could accidentally run more lines of code than you wanted. For example, suppose you had the following:

```
switch (myValue)
{
    case 45:
        NSLog (@"The value is 45");
        break;
    case -9:
        NSLog (@"The value is -9");
        break;
    default:
        NSLog ("There is no matching value");
        break;
}
```

If the value of myValue was 45, the program would just print this:

```
"The value is 45"
```

However, if you eliminated all the break statements and the value of myValue was 45, the program would print the following, which is probably not what you intended:

```
"The value is 45"
"The value is -9"
"There is no matching value"
```

Omitting @ and *

To identify a string in Objective-C, you must use the @ symbol in front of the string and then enclose the string with double quotation marks like this:

```
@"This is a string"
```

If you fail to put then @ symbol in front of the string or forget to enclose the string with double quotation marks, Xcode won't recognize this as a valid Objective-C string object.

Instead, it will treat it as an ordinary C string, which is probably not what you want since your program won't work right.

Whenever you use a class, such as NSString or NSWindow, make sure you use the asterisk (*) symbol to define a pointer. If you omit this asterisk (*) symbol when declaring a pointer, Xcode won't run your program.

Omitting Matching Pairs in Header (.h) and Implementation (.m) Files

Whenever you change something in your header (.h) file, make sure you make any necessary changes in your corresponding implementation (.m) file (and vice versa).

The header (.h) file typically contains Outlet variable declarations and an accompanying property declaration of that same variable:

```
@interface MyTestAppDelegate : NSObject <NSApplicationDelegate> {
    NSWindow *window;
    NSTextField *nameField;
}

@property (retain) IBOutlet NSWindow *window;
@property (nonatomic, retain) IBOutlet NSTextField *nameField;

@end
```

In this case, window is declared as a pointer to the NSWindow class and then defined as a property as well. In the implementation (.m) file, you must also define this pointer using the @synthesize command:

```
@synthesize window;
```

To modify a class, you must almost always change both the header (.h) and the implementation (.m) files. Because making one change involves editing two separate files, it's easy to forget to change two different files.

Logic Errors

A logic error can be harder to identify because you think you wrote your code correctly but your instructions may not be accurate or complete. As a result, logic errors can be frustrating to track down because you may not know where to look.

The simplest type of logic error is when you declare a variable but never use it, as shown in Figure 24–2. This won't stop or affect your program at all, but it's an error you should fix just to eliminate unnecessary code.

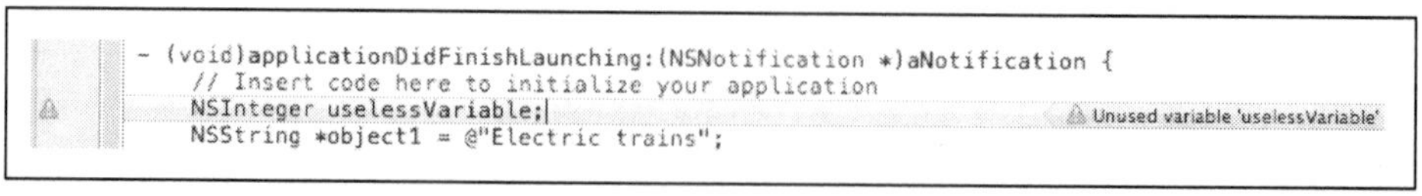

```
- (void)applicationDidFinishLaunching:(NSNotification *)aNotification {
    // Insert code here to initialize your application
    NSInteger uselessVariable;                          ⚠ Unused variable 'uselessVariable'
    NSString *object1 = @"Electric trains";
```

Figure 24–2. *Xcode can identify unused variables.*

One serious type of logic error occurs when your code does exactly what you want it to do but your instructions are wrong. For example, suppose you wanted to run a loop exactly five times using this code:

```
int i;
for (i = 0; i <= 5; i++)
    {
        NSLog (@"The value of i = %i", i);
    }
```

This loop actually runs six times like this:

```
2010-10-08 13:04:47.894 Demo[77461:a0f] The value of i = 0
2010-10-08 13:04:47.898 Demo[77461:a0f] The value of i = 1
2010-10-08 13:04:47.901 Demo[77461:a0f] The value of i = 2
2010-10-08 13:04:47.905 Demo[77461:a0f] The value of i = 3
2010-10-08 13:04:47.906 Demo[77461:a0f] The value of i = 4
2010-10-08 13:04:47.907 Demo[77461:a0f] The value of i = 5
```

Because you think the loop is repeating five times, you may not even consider that this loop is doing something wrong until your program runs and starts messing up.

Logic errors can be one of the hardest types of errors to identify and fix because you already think everything is working but it's not.

Run-Time Errors

A run-time error occurs only when you actually run your program and your program gets data that suddenly confuses it. For example, suppose your program takes a loan amount and divides it by the number of months of the loan, specified by the user. If the user accidentally types in a zero, your program will try to divide the loan amount by zero, and division by zero is impossible. As a result, your program won't work.

Run-time errors are another difficult bug to find and eliminate because your program may work exactly as you expect—except when the program receives the wrong type of data. Unless you test for all possible types of data your program might encounter, you can never be sure that you have eliminated all run-time errors in your program.

To identify possible run-time errors, test your program with a variety of different types of data, using extreme values. For example, if your program expects a number, see what happens if you give your program a huge number like 1 billion. Then see what happens when you give your program an extremely low value such as -0.0000009. If you want your program to accept data within a limited range, you may need to write extra code to check that all data falls within this acceptable range.

Viewing Problems When Debugging

When you build your program, Xcode can highlight two types of errors: warnings and cautions. A warning is an error that can keep your program from working such as a misspelled variable name or a missing semicolon. A warning is an error that won't stop your program from running but could cause problems while your program runs. Xcode highlights warnings with an exclamation mark inside a red circle and identifies cautions with an exclamation mark inside a yellow triangle.

To view each error message in your program, choose Build ➤ Next/Previous Build Warning or Error, or press ⌘= (Next) or ⌘= (Previous).

Simple Debugging Tips

There is no one best way to debug a program because every program and every bug is different. However, there are some simple tricks and techniques you can use to isolate problems in your code. Finding the source of the problem is the hardest part. Fixing that problem, once you've identified what's causing it, is relatively easy in comparison.

Comment Out Your Code

If you suspect that one part of your code might be causing a problem, the simplest way to test your suspicion is to delete the suspicious code. Of course, if the code wasn't the source of the problem, now you have to retype it all back in again.

A simpler solution is to comment out your code. Just turn the suspicious code into a comment that Xcode will ignore. Now if you test your program and the problem goes away, you'll know your commented-out code is the problem. If your program still messes up, then you'll know that your commented-out code is not the problem, so you can examine and comment out another part of your program.

For commenting out one or two lines, you can use the double slash comment symbols:

```
// int i;
for (i = 0; i <= 5; i++)
    {
        NSLog (@"The value of i = %i", i);
    }
```

For commenting out multiple lines of code, you can use a matching pair of /* and */ symbols:

```
/*
int i;
for (i = 0; i <= 5; i++)
    {
        NSLog (@"The value of i = %i", i);
    }
*/
```

> **NOTE:** You can also highlight multiple lines of code and then press ⌘+/ (in other words, press the Command key followed by the + key followed by the / key).

Check the Value of Variables with NSLog

One major source of bugs is when your program somehow changes the value of a variable in an unexpected way. To determine where your program might be changing a variable, you can insert NSLog commands in different parts of your program. These NSLog commands can print out the value of a variable at different points of your program. The moment you see a value change, then you'll know approximately where that change occurred and which code you need to closely examine to identify the source of that problem.

For example, if you suspect a particular method is inadvertently changing the value of a variable, you could place an NSLog command before and after the method call like this:

```
NSLog (@"The value of x = %i", x);
y = calculateResult(x);   // suspect method call
NSLog (@"The value of x = %i", x);
```

If the value of your variable is 10 before the method call and afterward the value of your variable is 8974 when it should have stayed 10, then you'll know that your method is somehow messing up that variable.

Using Breakpoints When Debugging

Ideally to identify problems in your program, you should be able to watch each step of how the program works and behaves at any given time. That way, you can see whether your program is skipping some lines of code by mistake or mangling the value of certain variables in unintended ways.

To give you the ability to examine your code, line by line, Xcode offers breakpoints, which you can place on an individual line of code. A breakpoint simply tells Xcode to run your program and stop when it hits a breakpoint.

Once you're stopped at a breakpoint, you can examine the current value of variables and then choose to step through your program, line by line, to see how the rest of your program works.

Placing (and Removing) a Breakpoint

You can place a breakpoint on any line of code, such as the first line of a method. To place a breakpoint, follow these steps:

1. Click a header (.h) or implementation (.m) file where you want to place a breakpoint.

2. Click in the vertical gray column that appears to the left of the line of code where you want to place a breakpoint, as shown in Figure 24–3.

```
- (void)applicationDidFinishLaunching:(NSNotification *)aNotification {
    // Insert code here to initialize your application
    NSString *object1 = @"Electric trains";
    NSString *object2 = @"Bicycles";
```

Figure 24-3. *You can place a breakpoint on a line of code by clicking the left margin.*

3. Repeat step 2 for each additional breakpoint you want to add to your code. You can add as many breakpoints as you want.

> **NOTE:** To remove a breakpoint, just drag it away from the left margin, and when the mouse pointer displays a puff of smoke icon, release the mouse button to delete your breakpoint, as shown in Figure 24-4.

Figure 24-4. *The puff of smoke icon lets you know that you just removed a breakpoint.*

Using the Debugger

The Debugger window gives you the option of watching variables and stepping through your code after pausing at a breakpoint, as shown in Figure 24-5.

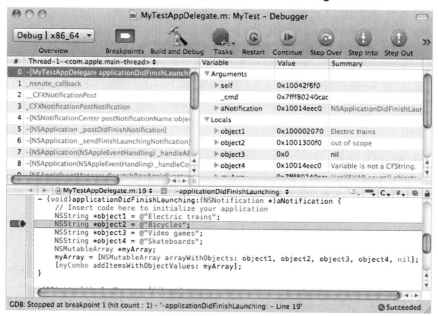

Figure 24-5. *The Debugger window can display the value of variables and let you step through your code one line at a time.*

To open (or hide) the Debugger window, choose Run ➤ Debugger. If you just want to step through your code and not watch how any variables change, you can also open the mini Debugger window by choosing Run ➤ Mini Debugger, as shown in Figure 24–6.

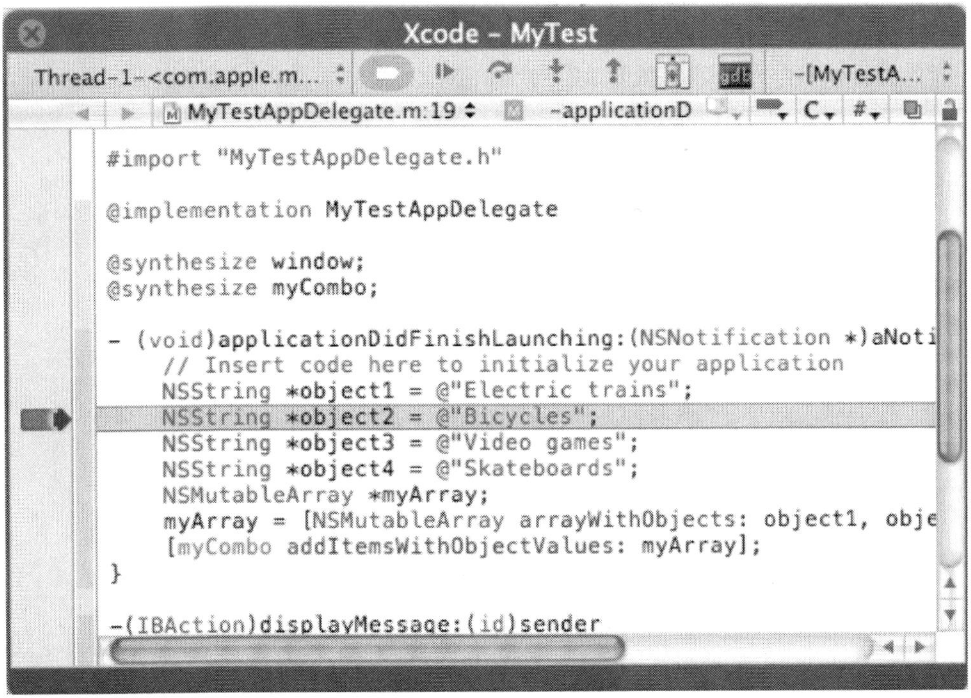

Figure 24–6. *The mini Debugger window lets you step through your code one line at a time.*

Stepping Through Code

After you place one or more breakpoints in your code and build and run your program, your code will temporarily pause at a breakpoint, which you can view in the Debugger or mini Debugger window. At that point, you have several options, as shown in Figure 24–7:

- *Restart*: Starts your program running from the very beginning.

- *Continue*: Runs your program to the next breakpoint. If no other breakpoints exist, it runs your program normally.

- *Step Over*: Steps through each line of code, skipping over method and function calls.

- *Step Into*: Steps through each line of code, but when it reaches a method or function call, it steps through the code stored in that method or function.

- *Step Out*: If you're currently stepping through code in a method or function, Step Out returns you to the code immediately after the method or function call.

Figure 24–7. *The Continue, Step Over, Step In, and Stop Out icons*

To see how the debugger works, follow these steps:

1. Create a new Cocoa Application, and give it a descriptive name like MyTest.

2. Click the MyAppDelegate.m file in Classes folder, and modify the code as follows:

```
#import "MyTestAppDelegate.h"

@implementation MyTestAppDelegate

@synthesize window;

- (void)applicationDidFinishLaunching:(NSNotification *)aNotification {
    // Insert code here to initialize your application
    int i;
    for (i = 0; i <= 5; i++)
    {
        NSLog (@"The value of i = %i", i);
    }
}

- (void)dealloc {
    [window release];
    [super dealloc];
}

@end
```

3. Choose File ➤ Save or press ⌘S to save your changes.

4. Click in the left margin of the first line (int i;) under the applicationDidFinishLaunching method (see Figure 24–4) to set a breakpoint. A breakpoint arrow appears in the left margin.

5. Chose Run ➤ Debugger to open the Debugger window.

6. Click the Build and Debug button. Xcode highlights a line of code, as shown in Figure 24–8.

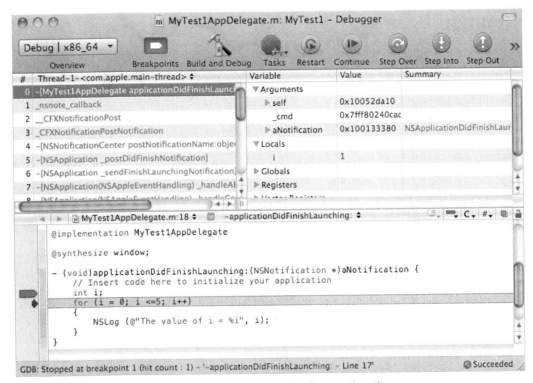

Figure 24–8. *Xcode highlights your code to show you which line is currently active.*

7. Click the Step Over icon to watch Xcode step through your code one line at a time. Notice that each time you click the Step Over icon, the contents of the i variable changes.

8. Click the Continue icon. Xcode runs your program from its currently highlighted line of code to the next breakpoint. If there are no additional breakpoints, the program runs normally.

9. Quit the program by choosing its Quit command.

By using the debugger, you can step through each line of code and watch how each line of code may affect your variables. The moment you see that a variable changes incorrectly, then you can pinpoint the exact line of code that's causing the error.

Debugging may be tedious and exhausting, but it's the only way to track down and eliminate as many bugs as possible in your program. The larger your program, the more places bugs can possibly hide, and the more bugs you'll need to track down and wipe out. Although you may not find and eliminate all possible bugs, make an effort to wipe out as many as possible, especially the ones causing your program to work incorrectly.

Summary

Even the best programmers make mistakes, which makes programming a constant trial-and-error process as you write your code, test it, and fix any problems with it before moving on to writing more code. Three common problems with programs are syntax, logic, and run-time errors.

Syntax errors are typically misspellings or misplaced (or omitted) symbols or punctuation marks that can keep your program from running at all. Xcode can often identify syntax errors so you can fix them.

Logic errors are harder to find and isolate because the code may be working perfectly, but it's not working the way you thought it would work. As a result, tracking down and eliminating logic errors is much harder because you first must identify what's causing the problem.

Run-time errors are some of the hardest errors to fix because your program may work perfectly, except when you distribute it to others who use the program in situations that you never expected or intended. When your program receives data that it doesn't know how to handle, it can cause a run-time error. Fixing such run-time errors can be difficult because you can never anticipate all possible problems your program might face when in actual use.

When Xcode identifies a problem in your code, it displays a message in the Issues window. The two types of issues are Warnings and Cautions. A Warning signals a problem that keeps your program from working at all. A Caution alerts you to a problem that won't keep your program from running but may cause unintended problems if you don't fix it.

Two simple ways to debug your program involve using comments and printing out values using the NSLog command. When using the NSLog command, you can view the printed results by opening the Console window (choose Run ➤ Console).

The Debugger window can display a variable watching window and your code with breakpoints so you can stop your code at certain points and step through each line to see how your program works.

When your program is working exactly the way you want, it's time to distribute it to others. Then you can sit back and look back on the long journey you took from learning about programming to writing your own programs to finally distributing your own programs for others to use. That's when you'll know you're a real programmer.

No single book can teach you all there is to know about programming, so now that you've reached the end of this book, it's time to start practicing writing your own programs, learning and sharing tips and ideas with others, and learning as much as you can from other books or attending conferences.

Since technology is always changing, you'll always need to keep learning something new just to keep up. The good news is that nobody can be an expert in everything, but many people can be experts in their own niche. Even though you may not think you know enough to be a programming expert, you probably know a lot more than you might think, and if you combine your programming skills with your current knowledge, you already know more than many people in your field.

Whether you plan on writing programs to sell, create custom programs for your work, or just enjoy making programs for a hobby, you'll find that computer programming can be a never-ending intellectual challenge that can keep you amused and mentally stimulated.

With your knowledge of Mac OS X programming, you can easily start creating iPhone and iPad apps. The future belongs to people willing to adapt to change and follow the market. By knowing how to program in Objective-C and use Xcode, you've just moved yourself into a select group of programmers ready to take advantage of the growing Mac, iPhone, and iPad markets. Within a short period of time, you may look back and marvel at how far you've come and how much you've learned, and it all started with your initial desire to learn the basics of programming the Mac.

Index

Special Characters

- operator, 78
- (subtraction) symbol, 13
& (ampersand) symbol, 193
&& (And) operator, 88–89
# symbol, symbols in Objective-C, 68
#define command, 76
#import "Class.h", implementation file, 177
#import <Cocoa/Cocoa.h> header file, 176
#import command, 68
#import directive, 178
#import "MyClass.h" file, 179
% operator, 78
%@ data type, 66
%f data type, 66
%i data type, 66
(id) sender portion, 242
-(id)init implementation file, 177
* (asterisk) symbol
    symbols in Objective-C, pointers, 70–71
    syntax errors omitting, 373–374
* operator, 78
*myArray pointer, 141
*testObject pointer, 179
/ (division) symbol, 13
/ operator, 78
// symbol, symbols in Objective-C, 68–69
[] symbols, symbols in Objective-C, 69–70
^ (Xor) operator, 90
|| (Or) operator, 89
+ (addition) symbol, 13
+ operator, 78
= (equal sign), 73
= symbol, and syntax errors, 372–373
== symbol, and syntax errors, 372–373

A

accessor methods, 196

Action method, 38–40, 42
addButtonWithTitle method, 318
addEntriesFromDictionary method, 162
addItemsWithObjectValues method, 292
addItemsWithTitles method, 272
addition (+) symbol, 13
addObject method, 150–151, 168
addObjectsFromArray method, 168
alert dialog boxes, 315–321
    buttons for, 318–321
    suppression check box for, 317
    text for, 317
alert runModal command, 318
algorithm, for programs
    defining, 354–355
    overview, 353–354
all-important semicolon, 66
allKeys method, 162–163
alloc method, 179
allowedFilesTypes property, 325, 329
allValues method, 163
Alternate field, 235
Alternate option, Attributes Inspector, 237–238
Alternate pop-up menus, 237
ampersand (&) symbol, 193
anchoring, objects for user interfaces, 227
And (&&) operator, 88–89
App Delegate icon, 219, 243, 245
AppDelegate file, 209–210
AppDelegate.m file, 64–65, 355
appendString method, 136–137
Apple Core Library, 54
Application file option, 217
Application icon, 219
Application template, 22, 331
applicationDidBecomeActive method, 213
applicationDidFinishLaunching method, 64–65, 74, 179–180, 192, 199, 207, 213, 272

E

Q

R

S

Breinigsville, PA USA
30 January 2011
254398BV00005B/73-400/P